G000124366

The Bonus of Laughter

The Bonus of Laughter

ALAN PRYCE-JONES

I made hay while the sun shone.
    My work sold.
Now, if the harvest is over
    and the world cold,
Give me the bonus of laughter
    As I lose hold.

John Betjeman

Hamish Hamilton : London

First published in Great Britain 1987
by Hamish Hamilton Ltd
27 Wrights Lane, London w8 5tz

British Library Cataloguing in Publication Data

Pryce-Jones, Alan
The bonus of laughter.
1. Pryce-Jones, Alan   2. Journalists –
Great Britain – Biography
I. Title
070'.92'4   PN5123.P73/

ISBN 0-241-11903-0

Phototypeset by Rowland Phototypesetting Ltd
Bury St Edmunds, Suffolk
Printed in Great Britain by
Butler and Tanner Ltd, Frome, Somerset

ILLUSTRATIONS

*

AP-J with Thérèse and David, Kent, 1942
AP-J with Somerset Maugham at Cap Ferrat, 1962

*

Mary-Jean, c. 1936
AP-J by Derek Hill, 1979

I

I ARRIVED AT Eton in the afternoon of January 22, 1922. My father, bowler-hatted, and my mother, carefully dressed down for the occasion, were with me, and we brought between us a hip bath of brown tin, a folding chair upholstered in red rep, and a few suitable pictures – by Cecil Alden it might be, bright with tally-ho heartiness.

It was not a happy day. My room in Cotton Hall House looked down on the lavatories, which echoed with regular regurgitations, and smelled commandingly of Jeyes Fluid. There was a folding bed in one corner, a deal 'burry' for clothes and books, a wall cupboard for tea-cup and plate, a red-covered ottoman for gym-shoes and flannel shorts, and by the grate a coal-scuttle, only filled three times a week for a fire to be lit in the evening. Four days of that week I could, in winter, write my name in the damp on the meanly-flowered wallpaper.

We had called on m'tutor, Mr Whitworth, a florid schoolmaster with a slightly dotty wife, and on m'dame, Miss Dix. I was the only new boy in the house, and so I was briefly an object of curiosity. I had never before been sent to a boarding-school, partly because my parents simply forgot, and partly because I was thought to be so precociously clever and so highly-strung that I was daily in danger of a brainstorm. That this was utter rubbish did not prevent my undergoing a lamentable apprenticeship to life, held back from any possible proficiency in learning, schoolboy athletics – in those days the main commitment of school existence – or plain awareness of the world, except from the hothouse comfort of an overheated nursery, or, worse, an overheated drawing-room.

So there we sat, in a miasma of Jeyes Fluid, while partly I dreaded the moment of being left alone, and partly I longed for it, so as to celebrate my escape into the society of other boys.

From this distance of over sixty years I look back on the three of us as though on a faded danguerreotype. My father is very much the colonel, with mouse-coloured hair and moustache, gold watch-chain – he considered wrist-watches, like suede shoes and, Heaven knows, pocket-combs, marks of the beast (an effeminate beast); my mother ran to strapped shoes, mink capes, a regimental brooch in diamonds – the Coldstream, of course – and sufficient but not obtrusive pearls; I, to judge by surviving photographs, have a deceptively angelic appearance, inevitably muffish and on this very day no doubt glandular with emotion. We sit by the empty grate with nothing much to say, while from the passage outside my room sounds the scuffle of small boys arriving after the Christmas holidays, the scrape of suitcases on linoleum, and a banging door or two. I remember hoping not to cry.

I suppose no parents can have tried harder than mine to deserve well of their children. They were endlessly loving and unselfish, endlessly, also, at odds with reality. That they had children at all seems to me today prodigious. True, my only brother and I were separated by eleven years, a world war, and a sequence of miscarriages. We did our best, my brother especially, to sing out our descant to the throbbing *vox humana* of parental love. But it was our parents' fate to repeat with their sons the impasse which blocked their pleasure in each other. Each was so set to fall in with some presumed desire that very seldom did either even approach the satisfaction of a wish. My father suggested plans, pleasures, excursions, because he thought they would please my mother; my mother agreed to something she did not at all want simply because she thought it would please my father. Both were wrong. And similarly my father was always putting himself out in order to teach me swimming, riding, shooting: all of which I detested, muff that I was.

Now that both of them have been dead for a generation, now that it is too late by so many years, I see them more clearly and love them more than when they were alive. On that particular day at Eton they must have been utterly themselves, my father casting his mind back to old cricket matches on Upper Club, hearing an ancient voice from the Nineties calling to the cricketers, 'Water Boils!' as the match broke off for tea, telling little tales of Toddy Vaughan, his housemaster, and of old Dr Warre, and of the day when he represented Wales at Queen Victoria's Diamond Jubilee procession through the streets of Eton and Windsor; my mother trying to slip into my hands unnoticed the little leather-bound book into which she had copied the ninety-first psalm as a talisman: had it not brought her brother safely through the Battle of Mons?

And then I was alone. One had a frugal supper, prayers, and lights out at 9.15. The next day the big boys of the school were to arrive, athletic giants of fifteen, and the day after the very big boys, among whom one, Dunglass, later Home, paid me a visit on the instructions of shared relations. He was in Pop, he could wear coloured waistcoats and seals on his top-hat, and he deigned to instruct me in the rules as they affected small boys: which side of the street to walk on, the need to keep a great-coat collar turned up, the simple procedures of fagging. No one could have done it better; he hit exactly the right note of friendly distance, and I could have foretold, nearly forty years ahead of the time, that one day he would be chosen Prime Minister.

My first years at Eton were happy ones. Hopeless at games, I managed to win a few silver cups – for shooting on a miniature range when my neighbour (I thought) accidentally shot bull's-eyes on my target; for winning a quarter-mile race out of plain agoraphobia (I ran fast in order to get away from the rest). I did very little work, but I had a talent for passing exams by cramming my brain at the eleventh hour, so that I soon acquired shelves of morocco-bound prizes, to the distress of Mr Whitworth, who knew perfectly well that though I might do brilliantly on Tuesday I should have forgotten my sudden skills by the week-end.

But after a year or two I became bored. My parents, expecting the worst, launched my school career by promising to take me away when I wished it. But when I did wish it, longing to learn a foreign language in France or Switzerland, they refused flatly. People would say that I had been sacked, they told me.

They reminded me of their sacrifice in keeping me at Eton; they reminded me how happy I ought to be, with my morocco-bound books and my tiny athletic triumphs, like winning the house fives only because I was partnered by the hefty son of a Bishop.

There were, of course, compensations. One was the friendship of M. R. James, the Provost, who used to ask me to dine in the shadow of Handel's organ, give me excellent claret, and send me back to Mr Whitworth at a delightfully late hour. Another was the occasional breakfast with the Headmaster, Dr Alington, marred only by his habit of picking on one small shy guest and reducing him to tears in order to amuse the rest of the company. And then there were the moments when one could forget one was at school: Sunday walks up the river, between banks of Queen Anne's lace, or under the great elms, now felled, which formed avenues up the Long Walk in Windsor Forest; or bicycle rides with dear Miss Dix, or illegal visits to raffish neighbours, like (surprisingly) Tallulah Bankhead, who gave us a Sunday cocktail before evening chapel.

Most of those who claimed Tallulah's friendship were caught by masters. They lined the streets by her house to protect the morals of the school. But I and my friend Tony Wilson used to order a taxi into the yard of the White Hart and travel on the floor with a rug over our heads, and we got away with it. For, as in all schools, outwitting the authorities kept us constantly happy. I remember being taken out by a raffish friend in his 45 h.p. Renault, a great yacht of a car with scarlet leather seating and a mahogany body studded with gold nails. Naturally, I insited on driving it, and on the outskirts of Maidenhead I was dashing along when I saw my tutor sedately bicycling just as he saw me, wobbled in rage, and fell off. I made my friend drive me at reckless speed back to Eton, and at once rehearsed a contemporary in a different version of the afternoon's activities. I had played fives. I had won the first game 15–7, and lost the second 8–15; I had all but sprained an ankle; and so on in careful detail. Eventually my tutor returned, and I was sent for. 'In Maidenhead, sir? But I was playing fives with Akers-Douglas.' 'Leave the room. Send Akers-Douglas in.' We were separately interrogated for half an hour, but as our rehearsal paid off, and we told exactly the same lies in minute detail, I got

4

away with that too. On such occasions one used to put one's face temptingly close to Mr Whitworth's right hand, because if he were to hit one he could be reported to the Headmaster. He became purple, his fingers stretched from his cuff, but hit one he never, alas, did.

And then there was the Cockpit, our quaint tea-shop in the High Street, presided over by the two Miss Masters, with whom we had an arrangement: David Herbert, Hamish St Clair Erskine, Roddie Henderson, Peter Beatty, James Lees-Milne, myself, and one or two more. We had our own room, protected by the two old ladies of the house, where we kept a forbidden gramophone, and secret stores to be shared with illicit visitors from London. Here we held court, eating baps and honey, swigging an occasional cocktail, listening to records of Edythe Baker playing 'My Heart Stood Still' on her white piano, telling each other lies about our parents' Isotta Fraschini, their villa at Cap d'Antibes, their partridge shoot in Suffolk – for we were appalling snobs.

It was usual in those days for anxious elders to accuse the public schools of almost universal sexual corruption, but in reality we were on the whole an innocent lot. More than sixty years later, I sometimes see an elderly gentleman, bald, stout, with a sad moustache, and I remember that once he was a self-conscious Adonis, top-hat to one side, proud of his reputation as a school tart. We believed in a system of live-and-let-live; we made vulgar jokes; we repeated ribald rhymes to show our sophistication; but very few of us translated vulgar ribaldry into action.

For my part, I remember very well the shock of an initiation which brought on uneasy consequences after I had been in the school for a year or two. One of our pleasures was to go to the rehearsals of the Music Society – a weekly event which gave us an excuse to leave our houses after dark in order to gather in the Music School and struggle through the choruses of *Acis and Galatea* and some four-square cantata by Grieg or Hamish MacCunn. One night, walking home with a fifteen-year-old, I must have revealed by an embarrassed silence that I did not understand what he was talking about. Once, on a golf-course, my father – equally embarrassed – had spoken incomprehensibly about bees, flowers, about anything rather than the concrete problems of small boys; and there the matter had rested. In the dark street Dandy Wallace had stopped and cross-questioned me. Surely I knew what used to be called the Facts of Life? I confessed that I did not, and Dandy took pity on me. The very next night I was to cut prayers, he informed me, and begin my education. He conducted me into the gloomy lavatories under my window, and there, dizzyed by Jeyes Fluid and the warming sense of a wide horizon, I was treated to a lecture which covered most of what I now know, since sexual mechanics are neither abstruse nor variable.

Under the Eton system, we occupied the same seat at meals, between the same neighbours therefore, and the following morning at breakfast I came under attack from the boy on my right, who had noticed my absence from prayers the night before, and also that Dandy was absent too. 'I know what you were up to,' he said, and turned his back. Usually he and I went down town between schools to eat a devilled sardine or something of the kind, but that morning he refused to speak to me. It was the same at luncheon, and at tea, which we ate together in his room or mine. After an entire day of ostracism, my nerve cracked. 'Yes,' I said, 'you are perfectly right.' My voice too cracked a little. I felt myself, in every sense of the word, totally abandoned. My friend, who was a fox-hunting type, already preparing for his eventual role as Lord Lieutenant of Warwickshire, was stricken; his only thought had been to tease me, and now suddenly he found himself with a cause on his hands. First he announced he would Kill Wallace. Then he imposed on me an alternative course of action. I must at once send for my father. And so cowed was I that I did. Come immediately, I wrote under dictation. Something frightful has happened.

I knew I could not tell my father about the matter in speech, so on the special grey paper we used for 'Sunday Qs' – a weekly examination in divinity – I wrote a delusive little essay, which I gave him to read a day or two later. He was standing on Barnes Pool Bridge, in Eton High Street, and I can see him now, wearing a rather clergymanlike overcoat, hanging straight from the shoulders, unwaisted, and of course a bowler hat on his head. He read, not understanding. 'You were in a lavatory,' he said, 'and there was someone else there too. Well? That happens, you know.' Faltering, I filled in the gaps, and my father laid his head on the parapet of the bridge. Would his hat fall into the stream? I wondered. He stood up straight, saying not a word, and we walked along the street to a teashop where my censor, foreseeing a difficult afternoon, had promised to meet us. We sat down to a banana sundae, choking, but ever silent. And then my father, still with no word, caught the London train.

He never referred to the matter – my mother wrote later that she could not imagine what I had told him, but that his distress on reaching home was equalled only by his reaction to my grandmother's death. However, the miserable aftermath of this confession was to undermine his confidence in me over years. I never dared ask a friend to visit me in the holidays for fear my father might yet again creep up to the room in which we were talking of Wisden averages or the prospects for the House Cup, throw open the door, pause, and glare, still silently.

As to my censor, I soon forgave him the jar he had given me. I even returned good for evil. Not long afterwards he came to me in agitation saying that his first cousin, from America, was about to pay him a visit at Eton. Up to the age of ten the cousin had lived in expectation of inheriting a peerage, a fortune, a great house near Kenilworth. Then Robin had been born to a senior branch of the family, and his expectations were erased in a flash. Robin told me that, when he was a baby, his cousin had put ground glass in his bottle, and a little later had inaugurated various gestures of a destructive kind: leading the little boy towards open manholes, sawing through the support of a swing, and so on. Now he was convinced that he would be poisoned, and he begged me to come with him to the White Hart and taste his food. I obliged. The cousin turned out to be a glamorous Hollywood success, a script-writer who needed no adventitious peerage, no abbatial Warwickshire seat. He seemed out to please rather than poison, but I credited my own presence with his forbearance, saying that he must have been nervous at the prospect of killing us both.

I did not long associate the Eton Music School with private tensions. I had been born with a musical gift – my mother in her day was an excellent amateur violinist – but I was not allowed to develop it. As always, I was thought too delicate for any concentrated work, so that only when I reached school age, too late therefore, was I given any training; I could play the piano tolerably well, but I never acquired more than an adequate technique. At Eton, music became more to me; at home it had merely signified pleasant sentimental noise, aspiring at best to the charming level of Mendelssohn's *Lieder ohne Wörte*. Now I discovered Debussy; I sat in a chapel stall and listened to the Brahms Requiem; in the holidays I went to the Queen's Hall and listened to César Franck and early Wagner – a limited list, perhaps, but I had nobody to help me extend it until much later.

It was the same with books. I read the whole of Scott, even to *The Doom of Devorgoil*. When I was quite small we spent a summer in Surrey and there, in my bedroom, was a set, bound in an ugly mauve which I found very beautiful, of the Waverley novels. I used to wake early, in order to finish *The Pirate* before breakfast and rush on to the opening chapters of *Quentin Durward*. One never recaptures the delight of literary adventure at the age of ten. The six o'clock summer sun lit the dew on the lawn; as a London child I was already intoxicated by the yellowness of cowslips and the intensive glow of dandelions in the garden below my window as I perched under an opened dormer, in a haze of pleasure which embraced *The Lady of the Lake*, and a swing by the tennis-court, and a dramatic railway tunnel nearby from which a plume of sulphur-smelling smoke and a windy rumble announced the invisible sudden presence of a train in the cutting. I had no guide to direct me in my reading. My mother – to my father's delight – still re-read the novels of her adolescence, with titles like *The Sweet Girl Graduate*; my father recommended Henty and *Masterman Ready*; my grandmother hid Ballantyne's *Coral Island* on top of the wardrobe as too exciting. So, on my own, I absorbed an odd diet of Novalis in translation, Johnson's *Lives of the Poets*, especially the short ones like Dyer and Garth (Richard Savage seemed altogether too long); I got by heart the poems of Herrick, out of another hideous little book bound this time in limp suede; I set on the same level *The Secret Garden* and *Treasure Island*, Alan Breck and Mr Scrooge: each seemed an equal part of a grown-up world which I never knew had ended fifty years earlier, for my entire family was comfortably rooted in the late nineteenth century, buoyed by confidence in an Imperial England which, it was assumed, would take even the First World War in its stride.

By the time I was fifteen I was dreadfully home-sick. Once I even wore the same woollen socks, day and night, for a week or two – baths at Eton in the 1920s were infrequent – simply because I had first put them on in my own room at home. Home at that time was a towering brick house in Buckingham Palace Gardens, a Willett row house in the London Dutch manner of the 1880s. One said of such houses that their glory was to be different: no two houses in the row were alike. I suppose, and hope, ours was unique. Much later the house was converted to offices, and one floor became for a time the headquarters of the National Trust. It had a dark hall, hung with the heads of animals shot by my father in Africa, stairs leading to a long even darker gallery, which linked two drawing-rooms, neither large nor well-proportioned, and then three floors of bedrooms, with a single bathroom between them. Over twelve years my mother's passion for box-rooms eroded what started, then, as a large house. A garden room on the ground floor first filled with junk; next, a bedroom here and a bedroom there. Deep closets were lined with medicines twenty years old; trunks of Victorian dolls' clothes were piled in with Worcester dessert-services and my grandfather's splendid dolman. The very top and bottom of the house were forbidden ground. In the basement lived Gallagher the butler, who slept in a kind of recess constructed to guard the safe; and from the top of the house there might at times be heard the sound of 'fourth floor laughter', in the expressive phrase which formed part of the private language put together by Lytteltons and Barings, and described the shrill hilarity of the maids.

From my Eton room above the sonorous lavatories I thought of all this with anguish. I wanted once again to be young enough to watch, from the nursery balcony, the Buckingham Palace guard marching out of Chelsea Barracks. They always changed the tune in front of our house – an event I took as a personal tribute to my father. I wanted to be younger, and so safer still; to relive the Proustian moment when my mother came to see me in bed and perhaps to lie beside me and sing 'Once in royal David's city' while I went to sleep. I was an odious child, and sometimes postponed this happiness by refusing to say good-night. 'Go away!' I would yell, and then my mother would descend three flights of stairs until I could hear the click of the drawing-room doors. 'Come back!' And back she came; perhaps twice or three times, until peace was made, and she lay on my nursery bed and started softly to sing.

II

I F WE CONSIDER living as an arc it is hard to say which of the
extremities that attach that arc to the general ground of
living is the more melancholy, whether the difficult beginning
or the difficult end. The end offers at any rate the consolation of
endurance. Though arrival only signifies a fresh departure, a
man has at any rate accomplished his temporal journey in one
piece. I can remember Osbert Sitwell, asked to describe the
trenches of the First World War, replying that at least they were
better than school. Although I do not look back with horror on
Eton, I find I have a recurring dream in which I am still there,
after fifty-eight years, lost, unable to find school-room, playing-
field or chapel, and saying to myself, I've been here for nearly
sixty years. Surely it must end soon?

The pleasantest things about Eton were those moments
when one escaped: sculling up river to Queen's Eyot, to eat a
duck's egg and gossip under the willows; to be asked briefly into
a private house, all chintz and roses and cucumber sandwiches;
to be taken on the Fourth of June to dine with one's parents at
the Guards Club in Maidenhead; better still, to be allowed out
on one's own. If I have said that we were sickeningly snobbish,
our snobbery was nothing to that of our masters. So, should
Aunt Elsie ask me to lunch on a Sunday at Burnham Beeches, I
was allowed to go because she was a Dowager Countess. More
resoundingly, one might be invited to play tennis by the Duke of
Newcastle at Forest Lodge. The pleasures were not, in reality,
so great. Aunt Elsie boasted that you did not need a good cook if
you had a chafing-dish, and accordingly she confected for

herself delicious little omelettes and the like, while her guests lunched off cold ham and an undressed salad. The Duke was not quite right in the head, and dwarfish in body. But both were a welcome change from Mr Whitworth and dear Miss Dix.

There was always the river. The crumbling banks of the Thames above Eton were planted with great arching trees which threw heavy shadows on the water. The water smelled brackish in the shadows, and there was always the chance that a swan might attack, threatening to tear the shiny fabric which covered the flimsy shell of an outrigger. I decided after one summer that cricket was not for me. I was probably the only boy unable to bowl whose batting average began with a decimal point. In the winter things were better. For years I ran up and down the field, playing our special Eton game of football, without ever discovering the rules. One could get away with this – though once, when an opposing side had been decimated by influenza, I was lent to them as a makeweight and on this single occasion could do no wrong, scoring again and again against my own side, so that in the evening I was beaten by one of the big boys for disloyalty. Usually, however, I ran up and down aimlessly, a technique unknown to cricket. And then, to my father's distress, I became a wet-bob; I chose to row. In a 'perfect', in a four-oared racing shell. Or to scull, with a wary eye to the swans, and a constant terror of turning too slowly under Windsor Bridge and being carried over a thundering weir.

It does not seem so long ago; and nursery days still cast a bright morning cloud, as if a lifetime of promise lay ahead. I can see Peter Scott in his pram from my night-nursery window and hear my nanny of the moment say what a good little boy he was. He never had a cold because his mummy – perhaps fired by memories of her heroic Antarctic husband – rubbed him in oil and left him naked in the garden whatever the weather. I hated him, because I always had a cold. Incidentally, I usually hated my nannies, nine of whom, since I was so detestable a child, I ran through in all. I remember two with pleasure: Miss Tomlinson, who, when she left after a year or so, departed in a taxi with yellow wheels, so that whenever I saw its twin in the street I used to be sick; and a huge lady who was sacked by my father when he surprised us by coming up to the nursery and finding me, on the table, patting her red face and saying, 'I don't love you, nanny, but you *are* beautiful.' This was a judgement summarily to be scotched, he thought.

Later, there were nursery governesses. One, a Christian Scientist, kept her teeth in a glass under the bed, and I at first feared they were a pet snake which one night would climb out and nip me. Another paid me out in my own coin by telling me repeatedly, and curtly, that she had no time for me, so that I used to sit bawling with misery, on the open top of a Bournemouth bus, begging to be given 'a second chance'. My mother took no part in these commotions once the war broke out in 1914, but decided she was not able to cope – it was simply, I think, that she missed my father, who marched away from Windsor with his battalion for France early in August. So I was left much of the time with my grandmother, while mama stayed upstairs with nurses or was passed from one fashionable nerve-doctor to another.

This, I repeat, was a very poor introduction to school life. I had, at the age of eleven or so, briefly gone to a day school in Sloane Street, organized by a sensible man called Mr Gibbs. His scholars, sporting red caps famous in their day, were mainly little fellows of six or seven on their way to boarding-school, so that hardly had I arrived than I became, from seniority only, head boy. My confusion was utter. I could not kick a football or bowl at a wicket because my experience of life had been limited to the interests of an old lady who took me in her electric brougham to 'leave cards' on other old ladies or to stay in country houses as if I were my own dead grandfather. I longed in vain to be like other boys. One day, shuddering, I pulled the tail of a kitten until it howled with pain, simply because I had read somewhere that nasty boys did such things and I ached to be a nasty boy. Likewise, a few years later, arrived at Eton, I seemed to myself to bring with me the cotton wool wrappings of a home life. Very early in my school career I needed some note-paper and found I had a few sheets of dolls' stationery and a miniature pink-edged envelope which had belonged to my mother. As an aide-mémoire I jotted down on the paper some elementary facts, such as '2 pints = 1 quart', or '16 oz. = 1 lb.' and printed carefully on the envelope the words 'Useful Information'. Months later the envelope turned up and someone had added to it 'Thanks for Information'. I prayed for death. I felt I never could live down the disgrace of the pink-edged envelope and its childish superscription.

The pains of adolescence have been so thoroughly researched that I do not propose to enlarge on my own experience. To my grandchildren today that experience must seem bizarre to an extreme, so utterly buried is it under the accretions of time, like some Mayan city under lianas of jungle. Like that city, too, the world I was born to has gone all but unrecorded. Journals and letters are no longer kept; moreover, the fossils I knew when they too were young were both unobservant in the main and inexpressive. Those who record their own lives usually follow much the same patterns. They started very poor and very unhappy, they ended richer and unhappier. My own case was different. I was born neither rich nor poor, and with a temperament rather happy than not. By the time I reached Eton I was beginning to climb out of the larva stage. But I had fitted so easily into the cocoon which enclosed my beginnings that my small wings found it for a long time both painful and unnecessary to stretch.

The cocoon was made of very different fibres. On my father's side, I was entirely Welsh. The youngest of eight children, he had been born to a classic Victorian magnate, who was the first to organize a mail order system and also a pioneer of the parcel post – unromantic activities, perhaps, but rewarding. Throughout the second half of the nineteenth century his fortunes grew. His Royal Welsh Warehouse, in Newtown, Montgomery, distributed his goods, and in particular the red flannel petticoat, all over the world. Clients ranged from Florence Nightingale to the Russian Government, and as he progressed towards his knighthood – his children said that he refused a peerage because he disapproved of hereditary honours, but possibly he was not offered one – he spent years in Parliament as Conservative Member for Montgomery Boroughs. When I remember him he was over eighty, and slightly dotty, an old gentleman in a donkey carriage who used to swoop upon me in the park at Dolerw, his Newtown home, and plump me down on his knee. For years I could not see without terror a coat topped by an astrakhan collar. My grandmother, called Noonie to distinguish her from my more familiar grandmother in Yorkshire, was a lively old lady with a great silver loaf of hair and a Welsh burr to her voice, as had some of the aunts, most of whom my father angrily disliked. There was Aunt Nell, whose vegetarian son refused to sit on anything made of leather; there was 'that little cat, Cis' as my father called her; Aunt Katie who had a mongoloid daughter; and Auntie Rose, whom my father positively liked. Flanking them were Uncle Pryce, he too a long-standing Member for Montgomery Boroughs, and a baronet; Uncle Bert, who also wore an astrakhan collar and had impoverished his entire family to a degree which brought on him my father's ready displeasure; Uncle Ernest, who was totally deaf as the result of treatment from some great expert after a little hardness of hearing had descended on him in youth. He had been, like Uncle Bert, an eminent rugger player – both, I think, played for Wales – and lip-read so perfectly that nobody noticed his deafness. As a small child I used to be disconcerted whenever he came to see me – which was not often – because my father could not be bothered to speak out loud to him but merely moved his lips, so that talk followed a pattern of silence on the one part, countered on the other by Uncle Ernest answering with enthusiasm. I could make no sense of this. There were consorts, too. Aunt Nell had a husband who was chairman of Humber cars – which meant that we had to buy a Humber from time to time because of the comfortable discount; Heaven knows who Aunt Cis's husband had been; Aunt Katie's husband, Uncle Archie, disapproved of me because I was always late for breakfast; Uncle Pryce's wife, Aunt Beatrice, was a demon on the tennis-court.

And then there was Aunt Ida, wife to Uncle Bert. My father's disapprobation extended to her, and he was especially vexed when, after losing her elder son in the First World War, she developed psychic powers. In trance, she required certain colours of pastel to be made for her, and later drew out lengths of fresco. These she showed to her friend Sir Arthur Evans, who found that they prolonged and embellished his piecemeal discoveries at Knossos. The disagreeable colour schemes of Knossos are thus, we were told, attributable to Aunt Ida's psyche. One day, in 1919, after tea, she slipped into a trance in my father's presence, covered a large sheet of paper with

15

charcoal, and then went over the sheet with an eraser. The result was a picture of the Russian Imperial family upside down. Even my father was a little impressed, since, when not in trance, she was said to be unable to draw at all.

By the time I was born, on November 18, 1908, at 17 South Street just off Park Lane, a house later pulled down, the fortunes of the Royal Welsh Warehouse were about fatally to decline. My grandfather had expanded into Canada and among other things had bought a great many acres on the edge of Calgary. After years, during which Calgary grew if at all in the opposite direction, he became bored and sold his land for what he had paid for it – a reaction which today fills me with sadness.

At home, he had discouraged all his sons from interfering in his business. They might go into the Army or Parliament; but they were not to enter the Royal Welsh Warehouse. With the consequence that, when he died at eighty-five, he left no effective heir and what had been for some sixty years a powerful commercial empire sank into obscurity.

With the years, therefore, we felt ourselves uncomfortably poor. From time to time my father would summon us to his room and give us a warning, 'I have done my best,' he might say, 'but now I can look no farther ahead than April.' He left the army, which he loved, and briefly 'went into the city', which he loathed. There he lost much of what money remained. Nothing ever changed, though. There was a Humber, it might be, and (since neither of my parents could drive) a chauffeur. There was a butler, and a cook and such maids as were needed. At the appropriate time a hired omnibus arrived from the Southern Railway and the servants and I and a great many boxes were loaded on it to make a short train journey towards a summer in the country. My mother handled this Hegira each year with skill. 'I can't face it, Harry,' she would say. And she went to her room, and pulled down the blinds while my father coped.

Herself was of a different stamp from my father, although for nearly fifty years they adored one another unreservedly. Mama was of Yorkshire and Northumberland stock, with a touch of Ayrshire thrown in. The third of four children, she had been brought up between Beningbrough, her father's home near

York, and 51 Charles Street, Berkeley Square. As Vere Dawnay, she had been devoted to her younger brother and her father, and very much less to her mother who in turn preferred her elder children.

Old pictures show my mother to have been graceful, charmingly pretty, and with a look of innocence edged by apprehension. This was a look which remained with her into married life, and, indeed, she did not expect things to work out happily, although in fact her life was, so far as exterior circumstances went, a happy one. It might have been happier still had she been encouraged to use her natural gifts, which were real and varied. She wrote a little and published a poem or two, she composed a simple hymn to her own words which brought in a comfortable sum to a military charity; she was much sought after as an amateur actress in days when great country houses put on performances of, say, *The Importance of Being Earnest* – her star part was that of Cecily. Uncharacteristically, she was a medal-winning high diver, and family legend had it that Queen Victoria came to the Bath Club where a special platform had been built for her, and sank forwards, murmuring My God! My God! as mama executed her swallow dive backwards.

None of these activities, however, was supported by her parents, except perhaps the diving. Her role was to hunt three days a week with the York and Ainstey, beside her father and her brothers – she had twenty-two falls, she said, before she was seven. She detested riding, partly because a weak spine made it painful to ride side-saddle, partly because her insides reacted so unfavourably to foxhunting that later in life she had a series of miscarriages. But it seems strange, not that at the turn of the century girls were still brought up after the fashion of a long-previous era, but that my grandmother, who was both extremely intelligent and in many ways unconventional, should have fallen in with the lazy procedure of forming not a clever daughter but a successful debutante, dedicated to the stables in winter and the ballroom in summer.

Many years later, after my mother's death, I came on part of a letter in a forgotten despatch box. It was from my grandmother to my mother. It said in effect that if my mother felt as she did it was well that she had spoken out rather than nursed her resentment in silence. 'Of course,' said my grandmother, 'I am not trying to take Harry away from you. After all, I love your father.' My mother was about sixteen at the time. And I understand that my father had been brought into her life by one of her brothers, also in the second battalion of the Coldstream Guards. My grandmother, who never doubted her own ability to charm, must have been attracted to this young subaltern, and asked him to shoot in Yorkshire. My mother, shy by nature and suspicious of the world, evidently fell in love, said nothing to anyone, observed her mother, and brooded. What is likely to have been an innocent friendship was coloured dark by her suspicion and eventually she exploded. But her own natural innocence must have made things hard for my father. In the same despatch-case I came on a correspondence with a lady doctor in Canada – safely remote – which was exchanged just before my mother's wedding. She wrote to ask what physical action marriage involved, and evidently she wrote in fear. The doctor's answers were reassuring, but suggested a calculated lack of ardour which would have made even an elephant impatient.

I adored my mother but I immensely enjoyed my grandmother. I was very small when my grandfather died and his widow moved to a house on the corner of West Halkin Street and Belgrave Square. In that house I spent an appreciable part of my childhood, and I still feel tenderly towards the life that was lived in it, towards such exterior props as the faintly violet-tinted glass in the drawing-room windows which dated from the early nineteenth century, the possible Greuze in the library, the whistle on the hall-table used by the butler to summon a taxi. I still remember tiny incidents which diversified the sequence of ordinary days, such as Princess Beatrice coming to tea and being hauled upstairs by me with the promise, 'I've got something to show you which you really will like' – in the event, a chair with a cane seat which could be lifted to reveal a chamber-pot; or the day when my grandmother was late for her own luncheon and arrived breathless to tell the guests, 'I saw a dreadful hansom accident in Belgrave Square. Two hansoms collided and fell down an area and both drivers were killed.' 'Gracious, Victoria, how awful for you,' exclaimed the guests. 'Awful it was,' said my grandmother, 'but if it had to happen it was lucky I was there to see' – a comment which conveys her flavour well: a flavour of vivid curiosity, compassion, and toughness.

Her life had been calculated to nourish these qualities. As the granddaughter of that Lord Grey who had nursed the Reform Bill of 1832 into law, she had inherited a taste for politics; her father, having brought the Prince Consort to England at the time of his marriage, had stayed at Court until his death, first as secretary to the Prince and then to the Queen; so that her early life was divided between Windsor Castle and St James's Palace; her younger sisters, Louisa* and Mary,† had played a part in the public life of their times, and so had her brother Albert.‡ During the nineteenth century the Grey family ramified vigorously throughout English domestic politics, and their cousinship, by the time I was born, was prodigious. In the England of fifty years ago, cousins were still the thing. My grandmother was not in the least snobbish. She had no reason to be. She had no social ambitions – how could she have? It was typical that someone who did have such ambition, like Lady Cunard, was known in my family as 'poor Maud' because she was a failure in the hunting field.

At Beningbrough she lived in an exceptionally beautiful house, presented with a careless and total absence of taste typical of Dawnays of her generation. She was a much-loved 'Auntie Tor' to her younger collaterals, and she carried within her the comfortable inner light of utter confidence in life. Thus, in 1917, while the war was going badly for the allies, she reinstated the custom of family prayers: we all repaired to the dining-room before breakfast, knelt in order of hierarchy, and invoked the Deity – a Low Church Deity, incidentally – to help our cause. A year later, when the war news improved, she abandoned this custom once more. She had done her bit.

I imagine that any intellectual interest I have inherited comes from the Greys. The Pryce-Joneses certainly had none; and the Dawnays did little beyond living prosperously in large country houses for a long time, sitting in Parliament and promoting their field sports. Though my grandfather was both

* Countess of Antrim
† Countess of Minto
‡ 4th Earl Grey

a Member of Parliament and a Colonel, he used regularly to be given months of hunting leave from his military duties. One brother did much the same. Another, bachelor Great-Uncle Francis, attempted nothing whatever, so absolutely nothing that my grandmother was spurred to prompt him, Why not go in to York and learn French? Only after his death did his lucky heirs discover that secretly he had played the Stock Exchange all his life and made a great deal of money for them. Great-Uncle Downe, like most eldest sons of that period, was encased in grandeur and so set apart; Great-Uncle Eusie was for me chiefly the very handsome old husband of Aunt Lena, a far from handsome old lady; Great-Uncle Geoff had somehow been unsatisfactory, perhaps only because he had not died; Great-Uncle Guy was indeed dead, and interestingly since he had been killed many years before by a buffalo in Africa. My grandmother told a lively tale of the buffalo suddenly appearing at the end of a long narrow ride, of the native bearers shinning up trees, and of Uncle Guy, weighed down by the accoutrements of tropical adventure, standing his ground until the sad and inevitable end – the sadder because obituaries pasted into family albums spoke of his great political future unfulfilled. When I went to Eton I was given my Dawnay grandfather's Latin dictionary, bound in full calf with a gilt coat of arms – his elder brother's similar school-books were additionally stamped with a coronet – and I heard that, when he arrived at the school in the 1850s, a chaplain was sent with him and lodged in the town for the next few years to watch over the moral fibre of himself and successive brothers. Finally there was Great-Uncle William, husband to Anne Addie, in her older age a lady so large that no hunter could carry her and so she followed hounds in a dog-cart reinforced by iron clamps – a far cry from the days when she had ridden out with her eleven brothers and sisters. There were also two delicious old ladies, lively and always dressed after the fashion of their youth in long braided jackets and sweeping braided skirts – Aunt Edith and Aunt Alice – who together in their bizarre clothes had much the appearance of a music-hall turn. Not content with mothering this substantial family old Lady Downe, left a widow, married her sons' tutor and produced three more children, of whom the closest to me was Aunt May Shaw-Stewart, who lived at Fonthill among

Beckford's ruins. To the distress of her relations, Aunt May became a Catholic and installed a Jesuit chaplain in the chapel of her husband's singularly ugly house, built in the Scotch Baronial style and never completed, so that what had been planned on an immense scale, to rival Fonthill itself, consisted largely of labyrinthine back premises, lit by fierce-smelling acetylene gas. I was not encouraged to stay there, on account of the Jesuit presence, my mother warning me that 'Aunt May will get you'. She did nothing of the kind, nor wished to, and I greatly admired her – not least the glittering sapphire clasp of her pearls.

It was a Dawnay axiom that nobody was so cherishable or interesting as a blood relation, and so it seemed right that we had such a number of them. They were, I suppose, a self-satisfied clan, not given to questionings or doubts, not intro-spective – though with an intermittent tendency to suicide – confident that God and the state were on their side. Many of them were frugal; when old Sir Hugh Shaw-Stewart travelled to Scotland he was made to do so second class and sitting up, while Lady Alice stretched out in a first-class sleeper. All of them put up with their marriages, their houses, their occupations, as if they were under an unbreakable contract to do so.

Because my father's not dissimilar family seldom left Wales I saw very little of it, also because my father liked to keep it at a distance. The only real link between the two sets of relations therefore was the Coldstream Guards, in which my father, my mother's two brothers and her father all served, and to which all were fanatically devoted. By the time I was old enough to be asked to debutante dances my mother used to look at me pityingly and commend my courage in accepting the invitation at all, 'because, darling, as you are not in the Brigade, nobody will dance with you'. Whatever the routine may have been in 1903, it was certainly not so twenty-five years later. Young Guards officers were looked on as bores by the beauties of the later day, who much preferred the company of such un-military party guests as Cecil Beaton and Oliver Messel.

I have said that I eventually grew tired of school, and longed to be educated in France or Switzerland rather than in Buckinghamshire. This was partly because, owing to the First

World War, I had no conception of any country outside the British Isles. To keep me quiet, my father, when I was fourteen or so, told me one day that the first foreign experience I was to undergo must be a visit to the birthplace of the greatest man in European history: Napoleon. He planned to take me to stay with Aunt May Shaw-Stewart, who had a villa in Corsica. We went. The expedition was not an entire success. My father had the set idea that all foreigners were thieves and corruptors; he therefore arranged that we should avoid setting foot in Paris by travelling from one station to another on the *Ceinture*. The trip was long; there was no food on the train; and by the time we reached the Gare de Lyon I said that I was hungry and I asked to go and buy something to eat at the buffet.

Fearing, I suppose, that I should either be robbed or corrupted on the platform, my father said crossly that he would come with me. But was my suitcase locked? No, I replied, I had no key. There was an explosion. I might have guessed, he snapped, that you would have no key. But he left the train just the same, and we were away some five minutes. In that time, a thief climbed into the compartment, opened my suitcase, saw that there was nothing of value in it, left it on the rack, and took my father's dressing-case, which had been carefully secured, and contained all his necessary treasures. I was delighted, I remember, but we reached Marseilles in a threatening silence, missed the Ajaccio boat, and had to spend the night in a double room, chosen for economy, where my father snored so angrily that I never closed an eye, and years later had not forgiven him.

On the return journey, after an agreeable time on that magical island, and fortified by small Napoleonic relics bought in junk-shops, we shared a sleeping-car and I announced that I wanted to unpack my pyjamas. There was another explosion. Why couldn't I sleep in my shirt? My father insisted that he alone could extract the pyjamas, climbed shakily on the lower bunk, lifted high the suitcase and dropped it on his head. In consequence, when at last we reached Victoria Station and were greeted by mama, asking eagerly if we had not had a marvellous time, she was again answered by total silence. My father did not speak for the rest of the day.

In retrospect, his silences appear more absurd than alarming. Fifty and sixty years ago, however, children held a father in awe. Mine, moreover, was a deeply disappointed man, and we all felt sorry for him. Life had begun so very well: he was a triumphant Etonian, an exceptional games-player who was equally successful at Cambridge; he cut short his University career so as to go with the Coldstream to the South African War, which he sincerely enjoyed; home again, he embarked on a happy marriage and revelled in his army life at Windsor or in London; he played polo, he was a fine shot; he was among the early officers of the Lugard period to explore the Niger, from which he returned with a quantity of animals living and dead. And then, in 1914, before he was forty, it all ended. Halfway through the war he was seconded from his regiment to Haig's staff, and thus disastrously lost regimental seniority. By 1918 he found himself facing a new world, the world of Noël Coward rather than Lily Elsie, of Ramsay MacDonald rather than Arthur Balfour, a world in which cousins played a diminishing part. He faced it, too, with a declining income, a wife in unsteady nervous health, and an elder son utterly unlike himself. No kinder, quieter man ever lived. By the time I left home and married I found this out for myself; but before that there had been difficult moments, largely through my fault, compounded by the fact that my father never adjusted himself to the twentieth century. His unique idea of pleasurable living embraced Purdey guns, I Zingari cricket matches, *The Pink Lady*, and an overall gloss of mild prosperity – he thought of outright riches as showing a lack of tact, if only towards himself. Towards me he was wary. Could I not, if I tried, grasp a mashie properly? Must I, gun to shoulder, always close the wrong eye in panic as a pheasant came noisily over? Following the big explosion, his frequent bouts of silence were due to inability to find the right words of rebuke – for he was a man of profound courtesy by instinct, and he would have wished to use only words of praise. But how could he praise a son who took taxis instead of the bus, who came home at four in the morning, and when chided for making the house ring with the dreadful cacophonies (as he found them) of Ravel and Stravinsky, turned odiously to piano arrangements of the overtures to *Zampa* or *Masaniello*?

He was a careful but not a practical man. For example, he made my mother keep accounts. Each evening she would open a tall ledger and question him about the day's expenses. Had he bought an evening paper? Had he taken the Underground? 'Oh, Harry,' I would hear, 'you must remember. Or my accounts will be all wrong.' Item by item, in an exquisitely legible hand, the pennies were jotted down; and only years later did I find that no page had ever been added up. The delicate copper-plate entries stood each on its own, so that no possible deduction could be made from nearly fifty years of record.

If I learned to be leery of my father's silences, I was equally so of my mother's nervous system. Her main symptom of distress was inability to meet any test, however small. She could not take a train, she said; she could not face strangers; she could assume no responsibility.

It had not always been so. When I was very small, my parents hired a house on the verge of Windsor Forest almost next door to the house, Queens Acre, made famous at that time by Howard Sturges, Edith Wharton and Henry James. A drawing-room window of our house looked towards the curve of the drive, and one day she was sitting by herself when she saw my father's commanding officer and his wife walking up to the door. She had no time to say to the butler that she was not at home, heard voices in the hall answer that the visitors would wait while the garden was searched for her, and in panic climbed behind a sofa which stood across a deep bow. The visitors sat on the sofa and began to discuss her in low tones. Yes, the room was quite pretty. Evidently my father's young wife had a little taste. Mama lay on the ground, until a pinch of dust brought on a sneeze. At which she rose up, as though it were the most natural thing in the world, and extended a welcoming hand, without comment. The guests fled.

Twenty years later, she could not have done this. I remember an evening, in Windsor Castle, where my parents lived in Henry VIII's Gateway, when they were asked, at a few hours' notice, to dine with the King and Queen. Mama at once became prostrate. She couldn't, *she couldn't*. But she did. And I remember sitting in a bathroom, myself distressed to the point of tears by her plight, expecting her to collapse, die even; yet awaiting her return a few hours later, in the best of spirits, having had a splendid evening – for, even in her moments of despair, she could rise above them to be excellent company.

There was a strain of eccentricity in the otherwise unsurprising temperament of the Dawnays. Mama, for instance, had a natural taste for martyrdom. She considered that she had been hardly done by, that everybody else was more fortunate than she. She observed with indignation that other contemporaries of hers were richer or grander than she, who knew herself to be more accomplished and certainly nicer than they. She was not so bizarre as her elder sister, Aunt Margie, who had married a clergyman whom she met on an East End soapbox – not necessarily a strange thing to do, but an act which gave rise to her father's remark, 'There are only two kinds of people I heartily dislike: clergymen and Buxtons. And dammit if my elder daughter doesn't marry the one and my elder son the other.' His dislike of Buxtons was quite impersonal. They were Liberals and that sufficed.

The clergyman was another matter. He was a handsome clergyman – the kind of ecclesiastic who turns up in high-minded Edwardian novels. The pleasing thing about him, in the eyes of his future in-laws, was that he was extremely, even fanatically, Low. Two candles on the altar, a plain, clean surplice, long impromptu prayers; such was his note. He was for a time chaplain at Sandringham, and later a canon of Bath, but he was not marked for preferment and ended his career in a remote Lutheran limbo, detecting the enemy hand of Rome all round him. My aunt was outright eccentric. Asked, for example, to one of the annual Buckingham Palace garden parties she would go in sand-shoes and wearing a mackintosh hat, but carrying better shoes and a smarter hat in a paperbag, only to be fetched out if the weather held. Like the black citizens of New York today, only half a century earlier, she wore a radio round her neck, and advanced on shopping expeditions to Selfridges, playing it loudly. She worried about money, without much reason, and I was not allowed to visit Sandringham after my nanny reported that I was made to share a breakfast egg with my cousin Alexandra: a parsimony paralleled, when she came to tea with my grandmother, by her habit of shovelling the cake, with quick dexterity, into a canvas sack, observed only by me, whose head at six or seven years old was level with the tea-table. She loved animals and from time to time had an instinct that somewhere an animal needed her. On one such

25

occasion she was asleep in Bath when the afflatus came on her, and she walked about the streets that night until she found a swan with a broken leg. Having no other resource, she tied the lace of one sand-shoe round its neck, helped it home – having bound up the leg with a second lace – and kept it in her bathtub until it mended.

Such, then, were some of the fibres which bound me to my home. And, to make me a still more unsuitable candidate for Eton education, I was both spoiled – in the sense of being humoured in every possible way – and neglected. My grandmother carried me about with her as though I were a *cavaliere servante*, and so I spent too much time with elderly people whom I considered my contemporaries. I remember walking round the lake at Buckhurst, and explaining to Sir Rennell Rodd, then ambassador to Rome, what he must do in the problem of the Alto Adige – I must have picked up my solution a week-end before. I was quite prepared to lay down the law about the bank-rate to the Governor of the Bank of England, or to explain the mechanics of recruiting to Kitchener. I did not, though, like to be put in a subaltern position. When T. E. Lawrence came to call on Uncle Alan and Aunt Elizabeth at three in the morning, I was outraged at being hauled down to the drawing-room, heavy with sleep, and encouraged to listen to accounts of desert exploits which meant nothing to me. All I recollect of Lawrence, after several such sessions, is the image of a small man talking a great deal and walking about the room, when what I wanted was either to explain to him what he should have done at Deraa, or be allowed to sleep in peace.

III

ETON IN MY time was not a very lively place. Because the stars of the 1920s were a few years older than I was I did not know them until after I had left school. Among them were Harold and Willie Acton, Brian Howard, Cyril Connolly, George Orwell, John Lehmann, Anthony Powell; but the only creative schoolboy I was in close touch with was Henry Yorke, later to become celebrated as Henry Green, but in those days a violinist in my house, not an embryonic fiction writer. He was not a good violinist; his only piece I think, was a version of Mendelssohn's 'On Wings of Song'. But I had to accompany him in that, and although he played a constant quarter-tone flat we won an inter-house competition. The Eton masters were too often heirs of the nineteenth century – the head of the science school had been there in my father's time, thirty years before. We were taught to turn Christina Rossetti into Greek iambics, a process which amounted to hemming together a succession of 'poetic' tags lifted to suit the scansion from a textbook. We heard a great deal about the age of Walpole – the phrase 'Peace, Retrenchment and Reform' was etched on my mind for ever as we marched back and forth across the same historical territory. We read Daudet's *Lettres de mon Moulin* laboriously: we owned, and used, a slide rule; once I made a crystal, and often I weighed small objects in water, but that was the extent of our scientific training. The only master I remember as a natural stimulator was George Lyttelton, who did more than make us learn 'Lycidas' by heart: he communicated a delight in writing and reading. And there was also the slightly cracked figure of

Arthur Goodhart, who could be trapped into abstruse predica-
ments and pronouncements by his ruthless class. 'Oh sir,' we
might say, 'can you explain cross-rhythm to us?' Goodhart was
an accomplished musician, and he responded at once. 'It is like
this. With my right hand I go one two one two; with my left, one
two three, one two three.' And loudly he beat the desk. 'At the
same time, with my foot I go one two three four five. Just listen,
boys.' And he set up a racket which had the untamed vigour of
epilepsy and deafened the class-rooms on either side. Or he
could be persuaded into saying things like, 'I might say yes, and
I might say no, and I might say nothing at all.' And, 'Certain
country gentleman know their Horace extremely well.' I liked
Goodhart very much. The moral tone of his house was deplor-
able, the pleasure-promoting devices of his pupils endless, and
I sadly regretted that I was responsible not to him but to the
austerer Mr Whitworth.

But under the Eton system, which gave one a room to oneself
from the very first day, one did make friends. In my own house
there was Graham Eyres-Monsell, an excellent musician, and
an improbable son for the Conservative Chief Whip, since he
early developed the art of rejecting unnecessary ties of thought-
less friendship and devoted himself whole-heartedly and generously to a very few chosen. There was Ian Akers-Douglas, a
superb games-player and a charmer almost as accomplished as
our contemporary Edward Underdown, who later played in
several Noël Coward successes but who survives in my memory
more vividly as a small boy in tears on weekly Sunday walks
along the river bank, because his family money had suddenly
vanished and his Norfolk home was being sold.

Beyond the resources of my house was Peter Watson, later
the financial force behind Cyril Connolly's *Horizon*, a notable
collector of pictures, and a slow-speaking, irresistibly beguiling
young man whose face was equally poised between the prince
and the frog. He was, from fourteen or so onwards, one of the
most sophisticated beings I ever knew: rich, funny, and wise
enough to abandon totally an early preoccupation with 'grand'
people, whose expenses he gladly underwrote for a time, in
exchange for a lively support of the better young painters of the
day. Yet I remember him, at the age of sixteen or so, slipping
me a note one morning which invited me to visit his room

between schools, leading me mysteriously to his bookcase, thrusting a hand behind the Latin dictionaries and extracting a little bottle, which he unscrewed in ecstasy, murmuring, 'Smell this: it is called *Quelques Fleurs*.'

There was Hamish St Clair Erskine, perhaps my closest friend, who had not been allowed by his father to accept a scholarship because he was not in financial need of it, and whose excellent brain, uncudgelled, began to atrophy at fifteen, so that the rest of his life was lived entirely on personal charm – a quality which may suggest, but not engender, happiness for the owner. There was Jim Lees-Milne, later an excellent writer and a lynch-pin of the National Trust; David Herbert, who was the despair of serious people and the delight of countless well-wishers; and a few good brains, usually in College like A. J. Ayer, John Carter, later a distinguished bibliophile, Roger Mynors, Roger Pettiward. There was also a youth disparagingly referred to as 'your friend Pinhead' by my father. John Morgan, later sixth Lord Tredegar, was indeed a rather silly boy, who had a sister Avis, and a father not subject like mine to occasional silences, but, out of rancour, silent round the clock. He used to invite John and myself to an occasional luncheon at the Orleans Club, a benignly fusty building in King Street, where one was offered delicacies like roast swan and peacock. Uncle Freddy, as I called him – he was in reality a very remote cousin – sat looking miserable while John prattled away; his misery was said to be due to the misconduct, and indeed disappearance, of his wife. It must have been her legacy that Avis looked like a tart, for Uncle Freddy might have been painted by El Greco; but her manner of life belied her appearance, and her company delighted me. Uncle Freddy had an elderly mistress, of whom Avis was fond, and so, between her hands and those of Miss Bassett-Boot, I soon fell with delight into dubious company.

Miss Bassett-Boot was small and pneumatic, with a head of marmalade curls and a bow-shaped mouth set in a face of snowy whiteness. She excelled at charades and at amateur theatrical ventures, such as scenes from Flecker's *Hassan*, run through in her Buckingham Gate drawing-room. We spent happy hours in Liberty's, in search of coruscating tissues for Turkish trousers, of jade pendants and gold lamé shoes, against

29

the day when she would assemble her group for a single performance, a group composed of a few similar ladies, a handful of elderly – to me: they must have been fully thirty-five – Italian counts of doubtful origin; and a few adolescents dazed by the incense-burner, the scraps of batik, and the modern Meissen shepherdesses perched on small tables touched up with gold radiator paint.

Uncle Freddy never came, and from my parents the mere existence of this society had to be hidden. But there was one absentee who interested me most deeply, after my father one day corralled me into his library and said, 'You are old enough to know that there exists a man named Evan Morgan. He is a first cousin of your friend Pinhead. And I tell you here and now that should you ever find yourself in the same room you are to leave immediately.'

This spurred me to pester John with requests to meet his cousin Evan, a meeting difficult to achieve because, as I later found, Evan shared my father's view of poor Pinhead. Nor could I extract from my father any reason for his interdict. He would tell me one day, he said, one day when I was older. Which suggested to me some link between Evan Morgan and an ageing gentleman I had seen one day on Lewes railway platform, where I was standing, aged twelve or so, with my parents and our host, Lord Monk Bretton. The ageing gentleman approached Monk Bretton and extended a hand, which was rejected. He murmured something, and received no reply, merely the stateliest of nods. He moved away. And later I wondered out loud to my father why our host, usually the kindest and politest of men, had rebuffed someone so sternly. Again I was told that one day I should learn why. For the time I had to be content with the information, 'His name is Lord Alfred Douglas.' 'But surely he lives in a Monk Bretton house,' I said. 'Why do you lease a house to someone if you are going to cut him in public?' 'You know nothing about it,' said papa, quite rightly. 'Now we shall talk of something else.'

When eventually I did meet Evan, with his cousin Avis, I was agog. Evan was at that time in his thirties. He was tall and very thin, with odd disarticulated movements, as if preparing to spread wings in flight. His nose was magnificently jutting, the skin stretched tight over an angle as if it had been broken; his

30

complexion was a little hectic – as a young man he had been tubercular and as an older one brandy did not help. His voice had a lilt to it, and his speech was often broken by a snort as he took another pinch of snuff. He appeared utterly confident, utterly relaxed, distant in a Firbankian way, but very evidently a man of vivid caprice and Arlecchino-like fantasy.

We took to one another at once, and until he died in 1949 I had no reason to be other than grateful to him for as much affection as his leprechaun character would bestow on a friend. Evan's misfortune was to have been born with far too much money, too little health, and no practical sense at all. His gifts were manifold. As only son to the chairman of the Conservative party, he had an easy entry into politics, and indeed was at twenty-four private secretary to the Minister of Labour. He stood for Parliament, but for Limehouse, in which borough his father was unfortunately a notable slum landlord; he drew, he wrote, he played the piano with facility; he was funny, and kind, and odd. For instance, he had an extraordinary power over birds. When he called 'Rosa, Rosa' across the lake at Tredegar, Rosa, a duck, came skimming out of the reeds. And in the cages at the Zoo, of which he was a Fellow, birds came crowding round him like spinsters round a popular preacher. He boxed with his kangaroos, he allowed himself to be teased by a formidable macaw named Blue Boy, which liked to bestow hammer blows at great speed between his toes, bare in the bathroom. And at Tredegar he summed up a disordered life by giving, week after week, vast and chaotic house parties. You might find, among thirty guests, Mrs Rosa Lewis of the Cavendish Hotel, the King of Greece, Yeats, the Metropolitan of Thyatira, a Berlin hustler, Princess Arthur of Connaught, C. K. Ogden, who helped to invent Basic English, a dog-breeding baroness from Hamburg, and so on and so on, while two distracted secretaries, Captain Weir and 'Mother S', somehow managed to make practical sense of what looked on the surface like another department of the Zoo.

What made Evan hard to know was his subjective view of the truth. Stories of egregious improbability turned out to be true; some likely tale was utterly false. Before he inherited Tredegar, he lived in a spacious Queen's Gate flat, in which he entertained the likes of Aldous Huxley, Nancy Cunard and Geoffrey

31

Scott, heady fellow guests for a teenager. There one night, among a small group which included Tallulah Bankhead in the first year of her fame, I sat over a cocktail or two until Evan invited us all to dine at Boulestin's, a restaurant he had lately financed. In the hall, as we left, there lay a note on a tray. He opened it, and blenched, rang the bell, and a footman appeared. 'When did this come?' he asked. 'An hour ago, sir.' Evan turned to us dramatically. 'This may have altered the course of history. It is a summons from the Prince of Wales to go at once to York House.' 'Well, go,' we said. 'Too late,' he replied, and sternly admonished the footman for not bringing the note at once to his notice.

After dinner, we were asked back for a nightcap. The footman, in indignation, had left the note where it lay and Evan picked it up idly and read it, as though for the first time. 'Really, Asprey's are becoming impossible,' he said. 'They send the bill before they deliver the goods.'

At such moments, his intention was not, I think, to deceive. It was merely that his inventive nature suggested to him a scenario which it was irresistible to act out. Instead of creating the poem or the picture of which he was capable, he used his gift to create an imaginary chapter of life for himself.

He also inherited his mother's eccentricity. Among her ways of showing it was her habit of taking, in hotels, the rooms above, below and on either side of her own. For she detested noise – which was why in her large house in Grosvenor Square she confined her existence to a ground-floor cloakroom without windows. Each spring she would make a sortie, in order to build a bird's nest so accurately derived from nature that it might have deceived any tenant, thrush, lark, or linnet, according to the year.

She lived apart from her husband, who preferred his vast steam yacht, *Liberty*, to the cloakroom, and various ladies to 'Aunt Cassie'. Their only daughter drowned herself, after a chaotic start in life, and Evan was severely frowned on by the one parent who could muster a frown. Instead, he was given an ultimatum: he must marry and produce an heir. Or else. And so, among my adolescent memories, is one of the Brompton Oratory – for Evan was a Papal Chamberlain of the Cloak and Sword – filled for his marriage to Lois Sturt, a most unwilling bride whose long affair with the Lord Pembroke of the day had been broken off when her lover decided to return to his wife, leaving her deeply unhappy. But the unhappiness of a broken love affair was as nothing to the unhappiness of the life she and Evan attempted to share, of which a single example can serve.

They lived for a time in St James's Place, and there one evening Evan invited Yeats to dine. I was brought in, and three or four more, so as to compose what was planned as a peaceful evening of talk. Unfortunately, husband and wife were already in remote communication, and Lois chose the same occasion to invite some of her racing friends – of the Silver Ring variety – and the secretary of the Zoo aquarium, for whom she felt a certain tenderness. Two totally different groups thus sat down in one dining room, and Yeats, who was accustomed to deference, was not pleased.

He was even less so by the end of the evening. Evan, as often when uneasy, treated the brandy like tap-water, and then, when the men were alone in the dining-room, rose to make a speech. It rambled, but cohered round an ironic peroration. 'I think,' he said, 'that we must congratulate Mr Boulanger. Thanks to his friendship with my wife, he can live in my houses as much as he likes, he can eat excellent food at my table, he can use my cars and my chauffeur. But I have to draw the line when he gives my wife the drugs prescribed for his fish.'

Hearing a voice drone on, Lois had crept downstairs, and was by the door, listening. At these words, she flung the doors open – she had her tigerish side – and pointed dramatically round the room. 'Leave the house,' she cried. 'All of you.' And herself left for the Ritz. But not before I had watched Yeats, stately as ever and in evident wonderment, being led by Godfrey Winn – then a very young and gossipy journalist – to the safety of the open air.

The 1920s were a good period for eccentrics. Self-expression was the note of the day; the rich had more money than ever before, and less inhibitions about what to express. Evelyn Waugh's *Decline and Fall* and *Vile Bodies* have been taken as satirical fantasies, but they describe a real manner of life with total accuracy. In those years I saw a good deal of another cousin, Elizabeth Ponsonby, who exemplified her period perfectly. The waste of time which took place was prodigious. One was always, in the silly world I moved in at the age of seventeen, dressing up for a party; indeed, one travelled with a dinner jacket and a *matelot*'s uniform, which we had found out to be the quickest and simplest form of fancy dress. Night after night, there was Elizabeth, often starting the evening with half a dozen of our friends in the Grosvenor Square house of the Arthur Bendirs (whose beautiful and silent daughter Babe Bosdari – much photographed by Cecil Beaton – shook our cocktails and helped us zip up our disguises) before we went on to Florence de Peña, or Gracie Ansell, or whoever was the hostess of an evening which invariably took in a stop at the Café Anglais, where Rex Evans sang at the piano, and an eventual eclipse at an unassuming nightclub behind Piccadilly Circle, the Blue Lantern.

Was this life totally idiotic? Not so. I am speaking of the middle 1920s, a decade which saw the sudden ascent of a new phase in British life. Not so long before, my grandmother would walk me up Box Hill in order to see the house of a great man, George Meredith; or she would insist on my going with her to tea with Lady Randolph Churchill, in order to acquaint myself with a one-time beauty still labelled 'dangerous'. Through an Eton friend, Angus Malcolm, I had the run of a pillared house in Onslow Square, decorated in apricot shades which I found intoxicating; and there, on deep silken chairs, I found Angus's mother, whom I thought – rightly – not only wonderful to look at but the possessor of a speaking voice even silkier than her chairs. There, too, though not often, might be *her* mother, the Jersey Lily, who seemed to me much less interesting. Or there was Mrs Gordon Woodhouse, the harpsichordist, taking us on the river at the Oxford and Cambridge Boat Race; and always the huge, seemly procession of great aunts and cousins. But these reflected the past, the world of Before-the-War. And what was exciting about the present at that time was that it had broken away from Before the War; to embrace the Russian Ballet, the music of Stravinsky, the harlequins of Picasso, Braque's guitars, the sidecar cocktail, the Bugatti car, the Sitwells, T. S. Eliot's *The Waste Land*, Noël Coward's *The Vortex* and Wyndham Lewis's *Blast*, Florence Mills, Lytton Strachey: a choice of scintillating appearances which have been written about far too often, but which had in common a quality which gave pleasure to my contemporaries – they all annoyed the generation of Before-the-War.

In the trough of such riches, the young acolyte like myself all but drowned. I had spent a good deal of time in the school library at Eton, at first because it contained English translations of Plato, Tacitus, Aeschylus, and the other classical writers whose texts I found especially hard to unpick – for at Eton in the Twenties it was the unpicking which mattered, not the synthesis of lilt and verbal music and meaning. Later I found the English Victorians, especially the poets, and spent happy afternoons in a pale light, breathing a smell of suede and morocco in the Library Gallery. I had written prose and verse of a sort ever since I could transcend the murky world of pothooks and hangers; by the time I was sixteen I worried my father by choosing the five tree-calf-bound volumes of Eddie Marsh's *Georgian Poetry* for a school prize, because he feared they might affect for the worse my little talent. I deduced that at first he suspected Marsh of compiling an eighteenth-century anthology, and my father well knew that the eighteenth century was no good. Later, when he discovered the George in question to be George the Fifth, he became even warier. Why, when Keats and Shelley were available, waste time on writers who could be lumped together with the cacophonous Debussy and the incompetent post-Impressionists, as 'modern'? My father was a Meissonier man: he liked pictures of quaffing cardinals only a little less; he had not opened Keats or Shelley in the twentieth century, and he thought them both foolish fellows at best. But at least they were not modern.

Mama was a little more adventurous. She liked, and noted, pretty contemporary poems such as William Kerr's beginning

> Chestnut candles are lit again
> For the dead that died in spring

while I was immersing myself in *Wheels* and dreaming of Dada. Not only did I experience again the Darien feeling – most young aesthetes, I believe, do that – in relation to poetry, but I found a Pacific to stare at in music, in painting, in religion, for the chief joy in being young is that one knows nothing of the way ahead but stumbles on, dazzled by hope, and never satiated by experience. My parents were alternately perplexed, enchanted, and anxious about this. Why was I so hopeless at rabbiting, putting, taking a half-volley on the tennis court? Why did I look downcast when they sent me out for a single with my teen-age cousin Bobby, whose tennis was of Wimbledon standard, so that he never moved his feet on one side of the net, while I ran about like a chicken in traffic on the other? They thought of riding, set me bareback on a pony and thwacked it into a trot. I saw the branch coming, ducked backwards instead of forwards, and was swept painfully to the ground. They thought of swimming, and, in 1915 or so, aged six, I was taken by my father, on a week's leave from the Front, to the Bath Club. 'Climb up that ladder,' he ordered, 'and slide down the chute. You'll find you can swim.' I climbed up, and, prudently, down. 'Do as I say,' he told me, and up I went, looking down on the water from what seemed to me an extravagant height. I climbed down once more. After the third try I was told coldly to go and dress; and, once I reached home, my elders were unanimous. 'You've ruined Daddy's leave,' they said: a verdict only to be understood in its full horror by those who knew a little of the woes inflicted by the Battle of Mametz Wood.

I kept my pleasures to myself, therefore, for fear of disapproval or the wrong encouragement. It was abhorrent to me when my mother, meaning well, said to a guest, 'Come into the next room, and we'll leave the door open, and perhaps Alan will play for us.' This was a veiled request that I should improvise on the piano, which I did with pointless fluency, bright with brave modulations, facile arpeggios and final chords in triplets of the kind Scriabin marks *ffff giobilosco*. My happy moments were when I was alone in the country drawing-room of one of our rented summer houses, playing Schumann's *Kinderszenen* while the smell of mown grass and lilac crept in at the window, and I caught brightly at the wonderful childish moment of power: 'I *can* play this; I am tense with pleasure at the thought of life stretching ahead in sunlight,' mixed with the tiny concrete pleasure of the moment – a visit to the Silent Pool at Shere, pretending my bicycle on the garden paths was a Mercedes, showing off to my grandmother's friends when they came to tea.

This diffused sense of happiness lasted all through my school days, largely because life was so ordered and predictable. At the time this vexed me: I hoped for surprises which never came. But, in retrospect, I see much good in an existence where love, kindness, generosity can be taken for granted, where it was unthinkable to be shouted at or hit – my father's snorts and silences stopped far short of harshness – and where the maintenance of such conventions as church on Sunday, temperance in all things, and good manners, was never questioned. Years later, Osbert Sitwell, who led a much less fortunate childhood than I, said to me that the great thing about such an upbringing was that it had been a wonderful rest, in preparation for the stresses of growing up. And it was.

Much that then seemed normal would be thought odd today. My father, recalling his Welsh childhood, recommended special reading for Sundays, and gave me annuals of Sabbath literature from his own nursery. Cards were not allowed on Sundays, and neither horse nor car could be used. Church, in London, meant the Guards Chapel in Wellington Barracks, and for this my father put on a tail-coat, a white waistcoat under a black one, and a top-hat. In the country, church usually meant Evensong, and I still see the motes of dust in the slant beams of a setting sun, still welcome the shortness of the 'Nunc Dimittis', and hear the richly melancholy threefold sway of 'The Day Thou Givest, Lord, is Ended' sung by a black-cassocked choir in some Butterfield chancel.

Secular matters might seem no less strange. It was not until the war of 1939 that my father offered anybody a cocktail, although he nourished the foolish idea that it was unfamiliarity which made young people drink, so that from the time I was allowed into the dining room at all I was offered whatever was given to the grown-ups, from sherry to port and brandy, all of which I swigged down with relish. To carve a ham in any house but one's own was an appalling solecism. Only the host or the butler could attempt this, and I remember on a visit to Kedleston, when I was a very young man, noticing one of my contemporaries cut himself a slice of ham at breakfast. Not only I, but our host, noticed, and the culprit was put on the eleven o'clock train. Then there was the question of reversing on the dance floor. My Egeria, Lady Malcolm, told me that Mrs Langtry, her mother, used to haul her off the floor if her partner reversed during the waltz, and even in my time parents gave warning to their children on this grave matter.

Such situations arose because in the 1920s England was still a club within a constituency. The members of the club stood apart. They made their own rules, they blackballed so many candidates that the vast majority of their fellow-constituents throughout the Empire never troubled to propose themselves for election at all. The members of the club banded together in closely-defined enclosures. We in Buckingham Palace Gardens, for instance, were at the extreme edge of one. Beyond us, from Eccleston Square to the Thames, was a closed world. 'The poor Berties,' people would sigh, 'live across the Bridge.' And when my Grey cousins moved to a beautiful Nash house in Regent's Park they were greatly pitied. 'The Greys,' people said, 'now have to live among lodgings North of the Park.' Most of Kensington counted as outer darkness. When, long before, my great aunt Sybil had died of puerperal fever, it was silently put down to living in the Cromwell Road. As to those parts of London to which people now expensively flock, Canonbury, Highgate, Clapham, Battersea, Barnes, they did not, for club members, even exist. I remember John Betjeman once asking the old Duchess of Devonshire, not long before she died, to what use their owners had put the splendid houses strung out along the Great West Road – Chiswick House, Syon, Osterley, Gunnersbury, among them. 'We used to drive out to our villas for breakfast,' he was told, 'after a ball.'

My generation was perhaps the first to condemn these attitudes out of hand, although individuals like Lady Diana Cooper had already planted the seeds of successful rebellion. We aspired to live in Bloomsbury attics or Chelsea cellars. But we were ruthlessly self-serving. Few of us had any money of our own, but we knew where money could be found, and we expected to be paid for. London and the countryside were equally full of large and hospitable houses, the hostesses of which needed the young to highlight their entertainments. Boredom was on the way out, often, alas, taking with it good manners. A formidable succession of great ladies, from Lady Desborough to Lady Cunard, from Lady Ottoline Morrell to Lady Wimborne, made it desirable to flash through the world like a firework, often leaving a smell of burning behind. An impish intelligence was the thing to aim at – not a solid, and certainly not a virtuous, intelligence. Henry James would have cut a far smaller swathe ten years after his death than in the year before the war. And those who were determined to set a standard were much likelier to adopt the standard of Bloomsbury or the Sitwells than of what struck my generation as Georgian stuffiness.

Looking back, it is astonishing how much we managed to do on so very little money. While I was at Eton I had no fixed allowance at all. I could charge my clothes and railway fares to an account which my father always paid after a scene, so that I soon associated shopping with rebuke but also with the confident feeling that somehow the matter would be dealt with. When I went to Oxford I was given an allowance of four hundred pounds a year, with no clear definition of what this was to cover, so that it all went immediately as petty cash. But I managed to buy Picasso lithographs at Zwemmers for a fiver apiece, and to take taxis rather than the recommended bus. Occasionally I asked someone to luncheon at the Berkeley – in those days an 8/6 luncheon – but there I always signed the bill until Ferraro, the benevolent guardian of the restaurant, who played a great part in the lives of my contemporaries, took me aside one day and said, 'I don't mind your signing the bill, because I know it will be paid in the end. But I must warn you that no bill is so depressing as one for food eaten a year before. Remember this when you grow up.'

IV

In 1926, at the end of the summer, I obtained my release. I was allowed to leave Eton, spend an autumn in Touraine – at that time it was planned for me that I might hope to be a diplomat – and go to Magdalen College, Oxford, the following year.

At seventeen, I had slid, rather than tumbled, into a schizoid state. On the one hand I wanted to be with new friends, such as the Morgans and Miss Bassett-Boot; on the other I had a childish impulse to cling to what was safe. Twelve years later I read with instant understanding Cyril Connolly's *Enemies of Promise* and recognized a more intelligent version of my own uncertainties. Of course: the one hope for people like Cyril and me was to conquer by cunning and by an amoeba-like ability to encyst and divide, rejecting the moribund part of a tiny personality, and building afresh on the ability to survive. I should never, I knew, be much like the schoolboy heroes who surrounded me. I should never fit easily into the slots provided for me by inheritance or environment. I foresaw that I should have to make my way in the world, since I could not retire into country acres and a little income, like another unambitious Robert Trevelyan, turning out unread poems and getting by as an appealing eccentric. I had no reliable moral scruples, but I had neither the looks nor the courage nor the will to float through life as a charmer – a condition which, even fifty years ago, required a few safe thousands a year for comfort. So one day I was a turbaned slave in Miss Bassett-Boot's oriental parlour, and the next I was a very well brought-up, clean-collared schoolboy, glad to be approved and invited by Monty

James the Provost, and by a troop of old gentlemen in the orbit of Eton; among whom H. E. Luxmoore was for long chief.

Luxmoore had been a famous housemaster, who, now in his eighties, had retired to a charming house on Baldwin's Shore, run for him by a sister. He had come to teach at Eton in the 1860s and never left. An ardent disciple of Morris and Ruskin, he had also been the Provost's tutor, and his active life had been consistently devoted to the good and the beautiful, as sought by Matthew Arnold and by Wordsworth's 'Plain Living and High Thinking'. He was himself, perhaps, the most beautiful old man I have ever seen, with long white locks curled up behind his ears and a great beaked nose. His voice was dark and resonant – a note on the 64-foot organ pipe – and to see him in the lovely island garden he had created – a garden which bore an appropriate inscription over the gate, *Et Amicorum* – was to be carried back half a century to an age of certainties and graces already half effaced by the attrition of the times. He liked me, often asked me to breakfast, encouraged me to walk in his garden and to swim in his stream. Alas, little by little the world of Miss Bassett-Boot took over. I went less often, and finally neglected him entirely: a desertion which earned me a letter that still makes me repentant – for he was an exceptional letter-writer, some of whose exquisitely scripted pages were privately printed after his death. They deserve to be exhumed.

He was also the moving spirit of the Shakespeare Society, and some of us were regularly convened to munch sponge-cake, drink coffee, and read aloud to him. This, for some reason, annoyed equally ancient colleague, Henry Broadbent, who, by contrast to Luxmoore's aquiline approach to life, resembled an arthritic cock-sparrow. One day we were privileged to hear the organ-note of the one, slow and splendid, set against the squawk of the other, thus:

Broadbent. Do you know what day it is today?
Luxmoore. I am not aware of anything remarkable about the day.
Broadbent. And you a Shakespearian. It is Crispin's Day.
Luxmoore, rumbling. You need not tell me what I know, Mr Broadbent.
Broadbent, cackling. Well, it isn't.

I was also taken up by the Lower Master, A. B. Ramsay, later Master of Magdalene College, Cambridge. He became aware of me because I was captain of the Lower Chapel Choir, an office I filled with unction in spite of a voice so small that my immediate neighbour in the choir stalls could never tell whether I was singing or no. Ramsay was a foolish old fellow, but not stupid. He made us speak only Latin in his classroom, and constantly interjected warnings, such as 'Cave virgas, cave ferulam,' uttered in the richest Italian manner. His dame – as the house matron is called at Eton – matched him admirably in foolishness, and was long remembered for breaking a silence at boys' dinner by remarking suddenly and primly, 'We ladies are always scrupulously clean.' If foolish, she was less eccentric than another dame, Lady Georgina Legge, who was reported before my time to have worn for choice pea-green football boots.

Then there was the Vice-Provost, Hugh MacNaughton, whose sensibility, we were told, was so acute that, whenever the word 'little' was spoken in his presence, he wiped away a tear. And, not least, there was John Christie, later founder of the Glyndebourne opera, but in my time a rather reluctant master, who used to cover the short distance from his house to his classroom in an enormous open car which he merely put into reverse when the time came to return home.

In one's last year at Eton one was accepted by all or most of these, and one had better chances of being taken out of a school atmosphere into houses and gardens which recalled home. I could never see a maid shaking out a mat, or a master mowing his lawn, or glimpse through some low window a tweedy wife buttering a scone, without longing to join a domesticity which might efface for ever the world of linoleum, soggy football fields, ink splashes on varnished deal desks, and clattering dinner-bells. I could, though, grasp at moments of oblivion: in the house of Hamish Erskine's disreputable aunt, Lady Angela Forbes; on some riverside terrace at Henley during the regatta; drinking iced coffee at Lord's in days when the Eton and Harrow match was still an event, complete with coaches and pale blue carnations and a Jack Buchanan musical to top it all off.

Finally came the day of release. I should by rights have gone to camp with the Officer Training Corps, but I pled successfully for leave, saying I was about to be sent away to learn French and needed a holiday. Avis Morgan was shortly to marry my friend Peter, the owner of the 45 h.p. Renault which had nearly collided with m'tutor some months before, and he consented to drive me in it to London. I have said that the car was enormous and made of mahogany. It happened that we left at precisely the moment the corps was marching along Eton High Street towards the railway station. Peter, who had not carried away happy recollections of his own schooldays, opened the cut-out, which produced a roar calculated to drown the band, if not break a window; and so we drove slowly by my exasperated soldier friends, giving them a deafening farewell, which prompted m'tutor to write to my father, 'I have known Alan behave badly before, but I didn't know he had it in him to behave quite so badly.'

I have written elsewhere of the idyllic months which followed. An elderly French doctor and his wife, childless and regretting their childlessness, took me in. They lived at Montbazon, in Touraine, and their house, like Chenonceaux, was built across the river bridge-like, so that the doctor, always clad in shawl and beret, could cast a line without leaving his bedroom. The household consisted of Ernestine, who brought me my morning chocolate, an invisible cook, and a youth who sawed wood, swabbed floors, and cleaned the two dogs, Muddy (so called because he had been a mud-caked foundling) and Tin Tin.

I have never been happier than in that late summer and autumn of 1926. The days, more than fifty years later, still glow with perpetual sunlight. The River Indre, on which I sculled a clumsy boat, Muddy and Tin Tin running beside, was much sweeter to me than the Thames. A pleasant girl, with that *léger duvet* on her upper lip which French novelists find irresistible, came to play tennis with me on a dusty court, and sometimes Madame Pépin organized a small hop round the tuneless upright piano on which she encouraged me to play her Granados's dances. She had run a little to fat, and wore a very heavy make-up, violet both in colour and scent. When the doctor gallantly lit her cigarette, she usually contrived to blow out the match, upon which he used to complain, '*Pauvre chérie, vous soufflez par le nez.*'

43

The great moment in their week was if we were asked to dine by 'Monsieur Dudley', a mysterious American who was restoring, almost single-handed, the ruined château above Montbazon. The Pépins looked on Dudley as a latter-day Heathcliff. He had been wounded in the war, trepanned, and exiled from America following a divorce the details of which were never clear but always dramatic. There was also a Russian lady, a Mademoiselle Narishkin, in the picture, whom later he married. Meanwhile he dressed as a peasant and enjoyed being thought *difficile*, a role for which he had exactly the right darkling appearance. We used to sit up late, drinking Vouvray when the Pépins stayed at home, and talking about sex, of which I had my first experience in Tours with a girl out of Maupassant, named Mauricette. For years I kept her card, hand-written in the kind of purple ink full of hairs chiefly found in French post-offices; much the same colour as the disinfectant which she poured into a bidet for me after our brief and unresponsive passage.

Day after day the sun shone. Angus Malcolm, preparing the career which led him to an eventual embassy, was learning French on the other side of Tours, and we bicycled from château to château. Or I took a minute local train from the little station of Esvres and explored the countryside by myself. Sometimes grand neighbours invited us for a night. There were the Carvallos at Villandry, the Brissacs, the Stanislas de Castellanes at Rochecotte. I remember arriving at the station at Angers on the way to Brissac, and being disconcerted by finding an immense coronetted yellow coupé for myself, and a brake for my luggage, which consisted of a single shabby bag. I remember, too, arriving at the house after dark and being taken straight to my room to change for dinner by a footman who waited to escort me through cavernous passages to a *salle de gardes* with figures in armour on horseback down the centre and a large family group of unknowns round a fire at the far end. Nobody moved, and I had to guess which was my hostess. This was the beginning of what turned out to be a visit of several days, in the course of which my hostess took me out hunting in a dog-cart – a test far more alarming than any whimsical hunter might have provided.

It is a wonderful thing to be young and to be aware of

happiness. Every day I knew this awareness, the more easily because Montbazon was still an unspoiled village, the country round was still idyllic, and Tours itself had not been defaced by German bombardment and wretched rebuilding: the France of Balzac's *Lys dans la Vallée* was almost unchanged; and in the slow rhythm of our days there was no interruption more disturbing than a visit to Niepçeron, the *patissier*, with Madame Pépin, or a round of his patients in the doctor's small boxy Citroën.

One day they asked me if I were a Catholic, and, lying, I said yes, of course. They appeared relieved, and I was amazed that I had troubled to lie. But a year or two earlier, during one of the icy Augusts I used to spend at Filey in Yorkshire, climbing along the Brig in driving rain, or (surreptitiously) escaping into the public lavatory on the sea-front to read immense *graffiti*, and wonder what on earth they were about in terms of real living, I had wandered into the little Catholic church, and suddenly had the sensation of discovering at once a question and an answer. I bought some pamphlets and later a rosary of blue beads, and before going back to Eton extended my explorations to Westminster Cathedral. In my ignorance, I supposed that one could enter a building a Protestant and leave it a Catholic, so I took my courage in my hand and rang the clergy-house bell. A priest, who named himself as Father Dove, came out, and I told him my wish. 'Have you spoken to your parents?' he asked. I said, 'Of course not.' He took me along a corridor into a library, and sternly sat me down. His verdict was that I must put my thoughts in order, and that the most he could do was to pray for me. It was some twenty-five years before his prayer was answered. But I have always been grateful for his good sense, and, from that day, never doubted that I should one day carry out an intention only delayed because of the pain I presumed it would cause my parents.

Also at Filey I caused them pain in an unwitting fashion. The anniversary of their wedding was due, and I decided to give my father a book, Michael Arlen's *The Green Hat*, which had received an outburst of praise in the Sunday papers. I had not read it, and knew nothing of it beyond the reviews, but I walked off to W. H. Smith, bought a copy and presented it.

Nothing happened for a day or two. Then, opening the door

of his smoking-room – he always had a smoking-room even in a hired house – he beckoned me in. 'Would you like to know what I think of your present?' he asked. I glowed, expecting praise. He picked up the book, advanced on the lit grate – at Filey in August one needs a fire – hurled it on the flames and held it down with the poker. 'I think *that* of it,' he said, pressing on the poker as though the book might escape him.

It did escape him. A book held down by a poker does not burn. For a minute or two he stood in an attitude of conscious rectitude, like St George above the Dragon, then picked the poor object out with a pair of tongs. It was barely singed.

Such an event at Montbazon would have been unthinkable. There all was sunlight, water lapping the reeds, hot chocolate, Muddy yawning at Tin Tin, and Madame Pépin eagerly reporting tiny pieces of gossip about our own grand neighbour, the Comtesse de la Villétreux, at Couzières. So delicious was the autumn of 1926 that I went back for a second visit the following spring, when I found myself sharing the pleasures of the house with an Eton contemporary, Robin Darwin, later a successful painter and Principal of the Royal College of Art.

Then, after some tedious months of illness, came Oxford. Part of the illness was an attack of iritis, so that for many weeks I went about with a patch on one eye – a circumstance which, for want of something better, made me conspicuous among the first-year men at Magdalen, some of whom went so far as to make way for me in the darker stretches of the cloisters.

In those days one spent a few days in College sitting for an entrance exam, and while I did so I had a curious experience. One of my uncles commanded the Officer Training Corps and had leased a house opposite Tom Tower on St Aldate's, said to be part of Cardinal Wolsey's palace. The owner had leased it on condition that he might use two rooms approached by a separate staircase should he have reason to be in Oxford during my uncle's tenancy. These rooms I was given during my stay. They comprised a panelled sitting-room, with a bedroom beyond it, only to be reached through a communicating door.

I went to bed early, with my Latin Grammar and other work books to occupy me. I heard my uncle and aunt come in from a dinner party and turned out the light with no thought in my head except of Tacitean syntax and Homeric aorists. Suddenly the room was icy cold and the darkness so hostile that I jumped out of bed and made for the communicating door. Once there, I became numbed with apprehension of something on the farther side, something that circled the room, always coming back to the door and pausing. I did not feel actively threatened, but I shrank back to bed and for the next hour read the only non-school book in the room, a once-famous anthology called *The Week End Book*. I read it through four or five times until, towards dawn, the cold and the fear vanished. I knew that whatever had been pacing by my door had gone away again.

That evening my mother telephoned to ask how my exams were passing off, and she asked me casually which bedroom I had been given. When I told her, she exclaimed. Had I had a bad night? For it happened that my father, the least psychic of men, had had precisely my experience in the same room a few weeks before. So my aunt was called and I was moved. Later enquiries brought out a story that not one but two wives of the owner had committed suicide in the sitting-room.

My eventual rooms in the New Buildings of Magdalen were far from ghostly, and I settled into them with zeal. Oxford undergraduates in the 1920s lived in a variegated world of luxury and squalor. The luxury lay chiefly in the fact that we had space and privacy, the squalor in the plumbing – usually hundreds of yards from one's bedroom and only to be reached after icy stretches of arcade and garden path. The University generation immediately older than my own had set a high standard of living, moreover. We spoke with awe of Edward James's exotic rooms, of Harold Acton's life-style, of Brian Howard's unsuspected skill – perhaps courage would be a better noun – on horseback, of Harry Stavordale's free-spending, and John Sutro's wit: by comparison, we looked on ourselves as mouse-like and, at best, derivative, the spendthrift inheritors of a bright Silver Age.

I look back on my brief Oxford career with vexation, for during the all-but two terms which I survived I wasted my time recklessly. My tutor was an extremely dull man, brother to a clerical Eton housemaster, who made a name for himself by giving absurd commands to the Officer Training Corps on field-days: commands like 'Squad! Into the bushes . . . scatter!' I never once visited my tutor, I never went to a lecture, I relied on an occasion which never came my way – a week or two of intensive work just before an eventual examination. If I still look back on my Magdalen days as a period of less than total disaster, it is largely due to a chance encounter which took place one evening soon after my arrival.

I was sitting in my room, wrapped in a towelling cloak and reading, when the door was opened by a third-year man, unknown to me, who was making his rounds on behalf of some university activity or other. I was embarrassed at being discovered in what I knew to be a ridiculous garment, but my visitor sat down and began a conversation which lasted, off and on, for over fifty years. His name was Betjeman, he told me: John Betjeman. He had moved out of College to rooms on Headington Hill, and he owned a Morris-Cowley touring car, to which, as to its owner, I can never be grateful enough. For to them both I owe a number of eye-opening adventures – the discovery of small Georgian churches like Chislehampton, of eccentric houses like Sezincote, of Victorian splendours from Keble College to All Saints, Margaret Street. I owe him some familiarity with names such as Voysey, Baillie-Scott, Mackintosh, among designers, Shenstone, Prior, Allingham among poets, Fuseli and John Martin among painters, not to speak of their more obvious peers, Soane, Lutyens, Pope, Tennyson (then out of fashion), Blake, down to an obscure undergraduate poet still at Christ Church, Wystan Auden. For the enormous pleasure of having one's eyes opened by John Betjeman was that he could move his lens in an instant from the great to the rewarding minor: at twenty he was already a formidable expert on the second elevens of art and poetry, so that he used to burrow into Dodsley and the Della Cruscans in search of the even more obscure, and dig among the book barrows of the Farringdon Road for the occasional prize of a Landseer drawing at seven-and-sixpence, or a set of Findon's engravings to Byron.

That was later, in the vacation, and in years to come when Oxford was behind us both. Meantime, in that autumn and winter of 1927, we were part of a company which rejected any idea of work, but absorbed a good deal of useful experience, taking in the beauty of College gardens and friable stone façades, and learning if not what was in the curriculum at least a certain amount of grace.

One could give a luncheon party in one's rooms, which meant long consultations with an excellent chef. One day I found a cache of Imperial Tokay from the 1880s unnoticed and so sold by the Junior Common Room at five shillings a bottle. I bought several before my cache was also discovered by the authorities and hurriedly withdrawn from sale, in case some crowned head might one day be entertained by the President.

There were Eton friends about, such as Angus Malcolm, Hamish St Clair Erskine, Peter Watson and Graham Eyres-Monsell. There were new friends like Osbert Lancaster. We thought our luncheons a failure if they ended before cocktail time, leading to dinner at the George – for we avoided dining in hall as often as possible. And there were a few dons, such as Maurice Bowra, John Bryson and George Kolkhorst, in whose favour we presumed to bask. So much has been written of these by my contemporaries that I shall not echo their observations – perhaps the best of them are recorded in Osbert Lancaster's *With An Eye To The Future*.

In this life women, and especially Oxford women, played a very small part. We were proud if we found our invitations accepted by Elizabeth Harman or Anne Huth-Jackson, but in general we associated girls with London, and moved in a strictly masculine but not necessarily homo-erotic world. It was *chic* to be queer, rather as it was *chic* to know something about the twelve-tone scale and about Duchamp's 'Nude Descending a Staircase'. But not everybody wanted to be *chic*. I suspect that some of those who left copies of Gide and Crevel about their rooms were more interested in Charlus as a baron than as a sexual archetype.

Certainly the Oxford aesthetes of 1927 or so all possessed much the same books, even if they did not read them. We found Firbank extremely funny. We admired and imitated the Sitwells. Like Robert Byron, we were Byzantinists, with a special addiction to nineteenth-century Greece. We waited impatiently for each new Aldous Huxley, though loyal to a man to *Crome Yellow*. We liked the travel writings of D. H. Lawrence better than his novels. We chose Gide's *Faux-Monnayeurs* as the latest masterpiece and made a heroine of Gertrude Stein. But we knew almost nothing of American writing, which was said to be provincial and imitative, though of course T. S. Eliot and

49

Henry James had shown some redemptive sense in becoming British. The cult of things German had hardly begun. Both Scandinavia and imperial Russia looked like honourable but unreal civilizations, if a trifle old-fashioned. Ibsen had done his work, and Tolstoy too.

But we had little patience with the heirs of the nineteenth century, whether native or foreign, whatever the art they practised. Out with Kipling and Galsworthy, Bennett and Wells. Out with Wagner and Elgar. Out with Sargent and Watts, Puvis de Chavannes and the Pre-Raphaelites. Give us Southern Baroque Art, we asked, and *Les Mariés de la Tour Eiffel*, give us Satie and Bérard. We were utterly inconsistent. We admired El Greco and Delacroix because they were suddenly *chic*, although we rejected in them the sublime at which they aimed. We sought out the small, the rare, the sketch rather than the finished masterpiece. Even had we been offered a performance of *Les Troyens* we should, I fear, have preferred *Les Biches*. We were in many ways a silly generation, with the exception of a few stern spirits, such as Wystan Auden, Christopher Isherwood, Stephen Spender, who kept a little aloof and mixed their own blends of medicinal high spirits and rather governessy doctrine. Not that we were silly in the sense of being blinded by the ease of life as displayed by the British and American rich – a display more fruitfully rejected by Auden and his kind. By the end of the Twenties, most of us were coming to terms with an impending *Götterdämmerung*: it was only a matter of when and from which quarter the blow would fall.

We could faintly remember from experience the world of Before-the-War, and we perceived that that world had gone for ever. Our elders, having known it for longer, grown up in it and accepted it as perfectly natural and right, were usually more optimistic than we. They believed in the League of Nations, in the liberal values, in the perfectibility of man; they could not bear to be cut off from the nineteenth century by vulgar barriers such as Fascism, Nazism, Leninism, which is why they often denied the existence of such barriers and claimed one or other of them, according to their own inclinations, as useful props the fault of whose architects was merely to be a little vexatious at times.

We who came of age in the late Twenties, finding the

post-War world in fragments, clung to whatever offered a sense of order. It might be the world of G. E. Moore, as filtered through Bloomsbury; it might be the Catholic Church; it might be some disciplinary enterprise like money-making or sport. Or it might be the inversion of order, exemplified by Dada and Surrealism. Most people, admittedly, feel towards life as plain folk feel towards art: they do not think about it much, but they know what they like. Moreover, at twenty, very few people have reached a steady view of either this world or the next. So that in the general intellectual chaos of the age it was not odd if I and my contemporaries veered this way and that, often doing silly things and briefly adopting silly causes. It was already a tragedy that the manipulators of our society were imprisoned by the past, like bees in amber. Our leaders, Baldwin and Chamberlain, had been born before the Franco-Prussian War; they had always been on the winning side; they knew almost nothing at first hand of other countries than their own. Like their immediate subalterns they operated within the framework of an indomitable empire: how could they make any accurate assessment of a foreign enemy?

Young men of my age, by contrast, travelled. They learned languages. They took third class tickets on the cheap New-haven boat to Dieppe, and spent vacations in modest pensions in Berlin and Florence and Athens. Some, like George Orwell or Henry Yorke, took trouble to find out for themselves what absence of privilege really meant. We felt ourselves bottled up by our elders, and bored to extremity by their tales of Passchen-daele and Mametz Wood. And so part of our silliness was in sheer reaction against the repetition of abstracts like victory, patriotism, never-say-die endeavour. We preferred to make horrible cocktails – never the same two evenings running – of ingredients like Crême de Cacao, Parfait Amour, or Vieille Cure, for the delectation of Miss Bassett-Boot and her *beaux* before one of our interminable luncheons.

The last of these marked my downfall. Towards the end of my second term the blow had fallen. No bills were paid, no work was done. I had become uncomfortably conspicuous as a first-year man with an eye-patch who dined at the George – a bad sign – or at the Spread Eagle at Thame – a worse one – who offered champagne instead of beer, who figured in our university scandal-sheet, the *Cherwell*: in brief as an eighteen-year-old riding for a fall.

My father was sent for by the President, Sir Herbert Warren, a snobbish and antique party, only the third in line to hold his office over more than a century (the first, Dr Routh, had reigned in Magdalen for sixty-three years). We lunched together, and my father agreed to pay my bills; the President gated me – which meant being in college by nine nightly – until the end of term; and all was forgiven, but not before my father and I had undergone a painful walk round and round the gardens of Queen's College.

At this interval of time, my sympathies are with my father. He had no idea how to cope with me, his ambitions for me were exalted, he was himself so self-denying, so circumspect, that my activities were incomprehensible to him. On that day I only wanted him to go away, and all the time we talked I had no thought but fear that he would make me late for a dinner and a dance some miles out of Oxford, to which I had been asked and to which I meant to go.

At last he left. I put on my evening clothes, climbed out of a window – since I was gated I dared not be seen leaving – and drove off to my party. Some time after midnight, I prepared to reverse this procedure, and to walk through Christ Church Meadows, so as to escape observation. I was not, though, to know that the night before a face looking out of its window and admiring the moon had been shot at by a passer-by, presumably a drunk returning to Merton. The face had been outraged, and had reported the matter to its Dean, who had arranged for a policeman to patrol the walk. I was therefore arrested on the technical pretext that I was trespassing. In my folly I offered an insufficient sum to the policeman, who carried me off to his police-station, from which I was returned to my college a little before dawn.

The rest can be imagined. Not more than twelve hours earlier my father had settled my problems with the President, and already the eirenic atmosphere was shattered. After a series of disagreeable interviews I gave my last luncheon, after which the guests helped me pack, and on my mother's advice I moved into the Randolph Hotel, where I skulked for a few days, not daring to go out for fear of being picked up by the proctors. At last my mother telephoned to say that as things would get no better I might as well return home, rather than run up a hotel bill for others to pay. At which, Peter Watson, saying that I could not possibly leave Oxford on a third class one-way ticket, appeared with a Rolls-Royce and drove me to London, insisted on greeting my parents with an air of hearty geniality and left just before the storm broke.

The Rolls-Royce was the last straw. Had it been John Betjeman's Morris-Cowley my welcome might have been less blighting. I was told that I was unemployable, that I could not live off my father any longer notwithstanding, that I could never marry, never go to the colonies (which did not welcome wastrels): in brief, that there was no future for me at all, because, though I had only been rusticated for a term, I should certainly not return to Magdalen.

Safely alone on the street that afternoon, I ran into an older friend who told me I looked unhappy. I explained the case. 'You have only one thing to do,' he told me. 'J. C. Squire, editor of the *London Mercury*, wants an assistant. He is having his hair cut at this moment in the National Liberal Club.' I followed this advice and found a benevolent, mildly intoxicated old gentleman – at forty-five he seemed old to me – sitting in a barber's chair. By chance, he knew my name. I had won English verse prizes at Eton, and someone had sent him a poem of mine. He put a fatherly arm on my shoulder. I was to start work on Monday, unpaid, but with the title of assistant-editor and the assurance that, using the magazine as a springboard, I should soon be able to pick up a few cheques on Fleet Street.

V

A HAPPY PERIOD opened. I stayed at the *London Mercury* for three or four years, while Squire opened one door after another for me and for the handful of mostly red-headed young women who also 'helped' in the office – among them Joan Haslip the biographer, and Anne Huth-Jackson. My predecessor had been Moray McLaren, an ardent Scots nationalist, and Robert Herring, who had been there before him and later became editor of *Life and Letters*, also gave me much kindness. The office itself was one of the few pre-Great Fire buildings to survive on Fleet Street, and in it I shared a double desk with Squire. Our room was at the turn of a very steep stair, unlit, with a loose bannister just at the turning, and according to our assessment of visitors we either did or did not voice a warning. On rare occasions, after some rough talk, we showed the visitor out and waited tensely. There was likely to be a skitter, sometimes a crash, and always a furious oath. We were perhaps rather young for our age. The great moments of the magazine were not spent, however, in the office, but in the pub next door, the Temple Bar. It was not an attractive pub, being designed in the washable tile style, with potted palms and windows at the wrong high level. But to it came, every day, a splendid group of visitors, headed by Hilaire Belloc, looking like a clerical butcher, Archie Macdonell, a sporting Fleet Street figure and author of *England, Their England*, J. B. Morton, who gave enduring delight through his *Daily Express* column signed Beachcomber; Squire's brother-in-law, the writer Louis Marlow, Edward Shanks, a very typical Georgian poet,

Dudley Carew, and Clifford Bax, who brought with him to the very tip of his beard a conscious air of carrying civilization to some outer tribe. Among the rare birds who came to the Temple Bar I remember the condor-like profile of Robert Cunninghame Graham.

Such visitors – and there were scores of them – were among the last of a now extinct race, much later denoted by John Gross as Men of Letters. They made a more or less meagre living, writing essays, and verses which rhymed, and little book reviews. They lived sparsely, they read a great deal, they aspired to the authority of Edmund Gosse at the *Sunday Times* or Squire at the *Observer*. They were totally unlike the pylon boys of the next generation, or the ever-spikier artificers who carried the torch after 1939.

There were also, of course, ancestral figures still alive in 1928. Squire used sometimes to descend on Thomas Hardy and once asked me to go too. I refused, thinking Hardy and I were divided by too many years, and I have always regretted it. But I did go with him to call on Robert Bridges and I still remember Bridges's magnificent appearance and the courtesy with which he greeted and sped us, jumping up each time although well over eighty. I also remember Squire sending him a letter of outraged sympathy when he was attacked by Horatio Bottomley for keeping silence too long for a Laureate, in an article headed 'King's Canary Refuses to Twitter'; to which Bridges answered by telegram, 'Blue Bottomley I call him. And the higher he climbs the more he shows it.'

Among his own contemporaries – Squire, I repeat, was forty-five at that time – his reputation was variable. Many of them, such as Virginia Woolf, found him coarse; they thought, with reason, that he drank too much; they had little confidence in the group, known as the Squirearchy, which surrounded him. They saw a slightly absurd, badly-shaven, confused-looking West Countryman – he insisted on that – but they did not see a man of great tenderness and generosity, an exemplary friend, and a poet who only lacked a sense of discipline, so that his successes, which still give pleasure, came into being like impromptus, often witty, often touching. He was amazingly fluent. Always late, he could write admirable prose sense at the printer's last minute, propped against a bar counter and despatching his copy page by page. He corrected proofs with lightning speed and total accuracy. And although to his own family he must have been almost intolerable – grubby, insolvent, spendthrift, unreliable, tipsy, absurd – he exercised spontaneous charm on a wide range of friends, especially great ladies, like Victoria Duchess of Sermoneta, who regularly tried to reform him by taking him into a different atmosphere. This sometimes had a disastrous effect on *them*. One, Miss Alice Warrender, who founded the Hawthornden Prize, took him semi-permanently under her wing. She was a lady of strict principles, who worried very deeply about his drinking. But in a few months Squire was quietly sobered up while herself succumbed to the bottle.

He took himself very seriously indeed. One evening he clutched my arm and suddenly said, 'You have no idea, my dear fellow, what it is to carry the whole weight of English poetry on one's shoulders.' Of Eliot he thought nothing. He never forgot a moment of nervous geniality when Eliot said to him, 'We ought to meet more often. We'll have beer. And whiskey' – a daily occurrence in his own life. He had admired Joyce's *Portrait of the Artist as a Young Man*, and wrote asking for proofs of any subsequent book. One day, therefore, I found the unbound pages of *Ulysses*, minus a fair-sized lacuna, in a cupboard behind my desk. I asked how they had got there, and was ordered, 'Burn them at once.' His secretary, Grace Chapman, had tried to carry out the same order but had only a tiny iron range, dating from 1870 or so, and also in the room, to burn them in, so that she had soon been discouraged. I have them still.

He was a constant victim of the absurd accident, as when a stranger got the point of her umbrella between his eyes and his spectacles and tweaked them off; or when a pheasant he had just shot landed on his head and knocked him out. But he was also at times a notable master over adversity. There was a meeting of the Johnson Club at the Cheshire Cheese, in Gough's Court, at which Squire was to make a speech. Shortly before dinner he fell on the floor, and though we thwacked him and shook him with a will he walked in covered in sawdust. To steady his nerve, he accepted another drink or two, after which he passed through dinner in a glazed state, saying nothing.

Until the speeches were announced, at which he rose with care, and spoke capably for twenty minutes or so, then sat down again, also with care, and the glaze took over. His only equal, in such moments, was Lord Birkenhead, the Lord Chancellor.

Little by little I brought some of my own friends into the world of the *London Mercury*. John Betjeman was among them, and published there a funny early story, 'Lord Mount Prospect'. James Stern also published with us, and one or two now-forgotten poets. But I was not often able to cajole the new stars of the day, already caught into a galaxy led by Auden, because Squire was suspect to them as a hearty, a cricketer, a reactionary who was selling out his early stock of ideas for a knighthood and for the kind attention of distinguished old ladies. He had never hit it off with Bloomsbury or with the Sitwells either, for he was totally out of sympathy with the wilfully and happily (on the whole) disordered life of Tavistock and Carlyle Squares. Or rather, he could not admit any idea which was not based on Victorian middle-class respectability, laced by strong waters. Not that he was prudish or illiberal; he simply did not wish to expand his views to a personal life beyond the remembered pleasures of turn-of-the-century Devonshire. It was typical that, when the Harold Nicolsons went one evening to dine with Jack and Eileen Squire in Chiswick, there should have been no dinner. The roast duck had been high, and the guests were treated to a cry of distress: 'I opened the oven door, and, oh, what an effluvium!' they were told, 'when all she meant was,' the Nicolsons explained later, 'that it stank.'

Yet you could not watch Squire in daily operation without forming for him a deep and grateful affection. He was, in all things, curiously innocent. Thus, his friends decided, in the early Thirties, to give him a dinner. This was designed to cheer him up, after the word had gone round that he drank too much, did too little, in brief that he was slipping. What had been planned as a quite modest affair expanded, however, as the hero of the evening took over the dinner himself. It had to be at the Dorchester. It had to include everybody of distinction whose names he could recall. Night after night, more and more haggard, he sat up with his devoted ladies re-doing table plans. Where to place Lady Hudson? How to include two Ladies

Rothermere? Whether or not to include the Lord Chancellor? Not surprisingly, when the dinner finally took place he was unmanned. For once the challenge of a speech failed to strike more than a brief spark, extinguished almost at once by champagne and tears.

Meanwhile, his juniors had a fine time. One evening Joan Haslip gave a party at which the guests played the childish game of Sardines, so that I found myself crouched in a cupboard under the stairs, for what seemed an hour of darkness, and squashed against Aldous Huxley. Another evening I had the satisfaction – since I found him an immensely dislikeable old gentleman – of seeing Belloc appear foolish. I had been asked to stay in Sussex with the Rosslyns, and on the second night Lord Rosslyn said to his son Hamish Erskine, 'I'd forgotten Belloc was coming to dine. He loves port and there isn't any.' He thought out a strategem, therefore, and bought a bottle of three-shilling ruby port at the local pub. At the end of dinner, a decanter was put in front of Belloc and a little speech was made. 'I have nothing worthy of you, Hilary, but I have at least a historic curiosity: the last bottle of the Rosslyn port laid down by my grandfather. It may be sugar. It may be vinegar. But at least it is unique.' Belloc rolled the port round his tongue, smacked his lips, and over the next hour drained the decanter, lifting his glass against the candle flame and exclaiming with every show of pleasure.

If I found Belloc dislikeable, he probably found me more so. A single aesthete in a brood of much older and more experienced hearties will always exaggerate his own aestheticism, and I have no doubt that I appeared intolerable except to a few, like Squire himself, whose inner kindliness and understanding of opposites made them amusedly tolerant. But even in the house of my mother's elder brother, who was both a published poet and a Major-General – it was Squire's contention that every officer in the Brigade of Guards kept a sheaf of his own poems in his knapsack – I found Belloc a most trying fellow-guest. I had to remind myself of his enchanting light verse, his parodies, his then-unpublishable squibs, his mocking ballads. His colleague, G. K. Chesterton, was much easier to bear with. I used to meet him with Evan Morgan: a vastly obese man with a squeaky voice utterly at odds with his appearance, and a very respectful terror of his wife. He barely troubled to notice the young but, so long as his wife was elsewhere and he had a glass before him, he was benignity itself.

Evan was also responsible for bringing Wells tangentially into my life at this time. I can see him at Tredegar, lying in a canoe on the lake correcting proofs, when a gust of wind took him by surprise, and in a moment proofs, Wells and all, were in the water. At the time I thought it a revenge of the Gods for a small outrage perpetrated thirty-four years ago on my father's solicitor, E. S. P. Haynes, then an Eton boy. Haynes had sculled up the river and was about to haul his boat through the lock at Boveney, when a youth his own age suddenly pushed him into the water. What concerned him was not the wetting, but that he had been in the act of looking at the watch in his hand. Years later he told all this to Wells who said, 'I remember. I was the boy. I gave you a push and I did it because I couldn't bear you to have a gold watch when I had not.'

One could write a good deal about Haynes, who was an admirable eccentric, with chambers in Lincoln's Inn and a house in St John's Wood. Transacting any kind of business with him was made hard by his habit of inviting clients to breakfast at home, or to luncheon at 3.00 pm at an oyster bar in Chancery Lane. I never saw him, I think, in his office. His own breakfast consisted of sherry and garlic cloves, his luncheon of oysters and white wine. If these business hours – and the reek of garlic – repelled business, it could also be transacted during long walks over Hampstead Heath. Haynes was a throw-back in manner and looks to the days of T. H. Huxley and Samuel Butler. He put on an excellent performance as a Victorian survival, crusty, encyclopaedic, and (to his own satisfaction) rational. It was typical of him to write an impulsive essay on *The Belief in Personal Immorality*, which arose from a printer's mistake in omitting the 't' from the title of a very different piece: *The Belief in Personal Immortality*.

At this time I also came at last into contact with those older contemporaries who had been out of my range at Eton or elsewhere: Harold and William Acton, Brian Howard, Cyril Connolly, Evelyn Waugh, John Lehmann, Eddie Gathorne-Hardy, Eddy Sackville-West. It is hard to define after so long the peculiar aura which emanated from the Acton brothers.

Half-Italian and half-American, they were most at home in England, but brought with them a Mediterranean fantasy and grace which were extremely un-English. Harold had more wit, more stability, a keener sense of purpose as writer than Willie as painter. And for a time they pooled their gifts – which included a genius for hospitality – in an immense house in Lancaster Gate. The rumour at the time was that they had persuaded their father, who had a large and distinguished collection in Italy, to equip it as a kind of show-case, appointing his sons as plenipotentiaries to dispose of expensive but surplus furniture. This gave the pretext for splendid parties. So far as I know, nothing was ever sold, and the house came to a very abrupt end a very few years later.

Meanwhile, it hummed with life. Oliver Messel and his sister Anne Rosse, all the beauties of the day, all the pleasure-seekers of the 1920s on their way to the Embassy and Rector's and the 400 Club flocked through it. And all over the West End of London there were similar centres of hospitality: Tallulah Bankhead in Farm Street, Brian Howard and Eddie Gathorne-Hardy in Bloomsbury Square, the Lygon sisters at Halkin House – just to name three or four such centres produces a kind of dazzle, as a score more spring to memory; not to mention the grand historical houses still in existence. Bridgewater House, Spencer House, Norfolk House, Warwick House, Derby House, Apsley House, Wimborne House: again the dazzle blinds recollection. All have been written about to satiety. The organizing ladies of Mayfair and Chelsea – Lady Cunard, Lady Colefax, Mrs Maugham – turn up again and again in the books of my contemporaries, and I do not propose to retread such familiar ground. But, for a young man in London before the Thirties passed into history, the possibilities of pleasure seemed unlimited, granted enough taxi-money and a resistant liver.

Nor did any but a silly few live entirely for pleasure. Even Brian Howard, who wasted so spectacularly spectacular talent, threw off an occasional spark; Eddie Gathorne-Hardy was a most skilful bibliophile; and, most gifted of all, Evelyn Waugh set us all an example by using the social life of his times as a precipitant for solid achievement in fiction.

Among all these I felt most at home with Cyril Connolly, who had not yet settled into the mould which, in middle age, made him often a difficult companion. He brought two opposed attitudes delightfully together. An eager heterosexual, he also cultivated those gifts, including sympathy, which made homosexuals appealing. He could be tender as well as funny, and was always at his best among male friends who expected nothing of him except that he should stay at his best as long as possible – friends like Maurice Bowra and Harry d'Avigdor Goldsmid. With women he was insecure. Some – the nicest – were touched by him; most, sooner or later, became exasperated. His moments of impotence always struck him on the wrong evening; his alternations of greed and austerity made him an exhausting lover; his alliance of extravagance to a wilful kind of penury confused all domestic life; his numerous bad days were not interestingly thunderous, but simply dark and silent. Either he sang for his supper or he sulked for it.

But the good days, now: how good they were! Then his sympathy reached out, his Irish gift for filling a stage set in motion a natural charm which acted on his hearers as if they had been touched by Puck's love-juice. The Bottom of the bad days was translated in the eye of every beholder, and some Titania of the moment was seen exclaiming, 'Thou art as wise as thou art beautiful.'

I have seldom watched anybody cast so strong a spell. Cyril had few inborn advantages. He was pudgy, rather graceless, careless in the sense that he seldom noticed the unlucky stain, the greasy smudge; he was not obviously out to please. Harold Nicolson tells of his marking the place in his host's book at the breakfast table with a piece of bacon. But, when he was in form, his small deficiencies mattered no more than had Dr Johnson's to an audience equally delighted to be impressed.

The saddest of these friends was also perhaps the most gifted by nature: Brian Howard. When he died, I wrote of him that he ought to have been the English Jean Cocteau. But between him and any fulfilment of his manifold gifts stood an impossible temperament, aggravated by drink, a tendency to lash out in words or blows, and a constantly frantic approach to day to day living. Yet he could be an enchanting companion, witty, forthright, erudite, courageous. His father and he were never in touch, his American mother compounded his difficulties by heaping money on him when she had it and then suddenly

61

cutting it off when he exasperated her. It did not cross his mind to earn a living. Was he not an artist? a poet? a dedicated, if eccentric, guru? He was unable to keep the affections he craved. And yet, when one saw him coming close, justified apprehension was tempered by a surge of hope. Perhaps today he would be all right. And frequently he was.

One often saw him with Eddie Gathorne-Hardy, whose monocle gleamed searchingly over manifold occasions. Eddie was a distinguished bibliophile, a caustic wit and a constant source of both worry and pleasure to his relations. Night after night at the Blue Lantern, he ran out of cash for the taxi home, and night after night rang up Daimler Hire, in the name of his elder brother, Lord Cranbrook, whose bills for Eddie's peregrinations after midnight were prodigious. He also had a maniac streak, as on a Blue Lantern night when he ordered a brandy and ginger ale in the small hours after the bar had closed. The barman brought the ginger ale only, so Eddie, choosing his moment, climbed behind the bar and snatched from the shelf a bottle of brandy, upon which, for the next hour, he became drunk. Not wanting to waste what remained, he left with it, and once in the street took a great swig. It was coloured water, a dummy hitherto disguised by ginger ale. At one moment of poverty about this time, when he lived in Maddox Street above the gallery where D. H. Lawrence's pictures had recently been impounded for obscenity, he was said to exist on the mushrooms which grew in the damp of the staircase well.

It was often a relief to move from these gaudy circles back to the world of Jack Squire, with its cricket weeks and its beery calm. Fantasies occurred there too. I recall a nice old lady coming to discuss a manuscript and suddenly saying, 'But we've met before. Only, where? Yes, I have it. In a boat on the Arno, with Piero della Francesca.' And there was also a day when Squire took me to lunch in Soho with old Mr Odham, of Odhams Press: an institution with which Mr Odham felt decreasing sympathy when it came to publish the *Daily Herald*. The old gentleman might have been a friend of Mr Pickwick. He had taken a private room at Kettner's, and had an upright piano moved into it because Squire had assured him that I might help write down a song composed by his late wife but recorded in memory only. Wrist tucked in the tail of his frock-coat, he sat me down, and began to sing. Or rather, he rumbled. With one finger at first, I tried to pick out a tune. Was it like this? or this? The rumble quavered a little, but settled on no precise note. After an hour, however, I had composed a song, accompaniment included, which gave satisfaction, and I was rewarded by a six-course meal, to Squire's admiration.

There was also William Cobbett, I think a retired tea-merchant, who had compiled a dictionary of chamber music. With an ancient wife, he lived in St John's Wood in a high-Victorian house, lavishly decorated in yellow silk. And there, again braced by an immense meal, I was ordered to accompany him in works far beyond my scope, such as Szymanowski's Violin Sonata ('Keep a steadier rhythm, Pryce-Jones, and not so fast') and a parlour version of Max Bruch's Concerto in G minor.

In those days music meant almost more to me than books. I have never possessed an adequate piano technique, but I was cursed with a horrid fluency which let me cheat my way through much which I ought to have avoided. Inevitably, I concentrated on thick, sonorous works – Szymanowski was a fine case in point – since I knew that I could not cheat on Bach, or Mozart. It was at this time that my one publicly performed composition saw the light of day: a tenor song to the words of Bridges, with a flute obbligato to amuse Robin Darwin. It was played at a concert of Old Etonian composers – a rash venture if we reflected that there was only one of any consequence, Thomas Arne.

Best of all was to find oneself in a society where all the arts were hailed with equal excitement. And this is what happened when I became friends with the Sitwells. Osbert was sixteen years older than I, but still under forty when I first met him, Edith was in her famous Moscow Road retreat, and Sachie, not long married, had established a degree of independence, but remained, publicly at least, one of an indissoluble trio.

It is hard to overestimate what the Sitwell example meant to me. Their background was not unlike mine: a background of country house security tied in with interludes of Eton and the Brigade of Guards. But they had already shown that it was possible to use just such a background as a springboard, to twist it into fantasy, satire, fresh enterprises of the imagination. Not

only were they older than I but also, I knew, much more gifted –
Sachie perhaps the best endowed by nature of the three – and
I soon found myself tagging along behind them in pursuit of
the baroque, of Italy as revealed in Lecce or Amalfi, of
Liszt's music, of Cuvilliés and the Bibbienas, of Caserta and
Würzburg.

Edith I knew much better later, and Sachie was essentially a
private person with small need of young admirers. But Osbert
became a true friend almost at once, and some of my happiest
memories turn on Carlyle Square and on Renishaw. My recollection of his father, Sir George, is rather different from the
picture put forward by Sir George's children. They have built
him into a great English comic figure, reliably the victim of
Laughter in the Next Room and lagging far behind his children in
the ability to tease or annoy. It must be admitted that Sir
George was in most ways an unbearable husband and father.
But he was not stupid; and, on the rare occasions when I
observed him in action, he struck me as a move or two ahead of
his children, who may well have felt compelled to foist a comic
persona on him, to dispel a constant aura of despotic malevolence. I used to be taken to call on poor Lady Ida, in a small
Dover Street hotel and in a constant state of bewilderment. In
the middle ground was a procession of vivid and talented
younger people, such as Willie Walton, Constant Lambert,
Tommy Earp, Adrian Stokes, Nina Hamnett, Rex Whistler, as
well as affectionate elders: Christabel Aberconway, Lady Wimborne and Mrs Ronnie Grenville. For Osbert knew 'everybody'. His hospitality was memorable, often washed down by
an 'old' champagne, not too old, but delightfully darker and
flatter than ordinary 'fizz'. The cocktails mixed by Robbins, his
manservant, were traditionally very dry, with a crust of sugar
round the rim of the glass, and I remember Osbert's concern
when he invited my mother to luncheon and she, who normally
drank water, downed three or four of these, plus whatever wine
was offered, and then some Cointreau with her coffee, before
setting off with alacrity to shop at Peter Jones, while Osbert and
I had to spend the afternoon lying down.

VI

To look back on those days from a safer plateau more than fifty years later is to be blinded, as if by looking too long at the unshaded sun. Images pierce through the glare. I am at Nore, Brian Howard's house in days of prosperity. It is six on a summer morning. With Eddie Gathorne-Hardy we have driven down from a night at the Blue Lantern, in a Daimler booked to Lord Cranbrook. We are drinking coffee on a terrace, to the bacchanalian music of Debussy's *Fêtes*. I am in the Queen's Hall, at the Delius Festival in which the master made his last public appearance, a wraithlike impassive figurine in a wheeled chair. I am in Wimborne House, at a concert of the Quartet Society, and every now and again there is a little squeak of pain as wax from a chandelier drops on a bare shoulder. I am with Nina Hamnett in the Eiffel Tower restaurant – what, I wonder, has happened to the Vorticist frescoes which used to adorn it? – watching Augustus John at one table and Aleister Crowley at another. Nina worries lest, if annoyed, the magician may evoke flames from his plate. She makes me look at the brass bat which clasps his belt. I am at the Beetle and Wedge, a Bohemian Thames-side inn, and I am amazed by the enamelled face – it took several hours to apply – of Hedley Hope-Nicholson, a middle-aged husband and father. I am at Knole, staying with Eddy Sackville-West, who complains, among the tapestries and the silver furniture, of the indignity of living in the suburbs, even protected by a deer-park. I am staying with the Dean of Wadham, Maurice Bowra, who opens a notebook and reads out solecisms from Eddy's novels, of which I only remember two: 'A large but strong box' and 'He literally tore his eyes off her and fixed them on a piece of cake'. I am at Long Barn with the Harold Nicolsons. I am at my desk in the *London Mercury* office, answering an illegible invitation to Jack Squire from Sybil Colefax: 'Do dine Tuesday. Just ourselves and Pirandello.' I am in my *matelot*'s uniform, not sober, dancing in the Chelsea studio of Madge Garland and her friend Dorothy Todd, trying to catch the attention of Peter Spencer only because my father had warned me so emphatically against him. I am in London night-clubs, in Paris night-clubs with Evan Morgan, in a BBC office being questioned by Lord Reith about my belief in God, as a preliminary to being offered some tiny broadcasting job; in more night-clubs, less sober; in the British Museum Library, trying to work. The dazzle grows. It is like being on a carousel: to be young, and to believe, falsely, that one has all the time in the world; to revolve, often to the sound of raucous music; to live splintered days, catching at this moth or that, to be unsure whether one aspires to be Heliogabalus, Plato, or St Augustine.

My still centre at this time was a very small Chelsea flat. It was my first independent home, in an anonymous brick block called Vale Court, in Mallord Street, off the King's Road. I decorated it after the Bohemian fashion of the day: silver oilcloth curtains, furniture of unpainted wood, drawings by Duncan Grant and Picasso dry-points on the walls, all done on a shoe-string, for I had very little money. My father, it is true, had relented and gave me an allowance, and I could make a thousand a year or so by writing. But living in 1930 was cheap. Even luxuries were possible when the Ritz or the Berkeley charged 8/6 for luncheon and 12/6 for dinner. And if I went to Paris I could stay comfortably in a small Left Bank hotel for less than a pound a night.

My parents had by then moved from Buckingham Palace Gardens to a flat in the Duke of York's Headquarters, which became theirs when my father gave up any pretence of making a fortune in the city and returned to his first love, the Army. In the city he only accomplished feats like raising as much capital as he could to buy German marks at the beginning of the inflation which made them totally valueless, or buying shares in a Mexican oil-well which forthwith began to gush sea-water

66

and continued to do so for twenty years. Now he took over the organization of the County of London Territorial Army, and at about the same time became a Gentleman-at-Arms, which gave him a gorgeous uniform to wear on state occasions, and also a tower in Windsor Castle.

This tower, Henry VIII's Gateway, provided me with another still centre. I made myself a second little room out of unpainted furniture and more oil-cloth, this time black, and shut myself up in it as often as possible. In those days, Windsor Castle was not at all the bedlam it is today. Nobody much passed through the gate, and as we were given the keys of the Home Park and the private terraces I had many of the advantages of a large country house. The brisk civil wars between ancient canons, military Knights, and resident courtiers kept me always entertained. And I also witnessed a still more comical war: between my mother and Mrs Stucley. My mother was a fanatical Coldstreamer, Mrs Stucley an equally fanatical Grenadier's widow. The war would begin by Mrs Stucley ringing the door bell with vigour. 'Vere, you should do something. The sentry at your gate is disgustingly drunk. A Coldstreamer, too.' My mother would bide her time. At length, she telephoned. 'Rosie, I have to tell you. The Grenadiers have taken over. And I do believe the sentry had a girl in his box when I came in on this dark evening. For the sake of the regiment, you must report this.' Neither ever acted on the advice given; neither even smiled about it.

In a nearby tower lived a splendid old cousin, Betty Montgomery, who entertained me even better. She had been a Ponsonby, daughter of Sir Henry, who had succeeded my great-grandfather Grey as Queen Victoria's Private Secretary, and sister of Sir Frederick, Lieutenant-Governor of Windsor Castle and later Lord Sysonby. She had married a general and lived all her life in Northern Ireland. But from what Proust called her '*belle solitude irlandaise*' she had for thirty years been in touch with all that was advanced in contemporary writing: with Proust himself, with Ezra Pound, Jean Cocteau, Marinetti, Raymond Roussel, André Breton: not when they became famous, but often years before the First World War, when they were young and unknown. She exchanged letters with them, they sent her their books – some of which I have today – but

she never met anybody outside the range of family and neighbours in Co. Down. Because she disliked the prospect of visiting
guests, she arranged her commodious house so that it had no
spare room but a dozen or so book-rooms, and in one of these,
arrayed like Klytemnestra in *Elektra* in scarlet and gold,
she received me from time to time for a little talk on, say,
Queen Victoria, to whom she had been Maid-of-Honour, or
d'Annunzio. I presume her to have had a romance with another
cousin, Maurice Baring, for I have a pocket Shelley, beautifully
bound for her in gilt-tooled vellum, with a loving poem on the
fly-leaf. I asked her one day, 'What was Queen Victoria really
like?' She replied, 'Not really our *type**, darling.'

Through Betty Montgomery I learned about the imaginative
side of my family, which sprang from frequent inter-marriages
between Greys, Ponsonbys, Dawnays, Bulteels, Barings,
Lytteltons, Beresfords. My mother's two brothers, both gen-
erals, were typical in that their very successful army careers –
one was Allenby's chief of staff, one head of the Staff College,
and both intimately connected with T. E. Lawrence's desert
campaign – were balanced by contrasting qualities. The elder,
Guy, founded a merchant bank and presided over large commercial enterprises. The younger, Alan, became a deputy to
Lord Reith during the formative years of the BBC. They were
handsome, with an attractive dilettante approach to matters of
importance which hid a great deal of acumen. My uncle Alan,
under a debonair exterior, shared the nervous tensions which
beset my mother, and eventually killed himself, as did several
members of his immediate family. I have wondered why. What
dangerous seed was implanted in these successful, worldly,
sporting Yorkshiremen? I remembered our Beauclerk relations, who inherited a far more dangerous legacy (we were told)
from the marriage of the ninth Duke of St Albans to Miss
Gubbins in the last century. I used sometimes to be taken by my
grandmother to visit their grandson, who lived in close seclu-
sion, sending out occasional letters on thick scarlet writing-
paper, with the rubber-stamped heading of a ducal coronet, or
postcards of Hastings churchyard on which was scrawled in
gold ink, 'Find the hare'; and indeed a discerning examination

* Pronounced, as in French, 'teep'.

68

could make out a faintly rabbity form, of which the gothic church door might represent an ear, and a tussock of grass the right eye. Surely the Dawnays of the early nineteenth century were far too proper to run a serious sexual risk? But I remembered their close affection for the Beningbrough gamekeeper, old Daniel, and then one day I looked at him closely and discovered him unmistakably a Dawnay. I thought it wise to ask no questions. The zest which became responsible for Daniel may have led some forebear towards disaster too.

A parallel disaster also afflicted my only brother, eleven years younger than I. This gap in age meant that he played almost no part in my life when he was young, for by the time I had left Oxford he was still in the nursery. Not only so, but my parents, perhaps fearing I should be a bad influence on him, kept us apart as far as they could, by building round him a nursery atmosphere only disseminated by the Second World War. He then matured abruptly; joined the Welsh Guards, and proved himself an excellent officer. He was an ice-skater of international standing, and later an acclaimed film director. But with time he took to drink. And, though he did not exactly die of drink, he died at forty-nine after mortifying bouts of nursing-home care and recurrent collapses. I shall have more to say of him.

In the middle ground of my life, from childhood on, stood a family friend, Robert Pratt Barlow. He had been a brother-officer of my father and my uncles in the Coldstream. They ragged him affectionately for was he not musical – a word which around 1910 also served as a euphemism for homosexual? He had published a waltz, much played in London ballrooms, at least one song set to words written by Alan Dawnay; his money had helped educate Noël Coward; he played the piano with rippling inaccuracy; he had inherited a fortune; he was a bachelor. No wonder his brother officers were a trifle suspicious.

So far as I was concerned they need not have been. Indeed, I owe him an extraordinary debt. For in 1931 he had planned to make a trip to the Far East with Alan Dawnay, and at the eleventh hour my uncle was put in command of the Staff College at Sandhurst, so could not leave England. The tickets were booked, and at that moment Bobbie Pratt Barlow remembered that my father's silences in my regard had been longer and darker than usual. Why should not I travel with him in place of my uncle? It was agreed; and in no time I was on my way to join my host at his winter home in Sicily.

I knew nothing of foreign travel. My father mistrusted all foreigners, unless they were Nigerians, of whom he kept a kindly memory, as one might of some ungainly but loveable pet. My mother had been once or twice with her brother to Monte Carlo, travelling with two cars – a Napier for the luggage and a maid, and a Daimler for brother and sister. She had stayed with uncles when they were Governor-General in Canada or Viceroy in India, but under circumstances which did not represent travel in general. I had been fairly often to France by myself, but only on one journey outside Europe, to Morocco, and then only because I was taken by yet another Coldstream officer and his mother – a concatenation which spelled safety to my father.

I reached Sicily under a temporary cloud. Told to get myself a ticket from Thomas Cook, I had accepted the suggestion of an old employee who organized Bobbie's travels, and found myself, not unwillingly, in a first-class single sleeper, when I ought, I was told on arrival, to have insisted on far more modest transport. But after that all was smooth sailing. Literally, too, for in a few days we were off in a luxurious liner, the *Ansonia*, from Syracuse to Alexandria.

During the next six months, we stayed in Cairo, leased a once-famous house in Luxor, the Villa Bella Donna, in which Robert Hitchens had written a best-seller of that name: travelled from Assuan to Jerusalem: on to Baalbek, Palmyra and Petra: sailed up the Anatolian coast to Cyprus: crossed to Athens and Vienna; spent a few weeks in the Salzkammergut and Bavaria; in brief, covered a good deal of ground with satisfaction to both of us.

I made this tour the theme of my first book, *The Spring Journey*; and so successful was the human element in our little adventures that we spent the two following winters together, in South America and Central Africa. No doubt this looked strange to some. I was twenty-two – Bobbie in his forties. He was a little like Gilbert the Filbert: sporting a very neat moustache; rather spinsterish – there were scenes in hotel restaurants if mustard was not already on the table – rather arch at times, with a head-on-one-side stuttery manner; dogmatic; witty; mad about the theatre; but above all musical, in either connotation of the word. He was also kind, supportive, and discreet. At no moment did his private life impinge on mine, while he was endlessly understanding towards the tiresome young man I must have been at that time. He was valetudinarian. My family told me that, in the Flanders trenches, he had been extremely brave, but always went into the attack with a rug, a gold box of aspirin, and an Asprey flask. There was nothing one could not discuss with him, for rigidity in his approach was confined to inessentials; shorts for instance *must* be truly short, and ironed so that the crease was down the side not at the front. He was a Catholic by adoption, temperate, at times governessy; but pleased, I think, to find himself half-tutor, half-parent and wholly friend to someone for whom he assumed no responsibility, but who shared his interests enough to be a companion.

Luxor in 1931 was a more peaceful place than it is today. The Villa Bella Donna was on the bank of the Nile, surrounded by oranges and roses. We lived there in untidy state, ministered to by a villainous Mohammed, who brought in a dozen or more of his relatives to create confusion in the house, and spent most of the money we gave him for housekeeping on drink. We had a boat with a blue and yellow mast, three donkeys named Marconi, Inghilterra and Lovely-Sweet, and horses at command, since in those days it was still easy to go sightseeing on horseback. In the Winter Palace Hotel nearby was a mixed collection of elegant travellers, among them Queen Marie of Roumania, Melba the singer, and a fabulous aged beauty, Marthe Letellier, the guest of a retired banker about whom clung a permanent but delicate whiff of *chypre*.

Madame Letellier was not very bright. She prefaced each trivial remark by saying to the old banker *'Ecoutez, Paul'* as though some pronouncement were to follow. And she complained more than once that she was never taken to the Casino. *'Mais, chérie, il n'y a pas de casino,'* her swains replied – they included a millionaire composer, Herman Bemberg, from Argentina, and also extremely old. *'Si, Paul, tout le monde connaît le Casino de Biskra.' 'Mais nous ne sommes pas à Biskra.' 'Ah-h'* and she sighed.

One night I found myself accompanying Melba on an upright piano when she felt impelled to sing Lehar's 'You are my Heart's Delight' to Queen Marie and to the assembled antiques in the deserted ballroom of the hotel: a bizarre musical experience. But it was not in the Winter Palace that I caught a little of the breath of life, but in Karnak, the Valley of the Kings – deserted for much of the day but for inevitable begging children, to be chased away by our private domestic beggar – and above all at a little table set among the roses in the exquisite early mornings by the Nile where I tried to work at a poem 'for Brian' – a notebook phrase which can only mean that Brian Howard had some plan to get it published for me.

I look back at myself, from this distance, with some interest and much distaste. I see a very thin young man, full of affectation – my parents preserved my letters from Eton on, and much later I read them with nausea: pretentious rubbish scribbled, often in coloured inks, on thick deckle-edged sheets. I was vain, I fancied myself as a coming poet. I took from the world what it had to offer and gave very little back. I was odious to my bewildered parents; slothful and not particularly honest. Thus, I might take a handful of small change from my father's dressing-table, or even Evan Morgan's, because I knew that I needed it and that neither would miss it. I was snobbish – I positively enjoyed accompanying Melba for the Queen of Roumania or being asked by the Lansdownes to a London dinner for King George and Queen Mary – but I was also quite unfit to take any part in the life that such occasions implied: too poor, too unsporting, too non-political, too unambitious except in the single realm of literature, and even then laziness and a natural triviality stood between me and fulfilment.

No wonder my relations were concerned. Before the journey to Egypt, my great aunt Mary Minto intervened to get me work with Winston Churchill on the book, *Great Contemporaries*, he was about to write. She had already tried to have me employed by a maharajah – was it Indore? – to spend a year in India and then go through Oxford at his expense, so that his undergraduate son might have at least one English friend. This plan was scotched by my father who entered one of his longer silences, heavy with offended pride. Had it been a Nigerian chieftain, now: but, no, it was an Indian to whom, in his view, I was to be a superior body-servant.

Aunt Mary returned to the charge, and, through her friend Eddie Marsh, landed me on Winston, who was at the time Chancellor of the Exchequer. My first assignment was to draft an essay on Venizelos, for which I was given *carte blanche* to buy any book I might need from Bain, a bookseller off the Strand. I bought, and read, copiously, and drafted some five thousand words, which I brought to the Chancellor's office. He was most welcoming, and prayed me to be seated. He then began unburdening his mind on the subject of a possible Wall Street Depression, on the unreasonable behaviour of the French, on the differences in character between M. Clemenceau, who had lately died, and M. Poincaré, on the faults of Lord Curzon as Viceroy of Indian as distinct from the merits of his successor, Minto. I could at best nod or open my eyes wide: there was no place in the room for a second speaker. Suddenly he stopped. 'Why are you wasting my time?' he asked severely. 'You are here to tell me about Venizelos.' This, though, with a twinkle.

When he had read my typescript he told me where it had gone wrong, and sent me away to redo it. After the third try, it passed. And then I found that he proposed to confect an entirely different script, sticking exactly to my structure, however. If I had Venizelos leave school half way down page two, his script followed this without deviation, only using other words.

I drafted one or two more of the essays, with the same result. And then it struck me that I was being paid five pounds a piece for what came to a good deal of work. So one day I left a note on the desk to say I should not return, and thereby, I suppose, lost an eventual place as minister, ambassador or son-in-law.

The last alternative I had probably already lost by my own ineptitude. There had been a dinner at the Astors' great house in Carlton House Terrace, a dinner before a ball. I had just left Eton and was placed next to Diana Churchill, and I flattered myself that dinner had gone well. I was asked to dine the following week at 11 Downing Street, and I was so carried away by the charm of my new friend that I wrote a facetious letter to Hamish St Clair Erskine, who was still at Eton, saying that we had talked about him, and agreed heartily about his many faults. It was the kind of unfunny joke that seventeen-year-old boys write to each other, and it did not cross my mind that

Hamish would take it seriously. However, he did. And went at once to Randolph Churchill, also at Eton, to complain. Randolph telegraphed his sister, 'Don't dine out on Hamish.' I knew nothing of all this, and arrived a week later in happy anticipation at 11 Downing Street, to be greeted in the hall by Mrs Churchill in the mood of a Maenad. How dared I show my face in her house? When she told the whole tale, I made to leave but I was told that to ruin a dinner-table as well would be the last straw; and so my punishment was to be glared at by mother and daughter not only that evening but for the next several years.

Incidentally, at about this time, I was present at the very start of Randolph's public career. There was a charming lady who lived in Montpelier Square and enjoyed the company of the young. He and I were both there one evening, when she wondered aloud why, if, as he said, he was constantly strapped for cash, he did not write a newspaper article. What about? he asked. 'About your father. About yourself as your father's son,' she suggested; and there and then she rang up a friend at the *Sunday Despatch* and fixed the matter. Randolph wrote the article, and never looked back.

VII

ONE OF THE pleasures of English life fifty years ago lay in its country houses. Their doom was already spelled out, but it needed a second world war to destroy the underpinnings of wealth, cheap labour and bad communications, on which they rested. Air travel was rare and for the few only; roads were narrow and serpentine; low wages made it possible to assemble large staffs inside and out. True, the days when my mother's nanny went as nursery-maid to Beningbrough at eight pounds a year were over. But there was still enough inherited money in the land to keep up Edwardian state, and sometimes more. My contemporary, Lord Jersey, pulled down a large house, Middleton Park, and commissioned Lutyens and his son Robert to build him one not much smaller on the site. Lord Faringdon, another contemporary, reorganized his family home Buscot, so that married couples were likely to have each two bedrooms, two bathrooms and a luggage room. And it was not long since Hever Castle, the big house I knew best in these years, had been overhauled and enlarged by the first Lord Astor at a cost of millions.

John Astor, chief proprietor of *The Times*, had married a first cousin of my mother's, and for a number of years we all spent Christmas together in that most hospitable house. I can still smell the burning cedar-wood wafted through the rooms to scent them before dinner, still see the groom of the chambers testing inkwells for freshness, and checking the supply of postage stamps on writing tables, still wonder at the stateliness of Albert, later butler, but then first footman. I can hear the

75

thwack of the balls against the cushion when we played billiard fives, the thud of other little boys' skulls on overhead pipes when George Mercer Nairne, stepson of the house, dared them to roller-skate in the dark through immense cellars. I can listen to Barrie reading aloud to us the stories he had woven round the house-party; marvel at the beauty of Lady Maidstone, round whom and our host we invented romantic tales. I can still prophesy of the young Anthony Eden that one day he would come to great things. For usually there were a few statesmen in the house, to whom we listened in awe over the port after luncheon. And, to amuse the young, there were nightly plots against neighbouring houses, Eridge, Penshurst, Ford – plots which might or might not be carried out but were planned in intricate detail: to paint a moustache on somebody's Holbein, or to pin saucy notes to a dowager's pillow. The engineer of these sorties, Captain Shaw, was John Astor's political secretary. He had a Mephistophelian face, an ingenious mind, and a Rabelaisian interest in Anglo-Irish affairs, which he had perceived both through the eyes of AE, Gogarty, James Stephens, Yeats, and of the American Lady Decies, who had for years filled his emotional life. I recall the exact tap of John Astor's wooden leg along the interminable corridors of the house at night – with horrid enthusiasm the younger generation whispered about assignations in remote bedrooms. By day we could notice the franker tap of the wooden foot on the pedals of an organ in the hall on which he loved to play.

Very occasionally, Nancy Astor or Vincent Astor might also be there. But there was no great love lost between the different branches of the Astor family, divided not only by the Atlantic but by conflicting prejudices. Violet, like Nancy, had great good looks, but her viewpoint was totally opposed to that of the Langhornes. The only trait, almost, they shared was a distaste, amounting to fear, for Catholics. Nancy took to Christian Science, Violet liked the kind of country clergyman who wears a number of medals on his surplice. Nancy liked very much being rich and powerful; Violet cared for such things not at all. She mistrusted brains, as did many of her relations. She would say of someone, 'I find him quite nice, but people say he is terribly clever.' And her Protestantism was such that, when she and Lord Astor planned to give Hever to their eldest son and move to France, she countered any suggestion about where they might live by announcing, 'The south, the Dordogne, the Loire Valley: oh dear, they all sound terribly R.C.'

One Christmas at Hever, Lady Maidstone was especially friendly. Before the party broke up, she asked me to visit her in London, and my heart bounded at the prospect. I waited for as short a time as I decently could – say, until mid-January – and then made my way to Manchester Square. The curtains were not drawn, and I could see her sitting by a fire, dark, beautiful and peaceful. I rang the bell and asked the butler, according to the polite formula, if she were at home. 'I'll go and see,' he said. 'Whom shall I say?' and then, returning after a moment or two, 'I'm afraid Her La'ship is out.' I can still feel the hurt of walking off into the dusk, while the firelight flickered on her face a few feet away.

I owe one house of special delight to John Betjeman, who drove me from Oxford to Sezincote, to visit the Arthur Dugdales, who at once became friends. Sezincote is a Gloucestershire house in the Indian style, a prototype of the Brighton Pavilion. The Dugdales were worthy of it: odd, engaging, unexpected. One night, Ethel Dugdale heard an unaccustomed sound in her dress-closet and surprised a burglar there. Her instant reaction was to say, 'My poor man, you must be very unhappy to be reduced to burglary.' He agreed. After some talk she suggested that he come back next day. 'Ask for my husband,' she said. 'And don't tell him you were hiding in a cupboard. We need a second footman.' The burglar did as he was told, found himself engaged, and left a week or two later with half the silver closet. 'Poor, poor man,' she sighed, 'he must indeed have been unhappy.'

Meantime, Colonel Dugdale, whose son John later, and uncharacteristically, became First Lord of the Admiralty in a Labour Cabinet, concentrated on other matters. He would set several decanters of port before us, and take our opinion on each. When we were right, in his view, and preferred a Rebello Valente, or a Dow '13, his delight knew no bounds. He used to shake enough martinis for the year and lay them away in casks in the cellar. In other ways he made few concessions to the post-war world. We asked him one evening how he had financed himself for a trip to Japan. Did he take a letter-of-

77

credit? or travellers cheques? He was astonished. 'Good God, man, haven't I got a cheque-book?' he exclaimed. And I could see him, every inch a colonel, coping with entire success with the problem of needing a thousand pounds in Kyoto, and having only a bank account in Moreton-in-Marsh.

Staying at Bicton was a more formidable experience. I had not long lived on my own in Chelsea when I was asked there for a summer week-end. My great-aunt Jane Clinton was not a special family friend, but for some reason I was invited, and found myself speeding up what I was told was the longest avenue of monkey-puzzles in Europe to a spreading classical façade, behind which were lodged a number of guests. I remember briefly the Leconfields, and Louise Wakehurst with her daughter Mary. I came down from my room for dinner and ran into an Abel-Smith, who looked at me with pity, and said, 'You'll be in disgrace, you're wearing a black tie.' Sure enough, when I reached the saloon, I found all the men were in tail-coats and white waistcoats. The year was 1929 or 1930; and, though a tail-coat was still usual in the theatre, it was not at a June weekend in Devonshire. I thought it best to go straight into action, and said to my host, Uncle Charley, 'I'm afraid I'm wearing the wrong clothes.' He flinched. 'You are indeed. Which footman have you got?' 'It's not the fault of any footman. I'm afraid I didn't bring a tail-coat.' He stooped towards me, and put a hand on my shoulder. 'Then,' he said, 'you must fire your man.' At the time I had a charwoman who once or twice a week swept vaguely under my bed.

The next morning at breakfast, I found in the dining-room two groups of identical cups, decorated in the Green Dragon pattern which Goodes, the china shop in South Audley Street, had made fashionable over many years. They were identical in size, but one group was of slightly thinner china than the other. I was pouring myself a cup of coffee when Uncle Charley cried out, 'Look what you're doing. That's a tea-cup. Not very pleasant for someone who drinks tea out of that cup to-morrow if you've drunk coffee out of it today.' I was not asked again.

By this time I had developed a passion for travelling. Why waste time on Sezincote, Bicton, and other such when I could go to Palmyra, Baalbek, to the Anatolian coast where waterfalls tumble over cliffs into the sea, to the castles of Cyprus and the rickety towers of Neuschwanstein?

The following year Bobbie and I set off on the *Almanzora* to spend Christmas in Rio, then continued south, crossed the Andes by train, and took boat up the coast of Chile, struck inland to Bolivia, spent a few weeks in Peru and Ecuador, and finally made for home through the Panama Canal. The whole journey took about four months, and I made it the substance of my second book, *People in the South*, which took the form of three novellas, attempting to catch the atmosphere of Brazil, Chile and Ecuador.

I was happiest in Ecuador, then an undeveloped country, the capital of which was reached by a single-track railway. One spent the night at Riobamba after leaving the steaming city of Guayaquil, and had the additional adventure of a wash-out on the line, so that a mountain had to be climbed on foot before taking train again on the other side. The porters, speaking Quechua and not Spanish, hauled our luggage over, and were much amused when sometimes a suitcase bounded out of their grasp into the river below.

To preserve my own I made friends with an Ecuadorian fellow-traveller of my age, who spoke the native language, and all was well. But much later, when we reached the tiny Hotel Sucre – the only tolerable hotel in Quito at that time – I was vexed when he knocked on my door and asked to share my twin-bedded room, because he had nowhere else to stay.

This was the beginning of a troublesome week. Young officers flocked through the room day and night; one was sick into my bed; others used my razor; others again brought in tarts and bottles of scotch. And when I protested my original friend looked hurt, and reproached me for ingratitude. Was I not now in touch with all that was amusing in Quito? Finally I turned him out – having taken refuge for a night or two with Bobbie on another floor – but lack of sleep made me unappreciative of the better things the city had to offer: La Merced, a salmon-coloured baroque church, with a red and gold choir gallery, and garlands of pink glass electric roses round the altar, switched on for me by an ecstatic half-Indian priest, illuminated himself by the wonders of electricity. Or the view from the Panecillo nearby, to the volcano Cotopaxi, across eucalyptus valleys and spreading green mountain ranges of the utmost beauty. Or daily meetings with a magnificent Edwardian admiral, Sir William Pakenham, who when Naval Attaché in Tokyo and an observer during the Russo-Japanese War of 1904 was said to have halted a naval battle because his white uniform had been spotted with blood and he was concerned to go below and change it. Certainly, he had remained a dandy. On suffocating afternoons in Guayaquil he wore a starched wing collar above a black suit and a Homburg hat; he carried a pigskin-handled umbrella from Briggs, with a gold pencil in it.

Peru had its pleasures too. In Arequipa we stayed at the Quinta Bates, a private hotel run by Tia Bates, the widow of a Scottish engineer, and a delightful old lady who stood no nonsense from anybody. A revolution was daily expected, Carnival was about to end, the Prince of Wales and Prince George, who had been paying a ceremonial visit to Peru while we were in Lima, were about to leave the country, in spite of urgent appeals to stay by the threatened President, Sanchez Cerro: it was exactly the moment for an uprising. And, sure enough, the rising came. There were shots by the Quinta Bates, and Mrs Bates, angrily waving a parasol, rushed out to complain. 'You know I won't stand this kind of thing,' she cried. 'Take those silly guns to the next street.' And sheepishly the insurgents did.

A little later we were in Callao, the port of Lima, where most of the fighting had taken place. A member of the English Club took me to see where a friend of his had been killed by a Government bullet as he advanced to the billiard table. Two shots had gone clean through his skull, shattered the left leg of Queen Victoria in an engraving on the wall and embedded themselves in the plaster just by the ear of two members sitting on a sofa and watching the game. It struck a very different note from the smiling figures of a few days before in the Country Club, milling round a shy Prince of Wales.

Had I known it, that spring of 1931 was a spring in which dragon's teeth were being sown all over the world. I remember watching an officer in Callao being brought into the fort by a large crowd. He was to be shot, we were told, and looked shrivelled and sulky but not particularly frightened. The escorting officer was telling him a joke. I found it extraordinary to be in sight of the moving limbs of a man about to be shot. Was it not 1931? Had war not been abolished thirteen years earlier? Were we not in an era of ever-increasing prosperity, international peace, and – at any moment – universal good temper? No, poor fool, we were not.

The third trip Bobbie and I made was to Central Africa the following winter. We stayed in Kenya with one of the founding fathers of that country, Lord Francis Scott, who had built a surprising house full of Italian furniture and set in brilliant gardens near Rongai, and then drove on through Uganda and the Sudan, to take boat from Juba through the Sudd. Kenya – and Uganda – were still very British, very much as perceived by Isak Dinesen. The people we saw in Nairobi were either the dedicated good-timers of the Muthaiga Club, or splendid eccentrics like the dowager Lady Seafield, who constantly travelled alone through Central Africa in mosquito-boots and slacks – a more unexpected sight then than now.

I had been warned against the Sudd. A week of it on board the river-boat would be a great waste of time, they said. But I found each day delightful. The bird-life alone was a dazzle of colour: subtle red wings, green backs, quick fan-tails and blue feathers sparkling like Amazonian butterflies. A small zoo greeted us: herds of elephant, crocodiles, antelope, eland. Dinka fishermen, grey and powdery from the ash of cow-dung, fished on one elegant leg. Our boat crashed into the banks of high reeds and elephant grass as we turned like a top to negotiate a corner; and at long intervals a clearing with a few battered huts had been hacked out of the wet emptiness lit by a sunless glare which turned the water to platinum, wrinkled by dipping birds.

Omdurman seemed a vast metropolis after long empty days. The shadow of General Gordon still lay on it. And then a few days later we spent a night at Abu Simbel, not yet violated by progress, and observed first in full moonlight, then at sunrise. Of all monuments to antiquity I have seen none equal it: not Palmyra, not Petra, not Tikal, not Sacsahuaman.

But more important to me than any monument was the fact that just before sailing to Africa I had fallen, for the first time, in love. A party was assembled in Worcestershire, a party of sixteen or so; and at the very last moment we were told that owing to an impending family death in the house we were all to be put up at the Lygon Arms in Broadway, in which a hunt ball was the pretext for our party. For a long week-end sixteen people of around twenty were left to their own devices; there was plenty of champagne; we breakfasted at 2.30 in dressing-gowns and we danced until five in the morning.

But I had no thought except for my absent hostess's daughter, Joan. She was very fair, with huge myopic blue eyes. Her voice had a delicious quaver – no, not quite quaver, an undulation rather, in it; her talk was unexpected, funny, clear-minded. She had no time for inessentials; though she was a natural enjoyer, she was also a perfectionist whom experience had already taught to be wary. I was twenty-three when we met; she barely twenty. For the next two years we spent as much time together as we could, hampered only by family disapproval.

In 1932 young people were still closely bound to their parents, even if bound by lip-service only. It would not serious-ly have occurred to either of us to break with our families entirely; we had not enough money, for one thing, and I certainly had no alluring prospects to offer a father-in-law. Nevertheless, my mother was at once outraged that anything so sordid as prospects should even be discussed by people who, she felt, in an access of family devotion, were lucky to enjoy her son's attention. The following winter I pursued Joan to Algecir-as, where I was made welcome by her mother, but her father remained (understandably) tepid towards me. A politician himself, he wanted his daughter to marry a Tory with a future, and the best that could be achieved was an invitation to Worcestershire to discuss the matter.

The first evening passed off quite well, though the gossip columns had made things harder for us by taking up our case under such headings as 'Love will find a way'. Unluckily there was also in the house a benevolent family friend who tried fatally to make things easier for me. When my host suggested golf, the friend exclaimed, 'But you can't expect Pryce-Jones to play with borrowed clubs.' Before I had time to speak for myself, he rejected tennis with equal finality. Finally, a walk round the lake was agreed on.

'I gather,' my host said, 'that you want to marry my daughter.' I concurred. 'Well, now, there are a few things to discuss.' I again concurred. 'Where is your place?' I said sadly that I had no place: my father was an eighth child, and it was very unlikely that his unappealing childhood home in Wales would ever be mine. 'And what job have you?' I told him. The dialogue continued until at last he said, 'And so, Pryce-Jones, having nothing, without prospects, without a home, you expect to marry my daughter, who has always had the best of everything, here, in Belgrave Square, on the yacht which a kindly Government allows me –' he was First Lord of the Admiralty at the time – 'No, no, Pryce-Jones, come back in a few years when you have something behind you.' The verdict was final. It in no way changed our affection nor our mode of life, however, and all went well until Joan's father carried her off with him to India, 'to forget'.

What were we to do? Neither family approved of the other, though the objections of my own parents reposed on nothing more solid than vague hostile recollections of an earlier generation when my mother was a debutante, coupled with resentment that her son had not been received with open arms. I decided to go to Vienna while Joan was in India, in order to show her that I had retired from a world which has been too often described – notably in Evelyn Waugh's *Diaries*, for though he and I were never intimate our lives were twined round much the same friends. And so I set up in the Schönburggasse, in rooms lately vacated by the philospher A. J. Ayer and his wife.

But first Joan and I had unclouded months among loving friends, chief of whom, perhaps, were the two youngest Lygon sisters, Maimie and Dorothy – Coote to her intimates. Their father, Lord Beauchamp, had moved to Australia after a scandal famous in its day, precipitated by the rancour of his brother-in-law, the Duke of Westminster. He left behind him Madresfield, in Worcestershire, a large corner house in Belgrave Square, and all that went with each: servants, cars, horses, oysters and chablis for light luncheons, excellent champagne when needed, and above all Maimie and Coote who made life wholly delightful for Joan and myself as well as for the more dashing of our contemporaries. For contrast there were visits to Cranmer, in Norfolk, the home of clever and delightful cousins, the Lawrence Joneses, and in itself an enchanting house, now, alas, pulled to pieces. Jonah, as he was called, had been successful but bored as a City figure, and was about to start a second and even more successful career as a writer.

When my parents wanted briefly to be rid of me – for a convalescence, say – they used to send me to Cranmer, where I was sure of finding affectionate intelligence from Cousin Evie, Balliol talk from Jonah (who was a little older than the Raymond Asquith generation, but cut from much the same cloth) and the company of five girls, one of whom, Dinah, who died young, was as nearly a sister as I ever knew.

Cranmer summed up an English experience once usual but now vanished. Evie's uncle, Sir George Holford, whose collections at Dorchester House and Westonbirt were outstanding, had no children, and so, on his death, Evie, among other relations, profited from a spectacular sale of masterpieces. Cranmer was taken back, after being let for years, and refurbished. It was a large house, but not crushingly large: of eighteenth-century brick; sunny; predominantly white inside; eminently welcoming. Those it welcomed were many, and none of them dull. Greys, Cecils, Palmers, Grenfells, Strutts, delightful neighbours such as Wyndham Ketton-Cremer from Felbrigg nearby, a selection of Central European stage folk – for Jonah suddenly elected to write plays – filled the house. There were dances, not too formal, for the county. People were expected to be sociable, more or less respectable, and conversible. They were not expected to be crass, aggressively doctrinaire, or censorious. There was excellent food, plenty of activity, enough servants, and a prevailing agnostic tinge to all serious opinions at a time when opinions were held, if at all, with violent prejudice.

There were also more Bohemian possibilities. I remember a summer weekend – in those days our parents still spoke of a Saturday-to-Monday. It must have been 1932, and the Cyril Connollys had taken a house at Rottingdean. Cyril picked me up at Brighton Station, and on the way out stopped at a wine-merchant's, saying he wanted to buy ingredients for a cup. On arrival, I found Peter Quennell, John Strachey, Brian Howard and Eddie Gathorne-Hardy, Piers Synott, later Under Secretary at the Admiralty, and a young man of great physical beauty, Nigel Richards, a central figure in Cyril's subsequent novel, *The Rock Pool*. There were also a pair of lemurs, which frolicked up and down the curtains, in spite of, or because of, a chronic looseness of the bowel. All went well until dinner, when I was given a glassful of a sweet foaming liquid out of a jug. I congratulated the host on his cup. 'It's not a cup,' he said. 'It's champagne.'

I had better luck at Renishaw, where the champagne was always delicious. Our party was usually the same: Osbert and Edith Sitwell, Christabel Aberconway, David Horner and Rex Whistler. Edith used to strike a chill by warning me to keep to the inner side of the staircase because of a malevolent ghost with a tendency to tip guests over the banisters. One day Christabel said she had passed a miserable night. It was as though her bed were covered in wet river-weeds, she told us, and Edith at once agreed. 'Oh, we know *that* ghost,' she declared. We ate memorably good food, walked a little – a very little – in the soot-encrusted woods, with the flare of the mines showing behind the trees as the afternoon darkened. We visited local houses: Hardwick, Bolsover, lived in not so long before by Lady Ottoline Morrell, Sutton Scarsdale, a magnificent classical house, one room of which I was astonished to find many years later, with an eerie pang, built into the Boston Museum of Fine Arts. I ran through the piano score of my old acquaintance Herman Bemberg's *Guinevere*, and recalled his voice from the depth of a bath-chair in Luxor. *'Je meurs, je meurs, et pourtant je suis si riche.'* We played paper games and the Truth Game – a dangerous pastime which compelled honest answers to difficult questions and ruined many a friendship. And I at least watched Edith glowering at any evidence of a close triangular friendship, however unalarming, between Osbert, Christabel and David.

VIII

I T WAS AT this time that I struck up a friendship with Willie Somerset Maugham. We first met through the now-forgotten writer Gilbert Cannan, and remained friends until the end of his life.

He was not an easy man to know, especially with an age difference between us of some thirty years. Some of those who have written about him subsequently depict him as a surly curmudgeon haunted by the fear that his homosexuality might be discovered. This seems to me rubbish. He was born at a time when men did not obtrude their peccadilloes, more from good manners than from caginess. It was rightly assumed that most sociable men are indictable for much the same reasons. They have experimented. They have chosen different life-styles to suit different purposes. Why, then, obtrude the same set of limited possibilities in love on the outside world? Certainly, Willie kept his deviations to himself, but he was perfectly adjusted to them and quite unworried by the fact that they were common knowledge. He was a shy man, and had he been born sixty years later, when closets were bobbing open all over the world, his reaction would have been the same, I think.

He was also, in the early 1930s, devoted to his daughter. Once or twice, when he suggested my visiting him at Cap Ferrat, he added, 'And try to come when Liza is there.' I remember, too, walking along Sloane Square on my way to lunch with Osbert Sitwell, and seeing Willie slip into a pub. I could not resist following him in and mocking him a little for what struck me as an uncharacteristic act.

He replied that his new book, *Ah King*, was out that day and that he was on his way to leave a copy on Liza. 'But,' he said, 'it s-struck me that I might run into Syrie, so I thought I'd f-fortify myself.'

We walked together along the King's Road, and as we reached Argyll House, where Syrie then lived, his pace slowed. 'I can't f-face it,' he said. 'You ring the bell.' And he darted away, leaving the book in my hand.

Much later, he did me a true kindness. My publishers, Cobden-Sanderson, a small firm which specialized in fine book-production, had made no money from my prose, so I hesitated to submit them my verse. I sent some poems to Harold Nicolson for advice, and he in turn passed them on to Willie. One day I received a letter. Willie said he had liked the poems so well that he had forwarded them to his own publisher, Heinemann, 'with instructions to go ahead'. Heinemann duly did so. Kindness alone could have prompted his gesture.

But he was not, as I have said, easy. However, on my first visit to the Villa Mauresque, he had endeared himself to me immediately. The party consisted of Gerald Haxton, to whom I took a strong dislike, the George Dorans, Willie's American publisher and his wife, and the Herman Rogers, who later played a part in Edward VIII's wedding plans. After a day or two all of these left with Gerald in Willie's boat for a week-end, and, to my alarm, I found myself alone with my host. I need not have worried. I was allowed in to the room where he worked, which had in it a fine Gauguin panel on glass picked up, he told me, in Tahiti by chance. He had hoped to find a Gauguin on the island, and after some disappointment was on his way to check a possibility when his car broke down in a rainstorm and he took shelter in a nearby hut. There, on a glass door, he recognised a set of Gaugin panels, the lower ones scratched over by chickens, but at least one upper panel intact. He asked the price, should the door be for sale, and was told that it would be high, because, said the owner, he would have to buy a new glass door.

The Villa Mauresque was delicious. Cool, extensive, full of moted sunlight, and kept in order by white-coated servants, it sheltered a most carefully-ordered life. People came to luncheon and dinner – not many of them, but never dull people.

Arnold Bennett, a cockatoo in voice and looks, and Dorothy
Cheston might be there; an old bird's nest of a lady, a Comtesse
Gauthier-Vignal; Princess Ghika; the Michael Arlens; Lady
Bateman: names not all of which strike a chord fifty years later,
but covering a middle-aged, prosperous life which seemed
delightful to a young man in his twenties. Edward Molyneaux
came from La Capponcina, Ethel Lloyd-Osbourne brought
recollections of Robert Louis Stevenson, Maxine Elliott added
a touch of legendary beauty. Or one picnicked in the mountains, aquaplaned in the Bay of Villefranche, and at last, alone
with Willie, talked over one cocktail, or at most two, before an
excellent dinner: talk about Spain, about Cervantes and Gon-
gora, about women like Juliet Duff and Barbara Back, about
the technicalities of success in life – a subject on which he
thought himself expert. Much of his leisure day was taken up by
tennis and bridge – areas of living into which I did not enter –
and in those areas he had an often-resident expert in Godfrey
Winn.

One evening he was ragging Godfrey Winn on his persistent
youthfulness. 'You must be nearly th-thirty,' he said, 'and yet
you pretend always to be nineteen.' Somebody in the house said
that, as we were in France, Godfrey must have a passport with
him. Could we not check? Godfrey soon slipped away to his
room. Next day he left; and we received a telegram from Calais,
saying, 'Please forward passport. Third shelf from top of
bedroom bookcase, behind French dictionary.'

It may have been that same year, after the party returned
from their yachting week-end, that there was a picnic on one of
the islands off Cannes. We sailed over, unpacked cold chicken
and fruit and champagne, when a violent storm blew up, and
we were immobilized until the small hours, our chicken coated
in blowing sand, the champagne warm and gritty. I remember
noticing how quickly manners, and in particular Arnold Bennett's, went to pieces, until what had begun as a festive evening
turned into a frieze of outraged elderly elegants, sitting solitary
behind rocks and angrily shaking sand from their hair, at two in
the morning.

One evening Gerald Haxton took us all into Cannes, to a
pornographic movie. The plot was mildly funny. A couple were
languishing with a son and daughter in the Bastille, and

concluded that their one chance of escape was to seduce the jailer. The marquise, then, must sacrifice herself. She tried and was rejected. Was she too old? Then Louise must have a try. No good? Perhaps the jailor had special tastes. There was nothing for it but to offer up Charles-Henri. Finally the whole family was at work, but the jailer, who had a strong impediment of speech, kept trying to speak and showed no active response to any advances whatever. Finally he got the words out. They were free. He had been trying to tell them so for twenty minutes. Willie, who took any reference to a stammer as a personal affront, sulked for the rest of the evening.

He was always fascinated by Spain, and in the early Thirties I spent a few happy days in Andalusia with him and Gerald Haxton, touring through the mountains in his redoubtable Voisin. Osbert Sitwell had suggested my spending a winter in Granada, working on a play which followed the pattern of many first plays – a promising opening act, a logical second one, and an abrupt collapse in the essential third.

It proved, however, an exhilarating winter. I took a room in a dependence of the Alhambra, barely warmed by a very smelly stove, and set to work. There was snow on the ground, but I used to sit in sunny corners of the gardens, by faintly scented box hedges, to counteract the stove, reading *Paradise Lost* and discovering Kafka's *The Castle*. For weeks I spoke to no one, until Willie appeared and carried me off. By that time I had succumbed to a psychosis which has never left me. In theory I love to be alone. But in a very little while I begin to feel mildly ill: a touch of headache here, a cold there, a brooding sense of apprehension – the whole dispelled at once by a friendly human presence. Willie provided that. He spoke good, rather formal Spanish, unlike myself, who had learned what I know in Argentina and so spoke with a colonial accent as well. He was an admirable guide, and an amusing companion, some of whose talk I noted at the time, sprinkled with observations such as 'There isn't, as you know, a hill town in Italy where some old Englishwoman isn't having an affair with her gardener.' Or, when we spoke of Lope de Vega: 'His latest play is delightful. T-typical Lope de Vega and extremely witty. It is not, h-however, by him at all.'

Later I moved on to Cordoba, Seville, Ecija, in days when

there were no winter tourists, and when explosions of contemporary horror like Torremolinos and Marbella were stretches of empty beach. I lived for a song in dusty Spanish hotels, furnished in deal and wicker – not much more, incidentally, than Spanish royal palaces; I revelled in country *fondas*, with horses snorting gently just below my room. I took loaded buses into the Cordillera: in brief, I saw an Andalusia which is fast disappearing today, when those who have represented it, like Lorca and de Falla, were still accessible and the dust of Alfonso XIII's fast cars still floated over the highways, when travellers still spent hours changing from one slow train to another in the eccentric junction of Bobadilla, and scarcely a breath, let alone current, of thought from across the Pyrenees ever penetrated the hermetic civilization of nineteenth-century Spain.

To finance this, and similar expeditions, I had a chief source of support, an elderly (I thought) lady named Mollie Seton Karr, who lived with her mother in a dolls' house off Chester Square and worked as features editress on the *Sketch*. The *Sketch* was a glossy paper, a junior sister to the *Tatler*, and Mollie Seton Karr wished to spruce it up by calling on some of the younger writers for stories and articles. Week after week I wrote for her, and her modest but regular cheques kept me alive. She was an editress of a kind that no longer exists: ladylike almost to a fault, tender-hearted, respectable after a Presbyterian pattern, but not above a wink; kind to mother; equally loyal to young friends and to the proprietors of the magazine: in short, a perfect dear.

When I reached Vienna I needed the cheques only slightly less, because of the cheapness of life there. I alighted in an ancient, shabby, more or less respectable hotel, the König von Ungarn, close by the Cathedral; then moved to the Schönburggasse, where I had two rooms in a flat belonging to Frau Jones, an elderly lady washed up in what must have been a creditable street, for it was quite close to the Belgian Legation. For my two rooms, heated, and swept by Anna during those rare months in which she was not pregnant, I paid some £30 a year. Meals were equally cheap. One could have an excellent luncheon at the Grand Hotel for a few shillings, owing to the depreciated currency of the country.

I at once took to the life of Austria. There was a handful of foreigners also in the city: Samuel Barber and Gian Carlo Menotti from New York among them, and Martin Cooper from London. Also a talented but by now unjustly forgotten composer, Stanley Bate, and a beautiful, already tumbledown scion of the Barrymore family, Robin Thomas, who shocked the conventional by going to Legation luncheons in sandshoes, and not entirely sober. With these I sat regularly at the opera, during the great years of Lehmann, Schumann, Mayr, Olczewska and – occasionally – Jeritza. We sat in a *Säulensitz** from which you could not see the whole stage, and we breathed the heavy smell of garlic sausage which intoxicated the upper galleries. We heard rarities, like Hugo Wolf's *Corregidor*, and most of the familiar repertory, magnificently done. Or we went to the Burgtheater to see Moissi and Thimig; to the Musik-vereinsaal, score in hand; to the Theater an der Wien and the Volksoper in search of Nestroy and Marschner. I never expected so abrupt an awakening to German feeling, so that, like Tosca, I can now cry '*Vissi d'Arte*'.

From time to time other visitors from London settled among us: John Lehmann, Stephen Spender, Robin Maugham and his Uncle Willie. For this was the Vienna of the Dollfuss period, and there still seemed a tenuous chance of it pulling through as a Christian democracy, in spite of the dark clouds already engulfing its German neighbour. These led to immense internal tensions. The remnants of Imperial Austria, now poor and unemployed, looked one way towards a less restricted future, the workers naturally another. The Hungarian minority despised the Slovaks, the Czechs hated the German-speaking Austrians, the Jews were uneasy and actively aware that most of what had been valuable after the decline of the Empire set in had been due to their special talents.

In this cat's cradle of warring stresses the only beneficiaries were those foreigners who, as in Paris during the previous decade, lived well on a depreciated currency. Our presence must have been exasperating to the natives, but they only showed this exasperation by the reasonable assumption that we would pay our way into their good graces. And so, for the first year of my Austrian life, I joined the crowd with gusto,

* a seat behind a column

maintaining a decent Left Wing attitude to local politics, but revelling in the very real pleasures of an Austria still mindful of the nineteenth century: in the butter-coloured castles, the pine-scented valleys, the chattering mountain streams, the peasant *Trachten* in the Tirol, the baroque abbeys, the unending gossip: the whole amounting to an aquatint world in which the characters of the *Commedia dell'Arte* still lived.

I saw a great deal of a remarkable character whose friendship I owed to Maurice Bowra. He was a large, comfortable man, who had been an exceptional classical scholar at Eton and King's, who talked with commanding brilliance, but who was chased, throughout life, by thoroughly deserved bad luck. A year or two later I wrote a pseudonymous novel about him called *Pink Danube*, safe in the knowledge that by that time he was a High Anglican monk, and so, I thought, unlikely to waste time on a piece of secular writing which could hardly have pleased him. For, with all his immense charm, Adrian Bishop was a difficult man to consort with. Totally unscrupulous about money, to a degree demanding, constantly forced to leave the city or the country – after the pattern of Norman Douglas – when he fell yet again into yet another scrape, unemployable except, at times, as tutor to some rich family until the fatal day when he became involved with his pupil, he was, all the same, an enchanter, whose entire life led to its climax, during the war. By then a senior Intelligence officer in Teheran, a hotel staircase collapsed under his weight, and he was buried beneath a toppled avalanche of debt, scandal, laughter, kindness, splendid jokes, learning and (at times) despair, aptly symbolized by an Edwardian hotel in ruins. Perhaps his years at Nashdom Abbey as Brother Thomas More entitled him to a welcome in the next world; alas, he had more or less exhausted the possibilities of this one.

The days flashed by in pre-war Austria. When the rain held off in spring and summer one drove over the dirt roads – not yet macadamized – to the most exquisite of pine-scented country-sides; one went on walking tours through the Wachau, sleeping in the guest-room of monasteries, and resting on warm afternoons under a foam of apple-blossom. One read Wildgans with Hans Doblhoff, a morganatic Habsburg, passing the time by rubbing bacon fat on too-new *Lederhosen*. One swam in icy lakes, sharing the religion of the sun with Tuke-like striplings who later turned out to be ardent Nazis.

In winter one went up to the Semmering to ski or skijöhr, often as the guest of an American Standard Oil heiress who was trying to decide whether or not she was a Lesbian – a decision which in some ways depended on Nijinsky's very trying wife. And at all seasons one tried to penetrate Austrian and German secrecies – a feat made the more difficult by the hospitable reluctance of Austrians to speak German to foreigners. We read Rilke and George with passion, we plunged into Novalis and Hölderlin, we admired the Sezession and discovered with excitement Klimt and Schiele. It was a happy time if one were twenty-five and protected by a foreign passport. And during my second winter I completed my own happiness by again falling in love.

IX

O N MY FIRST visit to Vienna, in 1930, Bobbie Pratt Barlow
had taken me to lunch with an old friend of his, a widowed
Baroness Fould-Springer. Her two youngest daughters were
with her at what turned out to be quite a large party, and I
noted in my diary that I very much liked my hostess and pitied
her for having such ill-mannered children, nudging each other,
mocking the company, lapsing into private laughter. They were
sixteen and fourteen at the time. Two or three years later, as I
got to know Austrians of my own age, I noticed that they spoke
often about '*les petites Fould*' and as autumn turned to winter
spoke with increasing excitement. They might turn up any day.
Their arrival meant the opening of a large house near Schönbrunn. It meant a rush of hospitality, not entirely unlike the life
of Madresfield, for the two girls came alone with their governess
and had at their disposal cars, servants, space, liberty – the very
things which we were to seek among the Viennese young at that
time.

The governess was a splendid lady. Every day at precisely
2.07 p.m. she was rung up by a much younger man, known to
her charges as 'Deux Heures Sept'. He turned forty when she
was sixty, and at that time she married him, concluding that
their age difference was no longer important. In 1932, however,
she had also other fish to fry, and attracted some derision by
contriving to fall into the arms of Chaliapin on an icy driveway
in St Moritz. I thought Marthe – for that was her name – both
sensible and affectionate towards '*les petites Fould*', and when,
sure enough, they arrived, the lodge-gates of the Tivoligasse

were opened, and I found myself in the presence of two girls rising twenty, funny, charming, utterly unlike the little wretches I had remembered them to be.

We used to skate in the early afternoon – a group of young people, most of whom were expert. They would seize one from behind and swing one into a figure of eight – the harder for me because my skates were ice-hockey skates anyway and I was not adept with them at best. My ankles swelled, and burned, and quivered. Very soon I found that Thérèse, the elder of the Fould girls, suffered as much as I did, and we crept away to the bar, to drink hot chocolate and rest our insteps. This was a course which led insensibly to the altar.

But the turning-point was the Jägerball of 1934: a social occasion on which we all were dressed as Tyroleans. I had been lent the right outfit by Count Rumerskirch, the father of my first German teacher, Marianne, and a man on whom we looked with excited respect, because he had been with the Archduke Franz Ferdinand in the fatal cortège at Sarajevo and his hair (we were told) had turned white in a night.

Thérèse and I danced. We sat among pine-branches under little candles. We talked about ourselves, we underwent that odd melting sensation which much later is seen to have been the moment of falling in love.

The home of the Foulds was in France, the so-called Palais Abbatial of Royaumont, the abbey built near Chantilly by Louis IX. There I found myself the following spring, and then again in Austria when I joined '*les petites Fould*' at the Post Hotel, Ischl, a small mountain resort on which still lay the shadows of the Emperor Franz Josef and Frau Schratt. And there, one September afternoon, on a hill above the Traunsee, under the lee of a baroque chapel, I asked her to marry me. She said yes with such decision that I broke my sunglasses in two and threw them, in what she considered an improvident gesture, over the low cliff into the lake.

Today, I suppose, things would have been handled very differently. But at that time we behaved with nineteenth-century propriety. The governess and the two nannies who were, after thirty years, still in attendance, betokened alarm mixed with excitement. Telephone calls to France and England were set in motion. We were guarded from one another by innumerable chaperones. Later, in London, it was decided that, because it was London and not Paris, Thérèse could visit me in my flat on condition that Marthe brought her and took her back to the Dorchester Hotel after precisely half an hour; during which time she discovered a box of unopened letters in my kitchen and seriously doubted if she could marry a man who took so little care of his mail – I have always flinched from opening a letter if I do not care for its face. Finally, we were married in Chantilly just after Christmas, on a sunny, snowy day, and driven up the avenue to Royaumont in a pony carriage, the spokes of its wheels plaited with white flowers.

Presents were decorously arranged; champagne popped; Paris ladies in Schiaparelli gowns and silver fox furs crowded round; until at last we left for the Crillon, and next day on the Orient Express for Rome, Athens and Istanbul, before returning to Vienna for the rest of the winter. In brief, a thoroughly decorous wedding of the period, equipped with the proper selection of rings, clips, vicuña rugs, crêpe de chine sheets for an eventual lying-in, Vuitton wardrobe trunks – which ruined our honeymoon by their size and weight – and travelling clocks from Cartier.

Naturally, during the weeks which preceded the wedding, I had time to study my new in-laws, and in particular Thérèse's mother. No doubt they devoted a degree of attention to me, for no more dissimilar backgrounds could be devised than Thérèse's and mine. Her father, Eugène Fould, had died some five years before. Her mother had lately remarried, choosing an extremely handsome Englishman named Frank Wooster. An elder sister, married to a Spanish diplomat, found her husband suddenly unemployed in Paris as a consequence of Alfonso XIII's abdication; and there was one brother, at that time unmarried, who found himself compelled, as an only son, to assume business responsibilities which were, I soon concluded, uncongenial. He should, by temperament, have been an architect, or a museum director. Finally there was my younger sister-in-law, Liliane, not yet twenty, and not less gifted than her siblings with intelligence and taste – two qualities to which she attached even more importance than they.

The four children were very close to one another, and bound the closer by two stalwart characters, Nannie and Jessie, each more English than the Queen – both literally and figuratively – each devoted to the children, and each extremely wary of the children's mother and step-father.

But it was that mother who, in her formidable extrapolations, embodied the entire family. When I first met her she was in her middle forties. I walked into the immense house in Meidling, quite close to Schloss Schönbrunn, and I saw a smallish, plumpish woman with, as chief physical advantages, most beautiful legs and hands, still beautiful nearly fifty years later. She had no classical beauty of face, but radiated, when she chose, an irresistible charm and a vitality which were balanced by an abrupt excess of nervous exhaustion from time to time. She spoke rapidly in French, English and German. I judged her, on instinct, to be wilful, generous when it suited her, formidable in displeasure, but also vulnerable. And when I learned a little more about her I succumbed to a fascination which lasted until the end of her life.

Her father, Gustav Springer, and her mother, Hélène von Königswarter, had been married seventeen years when their only child was born. Her mother died a few days or weeks later and Baron Gustav moved out of his house into the Imperial Hotel, leaving his daughter at home in the eventual care of a Scottish governess. He was a formidable personality himself: a banker, a coal-owner, a railway-magnate, a landowner, the owner of famous racing stables, a philanthropist. He had died in the 1920s, still rich in spite of recalling, I was told, two hundred and fifty million gold Swiss francs from Zürich to Vienna in 1914, on grounds of patriotism. But at his apogee, when he was the Harriman of the Austro-Hungarian Empire, he had been rich indeed, and so made it his business to educate his heiress in the management of a fortune. With her Scottish governess beside her, little Mitzi Springer was sent to the Dresdner Bank to learn about banking, to Poland to learn about coal-mines, to the Great Western Railway to learn about rolling-stock. Not surprisingly, she became bored, and fell in love, in her late teens, with my father-in-law, a witty, lazy, art-loving member of a family which had given France Achille Fould, Napoleon III's minister, the steel of which the Eiffel Tower is constructed, and, in a sense, Proust. Eugène Fould's mother was an Ephrussi, and one and all took much trouble

97

over a sociable young writer named Marcel who had many reasons to be grateful to Charles Ephrussi in particular.

Baron Gustav was not pleased by his daughter's choice. In his view Austria did not marry into France. But when she persisted he gave her, if as a dismissive gesture, the factories outside Paris which made much of the yeast of Northern France, and proved a financial godsend to her for the rest of her life. She was not greatly attached to her father. During the years in which his wife was childless he had fathered elsewhere children whom Mitzi had later to support. She even asserted that she had to move a wardrobe across her bedroom door to protect herself. But it must be added that she drew a tenuous line between the truth of fact and the truth of imagination. At least we may agree that it cannot have been much fun for a little girl to play hostess, Sunday after Sunday, to groups of bearded magnates, clouded by cigar-smoke, descending on Meidling for luncheon and an afternoon in the *Kegelbahn*.*

If such a life bored her it certainly did not bore me. To begin with, I was welcomed with touching warmth into my new family. And then I felt like a British Columbus to whom was opening an unsuspected, exhilarating world, peopled entirely by strangers.

My own family, at home, knew nothing about Jews. They were certainly not anti-Semitic, but they included Jews in the category of foreigners, who – at least in my father's view – were usually a trouble to know. When sometimes he spoke to my mother of a brother officer and said, 'Extraordinary thing. I do believe old Charlie's original name was Wertheimer,' he meant just that. Extraordinary that Wertheimer should become Williams. Extraordinary that Williams was so excellent a staff captain and owed so little to the example of his grandfather.

But now, of a sudden, I found myself moving among Todescos, Halphens, Heims, Rothschilds, Scheys. All of them were loyal to their past but few were noticeably orthodox. They had not exactly been absorbed by the societies in which they moved, but they had come easily to terms, just as Proust came to terms with the Faubourg. True, the Dreyfus affair shocked them

* bowling-alley

98

profoundly. My father-in-law, I was told, never felt the same about prosperous life in Paris once he perceived the treacherous volatility which underlay its pleasures. But Gustav Springer belonged, if exceptionally, to the Vienna Jockey Club. And his world was accepted, until Hitler's ascent, by the Kinskys, the Festetics, the Apponyis, the Mittrowskys, who shared his taste for horse-racing, Monte Carlo and the chorus line.

It would not be fair to say that Eugène Fould married his wife for her money. As a member of the family which had made a name for itself in politics, finance, art-collecting, sport, for half a century and more, he had no reason to better himself. But he must also, I think, have relished the opportunities bestowed on him through marriage, which included an Austrian barony given, to the mild annoyance of his French friends, by Franz Josef, to perpetuate his father-in-law's.

Then came the First World War. At that time, Frank Wooster was a young man in his early twenties. He had come into the world, along with a brother, when Leyland, the shipping magnate who commissioned from Whistler the Peacock Room, left his yacht in Ramsgate, went for a walk on shore and met the beautiful Mrs Wooster. He stayed with Mrs Wooster for two decades or more, refused a divorce by his legal wife, and settling substantial sums on his illegitimate children.

The legend continued: many years later he set off to visit his London lawyer and change his will in favour of the Woosters, and he died in the train. An embattled Mrs Leyland sped down to evict her rival, and in a very short time Frank lost the £100,000 settled on him in a few days' gambling in Monte Carlo. He joined the Army, and then in France met my father-in-law with whom he struck up a close friendship. He was captured by the Germans, and on release moved to Paris where he spent the rest of his life, never learning French, living as an amiable adventurer, either selling dubious antiques, in partnership for a time with Sir Robert Abdy, or carried along by admirers, both women and men, who happened to be elegant, notable, and rich.

For he was, as I have said, a man of exceptional good looks. Even in middle-age his appearance made strangers turn their heads in the street. A severe critic might call his looks a trifle Hollywood: the wavy hair eventually blue-rinsed, the straight, trim nose too defiantly triangular. His Charvet tussore shirts were too carefully ironed, the embroidered FWs on his pyjamas a shade fanciful, perhaps. And, to match this stellar presentation, he was often extremely silly, not least after a few cocktails. But he wished to please, and he pleased. He was kind. He was often funny. He was an excellent friend. And his positive qualities seem to have won my father-in-law's heart.

At any rate, he embedded himself in the life of the Fould-Springers, to the irritation of the children and, for a time, of their mother. But she, at least, saw clearly. What, she asked herself, is so attractive about us? And she answered her own question: my money.

And so she took over Frank's life. Knowing her, I very much doubt if she wished physically to absorb him. Her feeling was, at its most intense, a devotion like Carrington's for Lytton Strachey. And it evoked an emotional confusion which Bloomsbury would have understood. Eugène Fould soon wondered if he were not losing both a wife and a friend. Frank Wooster, beset by admirers of whom the Foulds were only two, basked in vicarious prosperity, and a climax was reached when he travelled round the world with Bobbie Pratt Barlow, and Mitzi insisted on following, with her husband and her eldest daughter, a week or two behind him, in case he fell ill on the way.

When the followers reached Saigon my father-in-law, by now a thoroughly unhappy man, himself fell ill, turned his face to the wall, and died. It took several years for the inevitable sequel to follow. My father-in-law had restored a handsome Louis XV house in the little town of Montreuil-sur-Mer, near Le Touquet. Frank persuaded his widow to buy up, and pull down, surrounding property so as to create space on which to build a large California-style house to his own design in a setting of gardens and pool. He was also installed in a Paris flat carved out of a house she owned near the Madeleine. The children watched, and sighed. Eventually my brother-in-law spoke up on their joint behalf. He spoke with vivacity as head of the family. A few days later his mother spoke up too. She thanked him for what he had done. It had crystallized her mind, she said. He had mentioned a family. There was no family, she asserted, merely herself. Now she had decided to marry Frank. And she did so.

By the time I came on the scene a year or two later, the Woosters lived chiefly in Montreuil and the rue de Surène; the children at Royaumont or in a large *appartement* in the avenue d'Iéna. From time to time the older, or (independently) the younger, generation went to Vienna or to one of several houses my mother-in-law owned or leased in Slovakia and Hungary. The surface of their lives was tranquil. The young were sent to Austria in a Rolls-Royce and wherever they might be were accorded total liberty. They had to go, if reluctantly, to Montreuil for an occasional week-end, and though their mother had no special affection for Central Europe she descended on them there from time to time. Family officers paid bills and regulated the details of living. The nannies conspired benevolently, the duenna, Marthe, kept decorum. But there was a good deal of whispering about Frank, and towards their mother a complexity of feeling on the part of the children, in which a stranger could detect strands of solicitude, resentment, apprehension, relief when things went well, tense again when they did not, at all times a sensitive violin-string tightness constantly being tested to discover whether family life were in tune or not.

X

ONE DAY IN January 1935, Thérèse and I stepped off the Orient Express to take up our new life in the Tivoligasse. We were met, no doubt, by a dark-blue Austro-Daimler coupé, upholstered in blue rep, with basket-work over the coupé itself, and carriage lamps beside the chauffeur. There would have been bowing administrators from the office to cope with the porters, Frau Hihn at the lodge to open the gates of the park, and Franz the butler at the door which he had already guarded for fifty years before I arrived. Fräulein Gusti, the housekeeper, must have been behind him, and a fat hall-boy, and fatter lady's maid, Mali, to unpack the dressing-cases. The wardrobe trunks followed.

It was a fanciful situation for a young couple to start married life thus wrapped in cotton wool. In the kitchen was the former cook of the Empress Elizabeth, whose Cumberland Sauce I can still taste. Herr Weingartner, the retired coachman, was around to open and close the *Kegelbahn*, the skittle-alley. If we needed extra money, within limits the office under Herr Brüll and Herr Mailáth-Pokorny was there to provide it. And over all the house itself, cut off from the outside world by a fifty-acre park, extended the benevolent shelter of a large building long half-empty of life, and until now totally empty of vitality except for a few weeks in the year.

It was an assertive house, much praised at the turn of the century, and even copied, we were told, by Balkan admirers. Its architect had hitherto built mainly theatres, and so the central hall was surrounded by a dress-circle, behind which an inner corridor led to a number of bedrooms. The stairs were set, as it were, on a stage between projecting boxes, and the whole was lit through a ceiling of coloured glass, for my late grandfather-in-law liked a display of light both blinding and polychrome. The Rote Salon led to the Gelbe Salon and to a dining-room redesigned by Eugène Fould, who had been vexed by the overall style of the exterior – Henri IV, more or less, with a surprising half-timbered kitchen wing and court after the Norman taste. Throughout, the walls were still hung with Lyons silks of the 1880s, sometimes quilted, and the furniture was very much that of a Vanderbilt house of the period in America; that is to say, expensive copies of French originals – a style which a slapdash Athenian, who had been hospitable to us on our honeymoon, once described without irony as '*système Henri Quatorze*'.

Our own rooms upstairs were more comfortable. There was a Telefonzimmer, with a Tissot on the silk walls, and a picture by one of the Koekkoeks, a marble bust or two on plinths, and chaises-longues spread with fur rugs by windows which looked up the park along an avenue. In winter, the double windows were stuffed by *polsters*, to keep out the draught, and white porcelain stoves reinforced the old-fashioned kind of heating which emerged sighing from vents in the floor. The bathrooms were especially welcoming. Immense baths were sunk below floor level, the porcelain stoves blazed, and the sofas were upholstered in towelling, so that an hour passed very swiftly in an Asiatic doze, book in hand.

Vienna in January is swept by winds off the Russian steppes. Wrapped in furs, we went for walks over the crackling snow. Indoors, the rooms shimmered with heat. In this hot-house atmosphere we discovered an immense happiness in each other.

But in that happiness there was a flaw. It had showed itself first in Rome, after we had been married a week or so. No warning shadow had darkened a honeymoon which promised strong and unclouded contentment. And then, suddenly one morning, Thérèse changed. She would not speak. She lay in the dark, she withdrew into a total desolation, prompted by no act or word, she became, briefly, a stranger; wanting no help, offering no explanation. Much later, there were tears. She was,

I saw, gripped by some force outside her will, and certainly outside her wish. As the years went by, I learned that this would recur every few weeks. And, when much later I read in detail of the recurrent anguish suffered by Virginia Woolf, I recognized every degree of an inconsolable pain; inconsolable because the shadows which engulfed them both were as mysterious and inexorable as the tides.

I do not claim that I said or did the right thing on every occasion. But I do know that the unhappiness inflicted on us both by this malady acted strangely as a link. I could not bear to see someone I loved in misery. And she, when the cloud lifted, could not bear to think that it had ever fallen on us. She was bewildered. She suffered as much from the bewilderment as from the cloud. Usually the most cheerful of young women, witty, tender, in love, adored by countless friends and an affectionate family, remarkably intelligent, and possessed of a life-enhancing spirit which made people of all ages and kinds turn to her for support and understanding, she had hidden in her a private hell, which terrified her, and terrified me. It never engulfed either of us, though we both suffered from watching for the abrupt onset of darkness.

I remember especially an evening the following summer, when we had briefly leased a flat in London. We dined in Hampstead, and walked away from dinner to find a taxi. Suddenly, in Arkwright Road – I can see the pool of lamplight on the roadway – she stopped. She felt ill, she said. She believed she was pregnant. And she said, in a vaticinatory tone of voice, as if looking into the future, that she knew, she knew what would happen. She could not bear the thought of being taken by surprise. A child should be planned for, dreamed of, aspired to. If she was right, she said, she foretold disaster. Her father and her elder sister suffered from a deficient circulation. She too would have phlebitis. She would have a major nervous collapse. I have never walked in Arkwright Road since. And she was right. Our son was born seven months later, with no difficulty; she was attacked by phlebitis soon after, and spent several months in a mental home near Paris, forbidden visitors, and at times in danger of losing a life to which, at the moment, she attached no importance whatsoever, so cruel, illogical, incoherent was her despair.

Thérèse was twenty-two, I twenty-seven. We were young, therefore, and I at any rate managed to salvage a constant hope, which by the end of the year became reality. Thérèse's health never quite recovered. She could never ski again, her pretty legs became less pretty, a posse of doctors totally forbade her to have a second child, and her withdrawals from life continued all her days, but little by little she regained health and courage, helped by an intense pleasure in the one child she was ever to have.

Most of our time until the outbreak of war was spent in Central Europe. This meant an almost complete break with English friends, although in 1937 we bought the lease of a Nash house in York Gate, so that our little son David should keep a foothold in English life. But so fascinating to me was the Vienna of the 1930s, and so strange the life imposed on us, that I came to look on Meidling as our real home.

It must not be forgotten that the 1930s were a bizarre decade. If one lived in Vienna, it was impossible not to see the disaster which loomed ahead. We lived directly in Hitler's shadow. My in-laws were Jewish. It was as if each day were salvaged from an inevitable wreck, and so we put off taking sensible steps as long as possible. I ought, as a responsible husband and father, to have taken up a paying job in London. We had very little money which was absolutely ours. But we were given every encouragement to pretend that we were very rich indeed. Houses, cars, servants, holidays, were simply there. We had loving families to promote what seemed to them our happiness. And it would have needed more moral fibre than I possessed to reject, in the cold name of good sense, an easy life freely offered.

So we had our box at the opera, our summer weeks in Strobl, and our autumn week-ends in Budapest. When we went to Paris or London we travelled in state with Mali the lady's maid to pack and unpack and a courier at the railway stations. True, we did not travel quite as grandly as my mother-in-law, who always sent her staff ahead to the wagon-lit which was set out with her own bed-linen, with the Cartier travelling-clock and the little photographs in silver frames by the bed, so that when she appeared at the last minute she might find herself in a setting identical, but for size, with her own bedroom.

Friends from London came to stay. Brian Howard refused to

be warned of the dangers of *heurige* wine and fell off the box seat of the Austro-Daimler after an evening in Grinzing, not before we had written a joint surrealist poem, 'The Electric Boot'. Derek Hill, then a very young painter, enchanted the girls of Vienna by making them Reboux hats out of domestic napkins in a restaurant. My father suddenly discovered, at our expense, the possibilities of the international telephone, and spent much time asking 'Whom do I know in Norway? in Bucharest?' Billa Cresswell* insisted on being taken round the nightclubs by Thérèse, six months pregnant but very willing. Theodora Benson asked me for a lift in our car to a charming little hotel in the Annagasse where I was to book her a room. 'For how long, *gnädige Herr*?' 'A week or two,' I said. *'A week or two?'* I realized that the neat eighteenth-century façade with its orange trees in boxes concealed a brothel, and kept Theodora in the taxi.

I ought to have felt cut off from my own generation of writers, for indeed they were sinking into the background of our life just when I should have been matching my wits and gifts against theirs. But the 1930s were a time of diaspora. People moved all the time – some, like Aldous Huxley and Auden, to America for good. I remember talking in London to Gerald Heard whose companion of many years, Christopher Wood, had fallen ill in California. 'I have to go and help,' he said, 'I shall be away quite three weeks.' And he was away some thirty years.

Only John Betjeman, consistent in his dislike of abroad, stayed in England for choice. Those who could not travel, pined. And a new quarrelsomeness entered social life as France and Hitler and Mussolini and Stalin played dice with one another. I remember an elaborate dinner at Londonderry House when a daughter of the house threw a silver cigarette box across the dining-room table because she held an opposite view to her vis-à-vis. This violence was new. The English do not normally become rabid in discussion. But, all of a sudden, well-brought up citizens, under the stress of the times, lost their heads. Oswald Mosley was only an extreme case.

In Austria, we moved in several worlds at once. Our family world was mainly Jewish. The collapse of the Credit Anstalt in 1932 had accelerated its financial decay. Three Rothschild

* Later Lady Harrod

brothers, Alfons, Eugen and Louis, shored up the ruins as best they might, and Alfons's wife, Clarice, still reigned over a sizeable kingdom: a mordant, formidable presence, equally redoubtable as friend or enemy. There was a whole group of old ladies living in mixed splendour, some of them helped by my mother-in-law, whose greatest pleasure, I sometimes thought, would have been to preside over the fall of her entire world, save only herself, still able to bestow or withdraw capricious benevolence. Viennese Jews of established respectability existed on the fringe of the good life. They were allowed to pay for Aryan company and Aryan pleasures, but not encouraged to go beyond the perimeter of Aryan society. The 'erste Gesellschaft', a hang-over from imperial Austria, simply marked time, too proud to work, too poor to dazzle. I remember the scenes made by an old Prince Liechtenstein when one of his sons decided to take a job in London or New York. Had he not just enough money to be seen in public once a week with the prettiest actress of the day? Had he any reason to do more in life than that?

The princes and the Grafs were usually extremely stupid, if also handsome, excellent shots, and lusty in bed. It was a typical Gräfin whom I heard describing her eligible son-in-law, 'Er ist ein gute Walzer, und Malteserritter.* By contrast, the Jewish world – at this level Jewish by race rather than orthodox religion – was often brilliant, creative and affectionate. Hofmannsthal was dead, but Alban Berg still alive and occasionally visible. We were to visit him one evening, knowing he had been ill, when he got out of bed to test his strength, and died: we felt half-responsible for his death.

The silliness of the 'grand' Viennese was summed up in an imaginary character, Graf Bobby, to whom were attached innumerable jokes displaying his ineptitude. But Graf Bobbys and clever Jews alike shared the Viennese passion for music and theatre. This was the great period of the Burgtheater, and the Opera, of Reinhardt in Salzburg, and the rediscovery of Bruckner and Mahler in the concert halls. Millöcker, Lortzing, Nestroy became familiar names to us, innovators like Webern and Schoenberg less so, because the Viennese public did not feel at ease with any work of art created since the fall of the

* 'He is a good walzer and a Knight of Malta.'

107

Empire. Yet if we gave a dinner-party it was still quite possible that a guest might bring his violin and another her cello, so as to run through a Beethoven trio after the cigars were smoked. And, all the year round, superb musicians, Chaliapin, Rachmaninov, Marian Anderson, Horowitz, played in public halls and private houses.

About this time the South African business magnate Sidney Beer fell into talk with Sir Thomas Beecham, who told him that 'What music needs is rich men like you and me'. This prompted Sidney to set up as a conductor, although at that time he could not read a score but learned his music from the gramophone. For his first concert he rashly engaged the Wiener Philharmoniker and Rachmaninov to play the latter's Second Piano Concerto. In the slow movement he lost his place, and Rachmaninov, more coldly saurian than usual, conducted the rest of the work from the piano, while Sidney stood with folded arms. The subsequent supper-party for both in the Kinsky Palais was not a success.

Another night, in a country Schloss, Chaliapin gave a party at which local singers performed. To their distress, he stopped them more than once. 'Not like that, like this,' he insisted, projecting a tremendous bass roar. We were given a peach *bowle*, and the peaches were overripe, so that, at the same moment, half the guests went scampering into the moonlit bushes. Brueghel would have enjoyed the evening.

Not more than a few hours' drive from Vienna were family properties in the Slovakian valley of the Theiss. Baron Springer followed an adage. '*Boden fliegt nicht weg*',* and bought land wherever he could. Unluckily, it lay along the borders of three post-1918 states, Austria, Czecho-Slovakia and Hungary. Family legend had it that at the Peace Conference my mother-in-law gained access to Lloyd George through an old friend, Lord Vansittart, and marked on a map where the new international boundaries should lie – so far as they concerned her. There was notably a large tract of land near Tepla Trenčin, and another on the Hungarian plain, towards Rumania. There was a Walter Scott Gothic castle halfway to Budapest, and another shooting-box in Western Hungary.

* 'Land does not fly away'

Life on these properties had scarcely changed since the sixteenth century. I noticed, for instance, that in a local cemetery it was impossible to tell from its design whether a tomb were brand-new or two centuries old. Marriages between her tenants had to be ratified by my mother-in-law in Paris. And, when we drove through one of her villages on the way to spend a week or two in the neighbourhood, it was not unknown to find flowered arches over the street inscribed ALAN and THERESIA, while the villagers paraded in their local finery.

When we reached the house, the superintendent used to ask what we wanted: a fur coat? a sheepskin cloak? embroidered vests? the people of the place were waiting to be put to work. There was to be a partridge-shoot, perhaps, or, in Hungary, a crueller sport. There the guns were hidden in a hay-wagon, while a great owl was tethered to the ground, upon which hawks swooped, to be shot as they did so. In Hungary, too, the news of our arrival would bring a gipsy band to the house, by nightfall. All round, the vast treeless plain, grazed by wild horses, extended, animated by the creaking of water wheels like those in Egypt. The zithers tinkled, the dancers warmed up, the night ran on, cheerfully.

It seemed to me absurd to have my part, however small, in these happenings without a smattering at least of languages. Magyar I never penetrated, but once back in Vienna I had a stately Dr Jokl come to teach me Czech – an accomplishment of which only one phrase remains after forty years, *Pokryvka je ružova* ('the eiderdown is pink' – a remark I have never had to make). Czech grammar is a diabolical puzzle, but at the time I acquired a small elementary skill.

There were social problems too. I begged the superintendent to stop each passing gardener printing a kiss on my hand while I was reading on a garden chair; but the superintendent pointed out that to do so would be insulting. The gardener would suppose that I thought him dirty.

All in all, I began to feel like a snake twitching out of its skin. The familiarities of English life became unreal, as I walked in the snow through the Gothick eccentricities of Laxenburg, or ate my *Garniertes Liptauer* in the Grünangergasse. For one thing my daily problems were so new. Could I continue to pay a young Austrian debutante for German lessons when I found, by chance, that she was passing the money on to the German Embassy to support Hitler's subversion of her country? How was I to be honest with a Spanish brother-in-law who worked for Franco in Paris when my own sympathies were with Wystan Auden, Cyril Connolly, Stephen Spender, Julian Bell – muddled sympathies which veered from Anarchy to Trotskyism – then stopped to reflect that Franco, after all, represented a degree of international order?

But that would not do. Mussolini and Hitler also represented order – of a kind. Or how about Czecho-Slovakia? Were there not sad stories afloat about the financial chicaneries of Prime Minister Hodža? The Czech Government had suddenly imposed a very large fine on my mother-in-law for unpaid taxes which lawyers denied she owed. Hodža, we learned, had approached her with a dubious personal bargain, and she was right to reject it.

What I wanted was to sit in my tower room and write a book or two. (I did so.) I wanted to play my piano, spurred on by the austere daughter of a former Ambassador who composed musical comedies in the twelve-tone scale, and put me through my paces in the Berg sonata and the Křenek suites. I wanted to be happy with Thérèse and our son, and also to follow the leads which fired my contemporaries to action. The arts, in the 1930s, connoted intoxication: good intoxication like the music of Stravinsky, Kokoschka's paintings, Eliot's synthesizing explorations; bad intoxications like Cocteau's *Opium*, Céline's fiction, the horrid vulgarities of Dali.

And then there were discoveries specifically Central European: Hölderlin, George, Stifter's *Nachsommer*, put in my willing hands by Eddy Sackville-West, Pfitzner's *Palestrina*, the drawings of Schiele. I bought one at this time for $15.00 and could have bought fifty. Thérèse and I became engulfed in the surviving vestiges of an imperial past. We spent hours in the library of Stift Altenburg, among its stacks of vellum-bound quartos; we explored the fretted and bastioned streets of Prague – barely put off by the extreme charmlessness of the Czechs, who, of all people, slammed one in revolving doors or stamped unwitting on one's toes in the bus, or in a passion of chauvinism chucked stones at a foreign car, especially if it carried an Austrian number-plate.

From a standpoint forty-five years on, I look back on my younger self with a good deal of distaste. Self-depreciation is a boring quality, but I have never been the kind of man, either in physique or disposition, whom I like. I get on my own nerves and I am always astonished if others do not share this reaction. By 1937, I had shaken myself out of total self-indulgence, since Hitler's intentions were by then obvious. What could I do? I joined the Liberal Party, because Sir Archibald Sinclair, its leader, was a supporter of Winston Churchill. I joined the Officers Emergency Reserve, which ensured being called up at the outbreak of war. But these were feeble gestures. And one, at least, was greatly frowned on by my father, who had long written Churchill off as an irresponsible turncoat – although not four years later, and with no apparent sense of incongruity, Churchill had become for him the saviour of Europe.

Thérèse was much more effective than I. She worked hard in London at placing German children in British homes, and later joined Lady Reading when the Women's Voluntary Services were founded. Up to the Anschluss, we spent part of the year in Vienna, but by then Austria had become a nostalgic dream, punctuated by gunfire round the Karl Marxhof, sweetened again by the miraculous beauty of the countryside, threatened alike by the zeal of Prince Starhemberg, the justified grumbles of the extreme left, and the ominous manoeuvres, just beyond the horizon, of the Wehrmacht.

But there were delicious interludes of self-indulgence. One of the family properties in Slovakia included Čachtice, a dramatic ruined castle which had been the home, nearly four centuries earlier, of Elisabeth Báthory, a female Bluebeard who for many years murdered the unlucky girls sent her as though to a finishing school for young ladies. Because she was a close relation to the King of Poland, only towards the end of her life did the authorities check a rumour that she bathed in the blood of her victims, and found this to be so. Even in our time the local peasants refused to cross the threshold of the ruins – which resembled Corfe Castle, and seemed to us in our innocence a ravishing site for a picnic.

Or we spent idyllic weeks in Bad Ischl, sometimes with my very un-cosmopolitan parents, who would have preferred the Leas at Folkestone, but bravely affronted the horse-flies which haunt Austrian Lakes, and the yodelling dancers in *dirndl* and *lederhosen*, after dark. Once I took them to an impoverished synagogue in Bratislava, where the sexes were segregated, so that my mother was swept up to a balcony and my father to a downstairs aisle, each very evidently expecting to be subjected to ritual murder.

After the stately pace of Central Europe we moved to a brisker tempo in England and France. Having joined the Party, I found myself vice-president of the St Marylebone Liberals and not long after adopted as Liberal Candidate for Louth, Lincolnshire, in succession to an embattled lady, formerly Member, Mrs Wintringham. The seat had a lively Liberal past, and although my links with the Fen country were non-existent the support of Mrs Wintringham gave a certain promise to my candidature. Its purpose was to help bring Winston Churchill to power, and my early steps towards that purpose were at least enjoyable. The villages round Louth were at first reluctant to show their hand towards me. I would go, with my agent, to some small market-place, set up a loud-speaker, try to avoid Thérèse's quizzical eye fixed on me from across the green, and begin my speech to no audience whatever. After a time, with luck, there would be a stir behind the lace curtains, a door opened ajar, and little by little a small, perhaps very small, crowd gathered, impelled by curiosity. There were meetings in village halls, where any success I might have was due to my playing 'The Blue Danube' on an upright piano. I stayed with saintly Baptist schoolmasters, and dined off tinned salmon at friendly kitchen tables. Occasionally a visiting star came too, such as a splendid figure, astrakhan-collared, and much more at home in Pratt's or lunching at the Ritz, Harcourt Johnson; and the equally splendid James de Rothschild. These, I suspect, were not vote-getters in Lincolnshire.

XI

LOOKING BACK ON my life at thirty, it seems totally artificial.
Cyril Connolly kept telling me that we were cut off from our
friends by living more luxuriously than they. We did but, as I
have said, we had very little money of our own and perched
precariously on the edge of splendour. Writers like Dylan
Thomas thought me able to help them with cheques, an
introduction (in his case) to Evan Tredegar as a fellow-
Welshman, or praise. We saw a certain amount of Stephen
Spender but the Pylon Boys, as at that time they were called,
lived lives separate from ours, and so did Bloomsbury, with the
exception of Raymond Mortimer and Eddy Sackville-West.
Harold Nicolson, Vita, Elizabeth Bowen, were much closer,
but long absences from London and an extreme distaste for the
tiny squabbles which nourished the Sitwells but poisoned the
springs of literary life made our time abroad a constant solace.
Yet artificial it was, as all exile must be. We spoke German
tolerably well, but never became an integral part of Austrian
life; nor, mindful of Austrian *Leichtsinn*, treachery – it was not
too strong a word – and leech-like cupidity, did we want to be.
At the same time England had drifted away. My father and
mother were happily self-sufficient. They did not need children,
although they looked on my younger brother, just turned
twenty when war broke out in 1939, as an agreeable toy. From
time to time they descended suddenly on Central Europe. I
remember my father joining a shooting-party of my brother-in-
law Max's in Hungary. It was very hot, and the other guns were
open-shirted and sweating. My father wore his Scottish tweeds,

remained perfectly cool as though in a chilly Yorkshire autumn, and shot, I was told, extremely well. The only moment at which he lost his sang-froid was when Count Haugwitz, husband at the time of Barbara Hutton, asked him after dinner, 'Would you care to see my jewels –' and then made a valet bring down his rubies, his sapphires, whereas my father flinched from anything brighter than good but moderate pearls.

My mother preferred to stay at home, writing her letters after breakfast, and keeping up the sixty or more identical leather volumes of a diary from which words which might bring bad luck were carefully banned. Thus, in August 1939, she was writing, 'How dreadful for Harry to start a w. feeling so desperately tired.' Not that war, for my father at sixty, was likely to be a repetition of 1914.

As to my brother, he was almost a stranger to me. When I married he was an Eton boy and, until the Welsh Guards claimed him on the outbreak of war, he was either at school or perfecting an Olympic standard of ice-skating – an art which threw my mother into ecstasies. She recalled her aunt Mary Minto as the Governor General's wife in Canada many years before, be-minked and be-beavered, doing her figures of eight backwards with admiring secretaries. Skating, then, must be a respectable activity, and she spent hours at Queen's watching my brother emulate his great-aunt with the international stars of the day. By contrast, my activities were thought not quite respectable. She was all in favour of her children gathering praise, and ran a surreptitious service of information about us among our relations. But her fields of possible triumph were still confined to the Brigade of Guards, the moors, and a small circle of dinner-tables. As she grew older, she withdrew. If the Lansdownes, say, did not ask me to dine a second time she looked sad. 'You see, darling, you're not in the Brigade.' If they did ask me to dine, she viewed the invitation with asperity. 'I can't think why Elsie should do this. *We* never go anywhere any more.'

Artificial though the framework of life might be, I did at least try to underpin it, if not with hard work, at least with a certain amount of thought. As a child, I had been inexpressibly bored by the automatic churchgoing of my elders. But I also possessed an *anima naturaliter christiana* long before I dipped into Tertullian

– or so I must suppose from the fact that I used to construct secret chapels in shrubberies and leaf through melancholy little books of household prayer in black leather bindings, left behind by great-grandparents in writing-table drawers. I have recorded a shaft of illumination which troubled me in the ugly little Catholic church at Filey; and now, years later, I found myself living in a Catholic country for much of the year and pretending to be a Catholic myself. This set up strong feelings of disloyalty. In England, I tried to make do with St Mary's, Bourne Street, with All Saints, Margaret Street, with St Cyprian's, Clarence Gate, where John Betjeman first introduced me to the inimitable work of Sir Ninian Comper. But it would not do. My feeling for Catholicism was much like that of Evelyn Waugh. I needed it as a force of order. I needed the Petrine rock to sustain me. And in those days Catholic observance was a delight. Benediction, Tenebrae, the music of Palestrina or Victoria, a numinous presence carefully evoked, spread glory over the liturgical year. It still took me a decade to convert a predisposition to a way of life, but at least I gained more from St François de Sales or the officially rejected Molinos than from my great-grandmother's dry little black manuals, or my father's top-hatted march towards the Guards Chapel.

Back in England, I nourished a slow-moving political career. It brought an occasional surprise, such as an invitation to luncheon with Lady Oxford in Bedford Square. I imagined that she was asking me in order to congratulate, stimulate – fascinate I took for granted – a recruit to Liberal ranks. I was thus a little surprised to find myself with one other guest, Mademoiselle Gogo Schiaparelli, and much more so when it emerged that I was thought to be a Conservative candidate, bent on putting in its place the party which twenty years before had betrayed Mr Asquith. Thus by pudding-time I was being treated as a fool if not a traitor.

Lincolnshire, however, was a delight. I could relax by making Tennysonian excursions to Mablethorpe – in midwinter a splendidly melancholy resort. Thérèse and I, fired by affection for Louth itself, visited one too-large but rentable house after another – all built after the style of Somersby but often withdrawn when it was discovered that I was a Liberal. In Marylebone things were livelier. Our president, Dorothy

Trotter, was a niece of Sir Herbert Warren, the President of Magdalen, Oxford, who had rusticated me. Disgrace in her uncle's eyes was a strong recommendation to her, and to her mildly rakish, dandified husband, Philip.

But, every day during the year or two which preceded the outbreak of war, all activities seemed more and more shadowy, all voices drowned by the radio tirades of Hitler, all hope eclipsed by distrust of a destiny presided over by Chamberlain, Sir Samuel Hoare, Lord Halifax and their colleagues. To make matters more oppressive, those who were taking the wrong decisions for their country were often part of the charmed circle of cousins whom the elders of my family for that reason accepted as oracles. How could Edward Halifax be wrong when my father had shot with his father at Hickleton thirty years before? True, Anthony Eden, who was on the right side, ranked as a cousin too, but even at that awakened the mistrust of my elders. Was he not a supporter of the unreliable Churchill?

Torn between conflicting aspects of disaster, normally sane people became rabid. A few years earlier Lady Winefride Elwes would never have received a postcard which I copied into my diary when her son Simon showed it me. It was elicited by an announcement in *The Times* that she had arrived in London from the country: in the event, to arrange for the evacuation of children should war break out.

'You – a devout Roman Catholic – to publish that notice in today's newspaper that you have returned to 31 Walpole Street from the country – you ought to be ashamed of yourself. You simply like a coward rushed away from London because you thought you might be bombed. A damned good job if a lot of you useless diseased old London females (no use for eating, no good for breeding) were put in a lethal chamber and destroyed. Yours etc. A Protestant Colonel (retired HAL) who with his wife and children remained in London. Great Western Royal Hotel. 3. X. 38.'

This was sent a few days after Munich – at a time when the peoples of Europe were prompted by terror, relief, shame, new resolution. Earlier, at the moment of the Anschluss, I had travelled at full speed from London to Vienna to find the balconies of our house hung with swastika banners. It was historically a Jewish house and invisible from the street, so this gesture struck me as bizarre. But the old servants were jubilant. Austria had been saved, they said, from destruction under Russian bombs by the arrival of the German army. For months they had been accumulating swastika banners in hope of this happy day. Then, the very next Sunday when they walked to mass at the end of the park, the Pfarrer* had expressed doubts. And at once they came to me again. The Pfarrer had said that German troops should be withdrawn. How were we to achieve this? Their reaction was typical. Having spent years plotting for a German coup, as soon as it took place the Austrians regretted it.

There was madness in the city. The manager of our family office had asked a German general or two, with their wives, to stay: no doubt as a precaution. I went to lunch there one day, and was seated beside a large lady who tucked into schnapps and beer and broke into a little lecture about the delights of living in Düsseldorf. There were speeches on the radio, she said, and marches, and processions, and more speeches in the evening. Everyone was illuminated by a new happiness and vitality. All the women were having babies. I interrupted to ask if she had a large family herself. No, she said, she had no children. 'But I shall, I shall,' she also said, defying the fact that she was well into her fifties.

A day or two later a voice from the family office informed me that I had a mission. It was at that time thought safer to keep money in Berlin than in Vienna, but money could not legally be transferred out of the country. I was told, therefore, that every penny of my mother-in-law's liquid cash which could be raised at short notice was destined to buy Mercedes-Benz patents through a trusted agent, and that my duty was to take the cash, illegally, to Berlin in my luggage. My mother-in-law was in a London hospital, undergoing a serious operation. It was anyway imprudent to discuss such matters over the international telephone, and I knew that the office manager was both empowered to act and determined to do so. All the same, the scheme struck me as absurd. I was to go to the airport and await a taxi with the money on board.

The day was stormy and the plane, which was very small,

* Parish priest

117

arriving from Budapest, was late. No taxi showed up, to my relief, and then suddenly it came, bringing a large paper parcel of bank notes.

These I placed in the rack overhead, as nonchalantly as I could. And at last we set off. Over the Black Forest the storm became so severe that we were forced to fly low above the trees. The little plane rattled about: a respectable matron in front of me sank on her knees, rosary in hand; and my parcel began to disintegrate. When I could, I stood up and poked little wads of bank notes behind holes in the brown paper, dreading our arrival and the, it seemed, inevitable disclosure. However, when we reached the Tempelhof aerodrome, I found that we had been given up for dead, because our radio had failed. And in the general relief nobody noticed my parcel. I left it deliberately on a seat while I went through the formalities of arrival, and trusted that no attention would be paid to so dejected an object while I sought out the agent who was to meet me with his patents. There he was, a solid Nazi official of inconspicuous probity. I exclaimed at my own stupidity: I had forgotten a parcel, I exclaimed, and I was allowed back to pick it up from the bench where it lay. It contained, I found, a very large sum indeed. I handed it over, I was given a drink by the agent, and that was the last ever heard of either money or patents.

A few weeks before war broke out we spent a summer holiday at Cap Ferrat. The Under-Secretary of State for Foreign Affairs, Rab Butler, was at the same hotel, and we had an agreement that he would tell us when to leave for England. It therefore seemed reasonable to keep an engagement to lunch with Willie Maugham. We found a degree of panic in the household. The yacht was being loaded, the servants were scampering about. Later I read in an account of his evacuation experience that our host had been shocked by the insouciance of a young English writer and his wife so unaware of reality that they positively had turned up for luncheon.

A few days later Rab Butler told us we must be off, and we drove north, I more fortunate than the others because I had a single suitcase which travelled with me, whereas they had more copious luggage which only reached them many months later. When Butler waved us off, I remembered being told by Cécile de Rothschild of the fluke which had brought him success in life. Years before her brothers Alain and Elie – later my brother-in-law – needed an English tutor, and their father had applied to the University Appointments Board. He had received several applications of equal promise, and so took the papers to the tower of Laversine, his home near Chantilly, and threw them off the roof with the notion that the first to reach the ground would get the job. The lot fell on Butler, whose public career developed from that summer assignment.

When I reached London I found an order posting me, with the rank of Captain, to Kandahar Barracks, Tidworth, where the 4th Hussars were to form a Prisoners of War Camp in which I was to serve as interpreter: not a glamorous job, but at least a practical beginning. I was loading a car to leave, and my father and mother were in our house to say goodbye when the first air-raid siren rang out – a famous false-alarm, as it happened. At the time, however, we were expecting annihilation, and our gas-masks were at the ready. The cook, the butler, the two maids, were white and tense, but my father, in the hall, gave an exhibition of stately calm by picking up some letters from a table and sticking stamps on them, punctuating each lick with a show of phlegm: 'The first time – I was blown through a window – was at Bapaume.' We had left our son David in the north of France, with Jessie his nanny, and in his grandmother's house. The theory behind this was based on the strength of the Maginot Line – of which Diana Cooper later said that if only it had been made of Scotch tape instead of steel the Germans would never have got through. We imagined a war of attrition in Flanders, during which I might have an occasional leave to join Thérèse and David at Montreuil.

For the time being, however, she and I stayed with Louise Wakehurst near Marlborough, while I kicked my heels by day at Tidworth, embarrassed by my military rank, foxed by the routine of saluting, and exasperated by Randolph Churchill, who spent all day in the telephone booth of the mess, noting down his own calls, 10 Downing Street . . . 11 Downing Street . . . Admiralty House . . . 10 Downing Street . . . *The Times* . . . 10 Downing Street . . .

The fact that we were technically, though not yet dangerously, at war; that my military duties were confined to giving, or acknowledging salutes; that I spent my evenings in a ravishing eighteenth-century house, Rockley; that part of each day was as serene as a September on the Downs could make it, gave life a kind of breathless suspense. I rode on the empty hills with my cousin Mary Loder, while Thérèse jogged behind – far behind – on a recalcitrant little donkey, Josephine; we picnicked with Robert Byron in Savernake Forest, he looking, as always, like Queen Victoria *en travesti*, choleric, clever, a faithful friend too soon about to die at sea. John Betjeman gave me the ideal present for a long war abroad, Hardy's Collected Poems. From time to time a neighbour turned up – Siegfried and Hester Sassoon from Heytesbury, Lord Ailesbury advancing up the drive in a tiny Trojan car with solid tires, advancing at fifteen miles an hour, and announcing what a little trump of a car it was, while his hostess, behind her hand, told us that his late wife when a girl was known as 'the maddening Miss Madden'. And then there were my brother officers at Tidworth, the senior of whom, with wife and son, were invited to stay at Rockley until we went overseas.

Our military unit was odd. We were a scratch lot, as a Prisoners' camp may well be. Colonel Wickersham was a nervous little man, whose authority derived from playing the part of butler in theatricals on the front at Eastbourne. His adjutant, a man of fifty or so, had served in the First World War, as had two ancient lieutenants, who might have done credit to Falstaff's irregulars. The Colonel was not at ease with Lady Wakehurst. He had looked her up in Debrett and ascertained her to be a duke's daughter, albeit, in life, a slightly eccentric dowager who took whatever privileges might be hers as a matter wholly settled but of no great importance. She had been a follower of Rudolf Steiner, and spent so much of her time on 'the other side' that finally she cemented herself firmly in this world alone – so as not to neglect her husband and children. Yet when my uncle Alan – her first cousin – killed himself she wasted no time before telephoning to my mother and announcing, 'Your brother is perfectly well. I've been with him through the first three spheres since he died – and they are the difficult ones. He'll be all right now, but I'm going to join him just to make sure, so I've no time to talk to you at the moment.'

After dinner at Rockley, she would settle Colonel and Mrs Wickersham at a round table and spread open a photograph album. 'Now, let's see. This is Hatfield – no, that won't interest you. Ah, and here is Evie Devonshire at Hardwick. But that will bore you. And, oh yes, these are the Dartmouths at Patshull. But that was many years ago, and you won't be interested, will you.' The evenings were not a success.

Few men of thirty were less military than I at that age. I was not exactly frightened, but I loathed being taken out of a happy family life and a comfortable home. When I went into Marlborough to order top boots – in the event never worn – or a valise: when I drove into Aldbourne or Pewsey, so peaceful, so welcoming, so embowered, I could not believe in the reality of my Sam Browne belt and my captain's flash.

And then one day we were at sea. It was still September, and Poland seemed far away as we disembarked at Dieppe and were billeted at – of all unwarlike abodes – the Grand Hotel. We had nothing whatever to do, for there were no prisoners and anyway there was no camp. I settled down as mess president, and luxuriated in the fresh and delicious food of the hotel chef. But in no time my officers came to complain. Why give us this messed-up stuff, they asked, all cream and strange vegetables, when we can have tinned Canadian salmon from the Naafi and apricots in syrup? I stood my ground, applauded by the Colonel, whose tastes had been deviated by Rockley life, and who anyway wanted to be in my good graces so that I could help him choose underwear, uncomfortably embossed and threaded with lace, for an Eastbourne *soubrette* who satisfied him, he told me, more competently than Mrs Wickersham.

Dieppe made as few concessions to war as Marlborough. I used to spend evenings playing bridge with Ethel Sands and Nan Hudson, two splendid old American friends of Henry James, upright in *guimpe* and whalebone, who had run their exquisite house at Offranville, filled with Sickerts, as a hospital in the 1914 war and were vainly bent on doing so again. They took me to visit Jacques-Emile Blanche, I remember, in a house redolent of the exiled Wilde and lynx-eyed Proust. They took me to see Mrs Romilly, sister of Mrs Winston Churchill and mother of Giles and Esmond, two conspicuous rebels of the day. Once or twice I drove over to Montreuil, to where Thérèse had moved so as to be with David. I was allowed to bring a car to Dieppe – a formidable Tatra equipped with what was then a novelty, an engine at the back. We had bought it in Czechoslovakia, a country in which my mother-in-law encouraged us to spend as much money as possible, because money could not legally leave the country. Unluckily the chauffeur who drove it from Bratislava to Paris omitted to buy oil, so the poor Tatra spent most of its young life in a repair-shop.

In some ways more amusing were evenings at the hotel, where the equally unemployed English nurses from a nearby empty military hospital came over to have a drink, flirt, and test my ability to accompany 'Ilkla Moor' and 'I have not brought my specs with me' on an upright Pleyel in the deserted ballroom.

Weeks passed. But at last deliverance came, as so often through the agency of a cousin, Sir Sidney Clive, a General, who arrived in Dieppe and took pity on my inactivity. He was on his way home from our Army HQ at Arras, where he had been amused by sparring talk in the mess. Lord Munster was on the staff of Lord Gort, commander-in-chief, known as Fat Boy, and one evening the talk turned to the possible inconveniences of bastardy. Lord Munster descended from William IV and the actress Mrs Jordan, and Lord Gort took this as a pretext to say, 'You must know something of the subject. After all, your family is illegitimate.' To which, apparently, Lord Munster replied, 'Yes, sir. And if we were not illegitimate I should be King of England. And if I were King of England you would not be commander-in-chief.'

Sidney Clive was able to arrange for me to be sent back to England, where courses for potential Gauleiters were being organized by Cambridge University. It still seems a brave sign of confidence that such courses could have been planned in 1939, but there we were, under the command of Lord Gerald Wellesley who, having been a diplomat or an architect until his middle fifties, joined his family regiment, the Grenadiers, and subsequently saw service in Italy.

Gerry Wellesley, later Duke of Wellington, was sometimes disrespectfully called the Iron Duchess, because of a certain spinsterish attitude to the modern world. He once spoke disparagingly of someone to Sachie Sitwell. The someone was, he said, impossible: the kind of person who spoke of 'a fruit salad'. 'But I always call it a fruit salad,' said Sachie. 'What

Vere Dawnay, AP-J's mother by
Ellis Roberts, c. 1899

AP-J's mother and father,
c. 1945

AP-J by Horst, 1938

John Betjeman, 1928

Robert Pratt Barlow, 1931

With the Cyril Connollys at Rottingdean. Standing: Nancy Quennell, Nigel Richards, John Strachey, Piers Synnott; Sitting: Eddie Gathorne-Hardy, Jean Connolly, Brian Howard, 1932

Thérèse, 1936

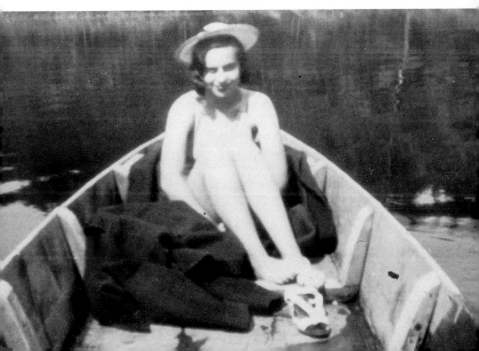

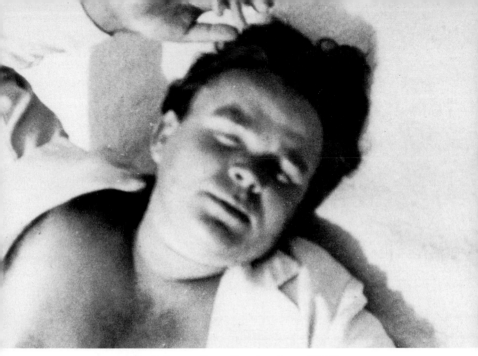

Cyril Connolly at Rottingdean, 1932

AP-J with Cecil Beaton, c. 1955

AP-J's mother-in-law, Marie-Cäcilie Springer, with her
Viennese court, c. 1904

The "atrium" at Meidling

AP-J, 1942

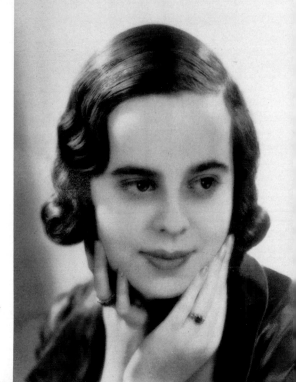

Thérèse at Royaumont,
1938

AP-J with Thérèse and David,
Kent, 1942

AP-J with Somerset Maugham
at Cap Ferrat, 1962

Mary-Jean, c. 1936

AP-J by Derek Hill, 1979

should I say?' And the Duke answered between clenched teeth, as if biting on a lemon, 'Macédoine.'

At Cambridge he had under his command Christopher Sykes and a score or more of officers for whom a courtyard at Trinity had been taken over. It was an exceptionally cold winter. In my rooms we studied under admirable teachers like Sir Ernest Barker and the economist, C. W. Guillebaud, whatever a Gauleiter-to-be needed to master. Yet so thorough was our grounding that with only a few weeks at our disposition we never reached beyond the eleventh century in any subject. We examined early Jewish migrations in the Crimea, we debated problems which died with the Merovingian Kings, we scribbled notes on the Pecheneg communities in pre-christian Hungary, but we never came to grips with the forces which have shaped Germany during the last thousand years.

My own days were slightly clouded by the reappearance on the course of Adrian Bishop, whose recent years had been spent as Brother Thomas More at Nashdom Abbey. I considered him to be safely immured there, and, as I have already mentioned, I had made him the centre of a short pseudonymous novel, *Pink Danube* – pseudonymous because it painted an unflattering picture of one segment of Viennese life and happened to be published soon after the Anschluss – a moment when it seemed ungracious to stress the faults of a volatile people. I recalled a meeting in a hotel in the Dolomites three months after the German occupation of Vienna. Thérèse and I were driving towards Hungary when we met my attractive young teacher, whom I had broken with when I found she was giving my money to von Papen, along with any help she could muster to unseat her government. I said to her, 'You at least must be happy. You have what you wanted and worked for.' She retorted, 'But the Germans in Austria are a disaster. They are ruining my country. I'm going to America.'

Pink Danube dealt in part with such infirmity of purpose, but it also painted a picture of Adrian Bishop in Vienna which did not give him pleasure, though his sensitivity soon absorbed a more interesting set of tensions, as the War Office kept changing its mind, and posted him one day as Lieutenant-Colonel and the next as Lieutenant.

XII

During the Cambridge weeks I assembled the small battery of facts, as opposed to opinions, which has protected me ever since; and they led me to reflect how much wiser it is to postpone a University education until life has shown a need for it – a reflection confirmed by the much later experience of my son, who packed two years of military service into the time between leaving Eton and going to Oxford.

At the time, however, I found myself an unwanted Captain, learned about the Pechenegs and the Merovingian Kings, but quite useless in areas of growing menace like Finland and Belgium. My weeks at Cambridge spared me Dunkirk, but they also separated me from my son, who remained in France as a pledge to enable Thérèse to share my Cambridge days but, in theory, to go back to Montreuil afterwards. Helped by my Spanish diplomat brother-in-law, we forgot the German army. The whole small family took refuge in Spain, then returned to the South of France until just before the German army occupied the entire country. My brother-in-law, a diplomat in Vichy, was by that time less well-informed than I, and I was in anguish until I learned that David and his cousins had left France on the last train, only because my brother-in-law had displeased Franco by helping fugitives cross the Pyrenees, so that he was demoted from Vichy to Morocco, much to my relief. From Tangiers I could organize the return of David, by now five, to England, where he made the headlines by announcing, on reaching Bristol airport with his nanny, that there was nothing to fear from the German army. He had seen them daily in

Cannes, wearing slacks on the Croisette, whereas the Portuguese – for he had been delayed in Lisbon – were a formidable lot: they wore feathers in their hats.

Meantime, I had been sent to other military courses – always in the Home Counties, in the daunting coniferous landscapes of Pirbright and Woking, where I rode a motor-cycle along sandy rutted paths; or listened to the advice of Sergeant (was it?) Malcolm Muggeridge while being vetted for the Field Security Police. Finally, I fetched up, by now a mere Lieutenant, in a branch of Military Intelligence, MI14, devoted to the German Army, and presided over by Major Kenneth Strong, a tall, lively man, who looked as though he were constructed geometrically round an imposing nose.

The star of our section was Eric Birley, a distinguished archaeologist at the University of Durham, who had made a special study of the German Army in order better to understand the Romans, his theory being that good armies at all times have much in common. His archaeological training, exercised on the Roman Wall, gave him encyclopaedic insight into German procedures, and he carried in his head a pattern of related facts I have never seen equalled. Should he learn that a captured Feldwebel had started his army career in Paderborn in April 1941 with the third Ersatz battalion of the sixtieth Pioneer Regiment, the man's subsequent career was at once clear to him. It happened that the Battle of France coincided with the first effective break in the German Ultra system. MI14 had the task of interpreting these breaks for the Chiefs of Staff and the Prime Minister as well as for the smallest possible number of commanders in the field – a scant list dictated for security reasons.

The advantage to me personally of this job was that for the rest of the war I, like my colleagues, was usually as well informed about the intentions, capacities, and reactions of the German High Command as Hitler himself. I was not a specially competent Intelligence Officer, but little by little I crept up the ranks, especially after I was sent to Bletchley Park as a link between the Cryptographers and MI14, trying to ensure that Bletchley and the War Office obtained what they needed from each other.

My first assignment, however, was a little different. After

Dunkirk, a possibility existed that the War Office might have to be evacuated. I remember late that summer being present at a meeting in which the Director of Military Intelligence told us that, if a single German division crossed the Channel successfully, Southern England would be lost. We were therefore to keep an eagle's-eye watch on shipping in the Scheldt. But we had to prepare for the worst. And my task was to go through the files of previous years stacked in the War Office cellars, and covering correspondence with the British Embassy in Berlin. This was a fascinating study. I carefully preserved the evidence of accuracy on the Military Attaché's part, and folly on the Ambassador's. The Military Attaché had perceived and reported the secret expansion of the German army, but his reports were minuted by Sir Nevil Henderson with comments such as, 'Major Mason-Macfarlane has allowed his military interests to affect his judgement, I fear.' Later, as DMI with the British Expeditionary Force, Mason-Macfarlane's judgement proved admirable. When Hitler's famous Yellow Plan was captured, and the ineptitude of the French revealed – for the British had relied on the French Intelligence Service and been sadly misled – it was partly Mason-Macfarlane's assessment of the likely plans for an attack formulated by army commanders whom he had known which enabled us to protect an escape route for our own troops. And in all this Birley played an invaluable part. He had for some time been convinced that French Intelligence was hopelessly faulty, and when he was proved right he turned overnight into an ultimate authority on the German Army. So much so that when, in 1943, American Intelligence was brought to Bletchley, the United States Army began calling up archaeologists in the hope that a posse of Birleys might emerge from their peaceful universities. The American contingent was headed by Brigadier Telford Taylor, later prosecutor at the Nuremberg trials, and in no time we established a harmonious partnership.

The War Office became a kind of home for the next three years. Our house in York Gate was burned by bombs in 1941, and for a year or so we lived at Athenaeum Court, Piccadilly, which was at least more solidly built than a Nash terrace house. The actual bombing took place at night while we were both out of the house. It was not pleasant to turn a corner and to see your home in flames at roof-level while the police, probably correctly, forbade you to try and salvage anything from the lower floors. At that time, we still lived in the house, sleeping at ground-level or below. And I have not forgotten a night of stress while we crouched under the basement stairs, and our man-servant suddenly said, in a calm butler's voice above the racket, 'I think, sir, I should go up and see if the upper floors are on fire.'

Frequent night duties in the cellars of the War Office brought to that ponderous building a certain homely quality. One brother-officer, Michael Holroyd, formerly Lecturer in Ancient History at Oxford, more or less set up house there, hung strings from pipe to pipe, and displayed on them items of melancholy underclothing. One might meet Tony Powell – whose *Dance to the Music of Time* contains much the best account of War Office living – James Pope-Hennessy, a refreshing new friend, who provided in those years a welcome note of Firbankian outrage among falling bombs; John Austin, later White Professor of Moral Philosophy at Oxford, and one of the ablest men I have known; David Niven. Life narrowed with the growing constrictions of wartime. Occasionally we dined at the Pastoria, off Leicester Square, one of the few restaurants which continued to offer tolerable food. And many of us discovered unfashionable Edwardian eating-houses like Frascati's which still sold magnificent ports and brandies at a shilling or two a glass to clients who appreciated nothing between beer and cheap champagne. We used to explore such places with Maimie Lygon, by then Princess Vsevelode of Russia, and I still cherish an invitation from her to dine: 'No party. Just ourselves and Greece and Yugoslavia.' She was concerned, I remember, with the difficulty of reintegrating Pavlovsk after the war – it had been her husband's childhood home and she expected its return after the Red Army had been defeated – in circumstances hard to define. The heating of so large a house would be a difficulty, she opined. And there had been some unfortunate building on the edge of the park. When I visited Pavlovsk thirty years later I noted that it had been totally destroyed in the war, but restored with magnificent skill by Russian workmen who think nothing of building a double staircase in lapis lazuli, but have much trouble in constructing a workable lavatory.

Athenaeum Court was well placed for excitement; our room looked down on Piccadilly, and when there were severe raids the view could be dramatic indeed. Once the street, which slopes sharply at this point, was turned into a torrent by burst water mains, and I can still see Raymond Mortimer looking out of the window, across rushing water to where fires burned in Jermyn Street and St James's Place, fires which threw a multi-coloured explosive glare against the night-sky. Raymond, rightly, treated this apocalyptic scene as an aesthetic experience. 'We need a touch of orange there, don't you think? and a *pale* green. Oh, that must be Stornaway House going up. All fireworks. But not quite the right blue.' On other evenings Harold Acton might be teaching my son, newly returned to England, a few words of Chinese. Or Brian Howard, in Air Force blue, dropped in from the Ritz, where he complained that the lift-shaft was jammed with rats driven out by the bombing of the tube station opposite.

As a very humble aircraftsman of thirty-five or so, he was not supposed to use the Ritz restaurant, but naturally rose above this and one day gave luncheon there to Meraud Guevara. He was telling her in vivid terms of the inefficiency of our air force. 'You see, my dear, we are given these *tiny* planes, *loosely* roped together with string.' A General at the next table overheard this subversive talk, whipped round, saw a middle-aged Other Rank who had no right to be there, and acted out his part. 'Stand up!' Brian, after three cocktails, stood. 'What's your name?' 'Mrs Smith, my dear, Mrs Albert Smith.' Then, sitting down again, 'As I was saying, Meraud, these poor little planes are *no match*.' His back by then was again turned to the General, who abandoned the case, speechless.

Less appealing was his rudeness to the American correspondent Quentin Reynolds. They met, by appointment, in the Savoy and, after the cocktails had done their work, Brian's character changed, as it usually did, and he began: 'It must be very pleasant for you, Mr Reynolds, to see the ruin, the disintegration of this country. The sound of the bombs must be music in your ears.' And so on. Third parties led him away, and expostulated. He must apologize, he was told. And they went to Mr Reynolds, saying that Howard's nerves had been dreadfully frayed by his experiences of late. He wished to apologize.

Reynolds accepted this with grace. They had another drink. And then the gramophone needle stuck in its groove, and Brian was heard saying once more, 'It must be very pleasant for you, Mr Reynolds . . .' Or he was in the Gargoyle Club late at night, when young officers newly emerging from the Dunkirk evacuation were trying to drown their sombre memories of the previous week. Brian went from one to the other, Harold Acton told me, saying, 'Dunkirky-wirky, my dear. We didn't do very well, did we now?' If hit, as he sometimes was, he hit back much harder. And yet, when all was well and the right mood was on him, nobody could be more appealing, witty, original than he.

One of the disadvantages of belonging to the inner Ultra world was that we were, so to speak, embedded in it by Churchill's order. Rather than risk our being captured, authority compelled us to stay where we were for the duration. Although I had no ambition to be a hero I was unhappy to miss a unique experience. I was unhappy to be a chairborne soldier only. Not until the very end of the shooting war was I finally posted to the staff of our 8th Army, first in Northern Italy and then at Caserta. But first I spent a year or two at Bletchley itself, though technically I still belonged to MI14.

My new home was in Ferry Stratford, close to Bletchley Park. It consisted of a little brick cottage on Simpson Road, which I shared with two brother-officers, one of them Edward Crankshaw, the expert on Russia. This cottage was icily cold in winter, and of a workaday ugliness which evoked high praise from John Betjeman when he visited me there. Our small party was cared for by a treasure named Honey, an elderly, lugubrious-seeming but benevolent lady.

The people I worked among were a wonderfully mixed bag. Others have written of the mathematicians whose cryptographic work justified the complex superstructures of Bletchley Park. But as the organization ramified it absorbed a noticeable variety of talents. Not all were happy in the monstrous surroundings of what had been once the creation of a Jewish magnate, Sir Herbert Leon. From time to time, for instance, the typists would exclaim, 'Poor Mr Wilson, he's done it again.' For Angus Wilson, understandably cast down, had jumped into a lake, fortunately only a few inches deep. Later we were told that his first, and brilliant, collection of stories, *Such Darling Dodos*, had been written as a form of therapy.

Then there was Lord Lamington, a senior member of the directorial staff, who from time to time had to be taken away drunk in a taxi. Later I came to see a good deal of his clever and attractive wife and to learn of two rare humiliations she underwent. They had long lived apart, but under the stress of wartime she decided one year to join him for Easter in Scotland, and to be in every way friendly and helpful. Lamington was near the Ayrshire coast and one day, on a morning of sleet and fog, her husband suggested a drive along the cliffs. This did not seem a good idea, but Riette remembered her resolutions and they set out. They reached a cliff path, almost invisible in the fog, and he suggested she walk a little way down it to a seat high on the cliff which had meant much to him when he was a small boy. She protested, but complied. As the fog swallowed her up, there was a loud laugh from the road, and a grinding of gears. After an hour or two alone in the darkness, she returned to civilization but not to Lamington.

The second humiliation was even worse. Riette had a love affair with Compton Mackenzie. For a time all went well, and then one night Mackenzie failed. 'But, Monty,' she said, 'you have never been like this before. Is anything the matter?' 'I can't think of anybody,' he replied in distress.

We had with us Morogh Bernard, a delightful dilettante, who once was heard saying, 'It is hard when one's mother is a Hoare and one's grandmother a Freke.' We had Willie King, not a dilettante at all – he was one of the chief experts of his day on porcelain – but an eccentric tippler, kept together by his wife Viva. She, incidentally, gave a useful phrase to the language owing to her predilection for homosexual friends, Norman Douglas in chief. This led to the euphemism, 'Is he a friend of Mrs King's?' – a question which made it possible for respectable persons to be explicit. 'Oh yes, he used to know her when he was young, but he doesn't at all care for her now.' Or, 'I'm afraid he's mad about her.'

We had Frank Birch, a Cambridge don who was said to be a uniquely talented Widow Twankey in pantomime. And F. L. Lucas, another Cambridge don, always to be seen in a blue shirt, fretting about the hostility of Osbert Sitwell. We had two

Air Force officers, Jim Rose and Peter Calvocoressi, both of whom achieved eminence in literature after the war. We had a sprinkling of very pretty girls, who worked on an encyclopaedic project known as the Index; and we had admirable Miss Botsford, an untidy, splendid lady who directed their activities, and through whom no fragmentary aspect of the Reichswehr, however arcane, was unverifiable.

Over miles of the hideous countryside round Bletchley hundreds, no thousands, of highbrows were billeted, though those working on the central Intelligence spine of the place, Hut 6 for cryptographers, Hut 3 for those who assessed the fruits of cryptography, were not very numerous. No breach of security ever occurred. We were forbidden to keep notes, to abandon Bletchley except on duty or leave, to discuss our work. We were very conscious of the Prime Minister's benevolent eye on us. But once or twice a week our duties took us to London, to the War Office or the Cabinet Offices, where it was sometimes my task to check the positioning of the German Army on Top Secret maps. The equivalent pin-pointing of the Russian Army was in the hands of a major and a captain, both of whom had lost large family brewing interests after the Revolution of 1917 – interests they were determined to regain. Although we had access to identical facts, my colleagues interpreted them differently, and so I might, one day, find that Baku had fallen to the Germans, when I knew it had not. This led to argument, to a most complicated clash of loyalties.

To those caught up in conventional military life, without the glamour of the Desert to enliven it, Bletchley looked like the promised land. One day I received a letter from Willie Acton, younger brother of Harold, who was guarding a petrol dump in Wales. He had been turned away from any contact with the war in Italy, on the grounds that his Italian was too colloquial.

I showed his letter to David Talbot-Rice, who was in charge of that MI department which dealt with the Italian Army. Could not Willie be employed by him? He said he did not like Willie Acton, nor did he approve of his ether-drinking habit, which had already landed him in trouble at Oxford. I insisted; and finally answered Willie's letter by asking him to luncheon with Talbot-Rice, adding that he only had to behave himself for an hour or two and his troubles would be over.

We lunched, the three of us, at the Travellers Club, and so powerful was the stench of ether that we were soon nodding, half-anaesthetized. 'I told you so,' said Talbot-Rice, and Willie returned to what was, alas, a short life at his dump.

For me, the main excuse for finding Bletchley tolerable as well as fascinating, was that I could fairly often get home to Kent for a night or two. It had not seemed sensible to install my small son in a Piccadilly flat, so I evolved a scheme. An Oxford friend, Sir Henry d'Avigdor Goldsmid, had a large property just outside Tonbridge. I calculated that, if I could have one of his farms for the duration, my family would have a better life than if I sent them to a safer place. Many of the locals would go west; there might be extra eggs and gallons of petrol; and by the law of averages we should probably not be killed. So we ended up at Castle Hill Farm, on the Pembury Road, a long low building, part brick, part clapboard, with an eighteenth-century core and Victorian additions.

No choice could have been better. From time to time a plane crashed on the farmland, from time to time a bullet pierced the roof – 'Drat that man!' David's nanny, Jessie, would exclaim as she looked up from her ironing – but for nine years we stayed at Castle Hill with immense pleasure, supported by the kindness of the Goldsmids at Somerhill, and by the Rae family nearby, by the Harold Nicolsons at Sissinghurst, and eventually by innumerable neighbours who made us feel at home in the Weald. There was a lively Roumanian princess, Anne Marie Callimachi, who lived near Goudhurst. In her day, she had been a great figure at the court of King Ferdinand, in bitter rivalry with her cousin, Marthe Bibesco. After the war they used to declare an occasional truce and meet for a night of Mitropan gossip in a maid's room at the Ritz. But at this time she lived, we supposed in sin, with a nephew, and regaled us with many accounts of Bucharest life. Her husband had his mistress, she her lover – both indispensable to a respectable court life, but both very boring to themselves. From time to time they would escape to Rome for a week or two of marital rapture before duty claimed them. She used to look at me with sorrow, while she confessed her peccadilloes. '*Toi*,' she would say, '*tu n'es pas fait pour la bagatelle.*'

The Raes were typical of a devoted, Protestant, prosperous

Anglo-American family. Father Rae came from California, where he had entrusted a fortune to his secretary while he spent many months in Europe with wife and family. On his return, he found that the secretary had started a process of embezzlement which it was not too late to reverse. The following year he returned to Europe, and, fired by Christian spirit, again handed his fortune to the same secretary, as a gesture of trust restored. That time the secretary got it. Mrs Rae, who reminded us affectionately of Céleste, the wife of Babar the elephant, and her sister Zaza shared the house with Gwynedd Rae, the very successful author of children's books about a bear named Mary Plain, and with a brother Kenneth, my first publisher at a time when he was partner to Richard Cobden-Sanderson. A whole tribe of Raes surrounded them and the family atmosphere was much that of a Louisa May Alcott novel. One day Gwynedd came in agitation. She had learned that rice was to be rationed. Why then, we asked, if there was still time, did she not buy rice? 'There isn't room in the house for another grain,' she answered in despair.

The steep valleys, the beechwoods swimming in bluebells each spring, the crisp snow along wooded winter rides, enchanted us. We became dedicated market-gardeners under the skilled eye of Mr Figgett, to whom Jessie, who never quite knew whether she was talking English or French, would shout from a nursery window, '*Jardinier, jardinier*, bring me some *pommes de terre*.' Thérèse used to thumb a ride into Tonbridge, finding the lorry-drivers much pleasanter than the private owners. For the first year or two of the war she worked with Lady Reading's Women's Voluntary Services in London. Then, when David returned to us, she moved to Kent and he, to his irritation, was accepted by a local girls' school which ran a special wartime class for small boys. His compensation was the excitement of lying in a ditch from time to time, his bicycle beside him, when a German bomber flew overhead. But by the time he was eight or so he asked me so seriously what he had done wrong to be punished when Charlie and Harry and Jack were allowed to go to a proper school, that we sent him away as a boarder. I have not forgotten our unhappiness as we put him on the school train at Marylebone Station, nor his beaming face as the train gathered speed, nor our attempt to conquer our foreboding (quite unnecessary, as it proved) by a bout of useless and expensive shopping.

Friends used to come for a quiet night or two, free of bombs. The only ones not encouraged to return were Patrick Kinross, a long-standing companion who had been best man at my wedding, but who had an unlucky gift – being tall and clumsy – for choosing a fragile chair to swing on, or a pretty ivory to use as an ashtray; and Cyril Connolly who, although there was a bathroom a few feet from his bed, regularly filled a chamber-pot and left it defiantly in the middle of the floor, for Thérèse or for me to empty.

Today I look down the pages of a visitors' book, and wonder what lay behind so many forgotten names. Vere and Honor Pilkington: that's simple. Vere had been the eldest of three brilliant games-playing brothers at Eton, to whom games came so easily that they could hardly be bothered to play them. Honor had been one of the daughters of Lady Kylsant, who demanded of her girls that they make fine marriages, and chose for Honor Gavin Henderson, a lively and even at times dazzling figure, but not by temperament marriageable. She told me once that after a miserable year or two she had woken in their Lord North Street house to hear a rhythmic knocking sound, and concluded that Gavin had hanged himself on the bathroom door. Should she cut him down? Should she stop the tap of his heels? She decided, no; then woke up thoroughly, with a start of remorse, to find that the tap was simply that of two heavy dressing-gown cords in a draught. After an annulment, however, and a devotedly happy second marriage, the two of them became excellent friends. Gavin took to politics, and became Postmaster-General in a much later shadow Cabinet, under Harold Wilson. He used to invite us to meet his colleagues at Buscot, the more than handsome house he had inherited in Berkshire. His political career was not advanced by a speech in the House of Lords, accidentally prefaced not by 'My Lords' but by 'My dears'. And I remember with pleasure a house-party which included the Aneurin Bevans, which Gavin's mother was invited to join for dinner. Lady Violet Henderson was a forceful lady, whose right-wing views were probably responsible for her son's left-wing career. Dinner at Buscot was always a trifle odd. For years, when such auxiliaries existed, there were footmen, there was silver gilt scattered on the table. But the guests dressed down – into sweaters and flannels – rather than up. On this occasion, Lady Violet, very much not in flannels or sweater, turned to Aneurin Bevan and asked him why he permitted Welsh miners to strike. He replied, patiently, that a coal mine is not an agreeable place to work in and that the rewards are meagre in relation to the hardships. 'I don't suppose,' he began, 'you have ever seen one. But it is hot down there, and steamy, and there is nothing but a very dim light.' Lady Violet let her pearls fall with a crash on the table. 'I know exactly what you mean,' she said. 'A number of my friends pay two pounds for the pleasure of using such a place. They call it a Turkish bath.' Her aim was to annoy, and she succeeded.

We seldom spent a night in London. But I remember two: both in the Regent's Park house of Elizabeth Bowen. The first time, there was a little dinner: Elizabeth and her husband, the Stephen Spenders, Stephen Tennant – who had the habit of refreshing his fair hair with a little gold dust – and ourselves. While we were sitting down to dine a raid took place. Heavy crashes resounded, the curtains swung on their rods, the soup on the table broke into small waves. But the raid was never referred to. Talk turned on, say, Thomas Love Peacock, or the rhythmic subtleties of Meredith's 'Love in a Valley'. Thump, whee-ee, thump, from outside proclaimed war. But within Elizabeth was saying, 'Emily Eden really ought to be reprinted. She is as good as Maria Edgeworth.' On the second occasion I was given a room under the roof. Suddenly, Elizabeth came in to it, at about one in the morning. She was wearing a helmet and carrying torch and axe. 'Before I go on duty,' she said towards the darkness of my bed, 'I must tell you what to do if the house catches fire.' It may have been that same night that Stephen Tennant arrived from the country at Claridges, and kept a hired Rolls-Royce waiting at Elizabeth's during the raid, chauffeur presumably on the box. I never knew him well, but the rest of his family were family friends, and to some extent 'family', since his mother, Pamela Glenconner, had married Lord Grey of Fallodon. He himself had been a young man of extreme good looks and much talent, and he did not allow increasing age to daunt him. Once, during the war, he reached Wimborne station, on his way to stay with Raymond Mortimer at Long Crichel. The black-out was on, there were no porters, and neither host nor guest felt able to haul the suitcases to a car. So all was left on the platform but for the make-up box, itself neither small nor light.

Movement in wartime was obviously limited; but we spent one leave in Devon and Cornwall, saw Clovelly without a single tourist, and walked at Land's End and Zennor entirely by ourselves. Another time we drove to Wales and lunched in Shrewsbury at the Angel, at that time run on old-fashioned lines with a single table d'hôte presided over by a lady in black bombazine. I had telephoned in advance, so my name, with its Welsh connotations, was known. Suddenly a lady in fox furs arrived, demanding a table to herself. She was told that this was impossible, and an argument followed, in the midst of which a little waitress murmured to me, 'Anyone can see she's English.' Later, we lost the way, confused by the wartime practice of turning signposts the wrong way about, in order to perplex invading Germans. Two old ladies were mowing a churchyard, and I stopped to ask them how to get to Newtown. They looked at one another. 'Shall we tell them?' one asked. I said I was a British officer. 'You're not in uniform,' they retorted, and that was their last word.

But such small diversions barely broke the sameness of a life chiefly spent between the basement of the War Office, Bletchley, and Kent. Forty years later I find it hard not to confess that I thoroughly enjoyed my war. Undramatic, un-heroic, it certainly was, but seldom dull. There was the day when, in the heart of a Russian winter, radio signals went mad, and those designed for communication between one German tank and another, over a few hundred yards, and so not even encoded, were received on British soil. There was the day when Professor Norman, our local authority on futuristic German weapons, first drew our attention to Peenemunde, and other bases of the V1s and V2s still lying in the future, and unheard of. There was the day when Lord Mancroft, acting as duty officer, was rung in the middle of the night by a voice which he recognized as Churchill's and asked to provide an immediate answer to some such question as, How long will it take for three German armoured divisions to reach the Don? To which he replied that he had not the slightest idea and had no means of

136

finding out before morning. 'Do you suggest,' asked the voice, by now angry, 'that I should let you sleep in peace?' 'Yes, sir,' Churchill was told, 'and so I believe should you.' It was reported next day that a horrified senior officer had ordered him to apologize; but that the Prime Minister had in fact been much amused.

XIII

ONE DAY, EARLY in 1945, there appeared at Bletchley Harry Hitchens, a schoolmaster turned Brigadier and a splendidly sardonic observer of humanity. He was assembling a small staff to meet a situation which in fact never occurred, for at that time it was believed that Hitler might form a redoubt in the Austrian Alps, and Hitchens's function was to prepare the Intelligence pattern to this.

And so I escaped from Buckinghamshire to Italy, first to the Trentino and later to the Palace of Caserta, where were the headquarters of the Allied Forces. A new world surrounded me, one which, as I had not, had experienced the stresses of North Africa. I found friends old and new: Hamish St Clair Erskine, who had had an admirable war with the Brigade of Guards, even though it had started strangely for him when he went overseas, taking only such luggage as Lord Rosslyn's silver-gilt picnic-case, on the grounds that you can always find essentials, but not luxuries; John Willett, the translator of Brecht; Archie Colquhoun, translator of Manzoni, who, as a dedicated Marxist, had an inconvenient vision flying over Lourdes and ended his days in a monastery.

The war was virtually over, and though I was a mere Lieutenant-Colonel – a basic rank by 1945 for those who had been in the army more than five years – I had access to delights such as visiting Duino, briefly a corps headquarters, borrowing the Commander-in-Chief's suite at the Grand Hotel in Venice and using on any reasonable excuse an aircraft or a captured

Mercedes, or a German army horse, the discomfort of whose saddle is with me still.

Years before, Jack Squire remarked that every officer in a good British regiment carried a manuscript in his knapsack, very probably a sonnet sequence. And certainly at Duino there were copies everywhere of Rilke's *Elegien*, discussed in the mess from behind a clipped moustache. It was not quite the same, I later found, at Caserta. One evening, in that most splendid of palaces, an unknown major began to discourse on the building, its size, its marbles, its cascading staircase. 'If you're so interested,' I ventured, 'you must have read Sacheverell Sitwell's *Southern Baroque Art*.' 'Art?' he snapped, 'Art? I became interested because I took the palace drains as a special subject for my promotion exam. I'm a sapper, you see.'

The highlight of our months in North Italy came when the Russians finally allowed an inter-allied mission into Vienna, to negotiate boundaries between the different zones, and similar matters. We were kept hanging about for weeks until the prospect of a starving city became so actual that the Russians decided to bring in ourselves, France and the United States, so as to spread disaster thinner.

But first we had celebrated VE-Day, in my case in Rome, in the company of Peter Acton, a very dear friend not long after killed together with his wife in an air-crash: an example of Providential forethought, for neither could easily have survived the other. On the day itself we walked up to the Officers' Club, while fireworks burst overhead and the streets below were jubilant. Only the cloak-room girl looked glum, and Peter spoke to her about this. To which she replied, sensibly, 'You might not look cheerful if you had just lost the greatest war of the century.'

Rome in summer, experienced from within an army tunic, can be unbearably hot. Moreover, there were not many amenities in 1945. I was lucky, however, to have a cousin Michael Dawnay, who was a friend of Annina Badoglio, daughter-in-law of the Marshal who was then ruling Italy. So, while the city sweltered, we lay by a roof-top pool in the palace, flanked by trophies taken from Ethiopia in the Thirties. The city was not starving, but it was very poorly supplied. We, however, on our sunny roof, had every luxury, shared with a scattering of sunburned beauties. There might never have been a war, never a more serious purpose to life than to reach out for an iced glass of champagne and peach-juice.

However, word came at last that we were to leave for Vienna. And so the J Mission formed up at Klagenfurt early one fine morning. The roads were abominable, and it took all day to reach the city, where we were put up in commandeered villas in the suburb of Lainz. The unlucky owners, short of water and threatened by the total breakdown of an already scant civilization, had been turned out only that day and they crept back one by one to ask a small favour, or to report a rape, a fresh case of syphilis, not complaining of the Russian fighting troops but of the Tartar occupying forces. We ourselves were informed that we were to dine with Marshal Tolbukhin within the hour. We were covered in dust, there was no water, our baggage wagon had temporarily disappeared, but we brushed up as well as we might and took off for a large villa where the officers of the Mission were met by, in each case, a Russian of equivalent rank.

It was a big party which sat down, at about ten o'clock, to a table presided over by the Marshal, resplendent with medals. Each guest was given three glasses, into which liquids were poured by colour. Thus, one glass might contain claret and cherry brandy, another, gin, kirsch and vodka, another hock and Grand Marnier. Toasts, with no heel-taps, were numerous. I and my cannier colleagues managed to spill or hide our glasses, but those who tried to show good fellowship by swigging the contents down were soon in a very poor way.

At the end of dinner, a band struck up, and we were seized by our Russian vis-à-vis and waltzed briefly round. I have not forgotten the expression of our senior officer, a genial but somewhat hidebound cavalry General, Sir John Winterton, in the enormous white-uniformed arms of Marshal Tolbukhin. After a few turns, the Viennese maids were brought on, we were released, and those who could still stand took more usual partners. My appointed Russian friend, who had been perfectly genial throughout dinner, turned on me at this point, and accused me of eavesdropping. He had seen, he said, that I lied when I denied any knowledge of Russian: I had listened to every word, and taken notes, no doubt. At such moments –

on subsequent days – the situation was saved by one of our interpreters, Natasha Benckendorff, equally skilled in linguistics and diplomacy.

Our work began after an almost sleepless night. The powers that be had given us Russian speakers, but they had forgotten that German would also be used, and so I found myself called on to play a part for which I was wholly unfitted. I cannot fluently discuss refrigeration-plants, sewage disposal, or pest control in English, let alone Viennese. And the situation was made harder by the fact that we never talked with the same Russians twice. Each day there was a huge luncheon and dinner; each day our hosts, knocked out by high living, were replaced by fresh officers. We, however, remained the same, so that when we reached Italy again some time later, most of us went quietly to bed and stayed there.

When we were not conferring, we drove through the city. I took our General to Meidling, of which I had had no news since the outbreak of war. From the street the house was hidden by trees, but the lodge was intact, and at first sight, as we mounted the drive, everything seemed normal. The statues set in the façade, the hideous polychrome roof, looked as they always had looked; but closer inspection showed that the house was half in ruins. A bomb had fallen through the skylight above the central hall. A Blüthner piano which had stood under it had been hacked to pieces with an axe. In the room where my son had been born a Russian soldier was asleep, drunk. Later I found that for the first years of war the house had passed unnoticed. The old servants collected their pensions from the family office, and, hidden behind its trees, the house itself was not perceived as a British property. Suddenly the authorities discovered it. The silk walls were ripped down, the panelling stripped, showers were installed, dormitories laid out, and a school for Gauleiters created. I found on the floor some foxed picture postcards of the 'Gauschule Schönbrunn'. I had left behind a portfolio of Kokoschkas, which had been destroyed as decadent art; but most of the pictures survived. For the time being, all I could rescue was four bottles of 1820 brandy, salvaged by Franz the butler, and later consumed by the General and myself. In earlier days I had noticed that whenever a bottle of this brandy was opened – something which hardly ever happened, since it was both precious and the property of my mother-in-law – it was never seen again, however little had been drunk. I had spoken to Franz, saying delicately that he must be responsible for safeguarding it. He was indignant. 'How far do you think one little bottle can go? After all, there is myself, and Fräulein Gusti and Herr Weingartner and Franz Hihn and the chef.' I begged him to take the Kümmel and the crème de menthe instead.

During our peregrinations in the city I was made aware of a British jeep which did not belong to our mission. I tracked it to the Clam Gallas Palais, and found two young officers who had become bored in Holland and decided to go what was called at the time 'swanning'. After all, Russia was an ally: why not drive to Russia? I had to tell them that their choice was a simple one: either drive back to Amsterdam or be court-martialled. They revealed, however, the presence of a refugee Polish countess and her two sons, hiding in the house, after what was by then a normal experience. Their property had been devastated by Germans and by Russians; they had fled to Hungary; and now dared not venture from the palace which hid them. The countess said she did not care for herself, but she fretted for her sons and for the family jewels. I was able to conceal both young men and jewels under a pile of blankets when finally we left Vienna, and hand them over later to their father, who was on General Anders's staff in Italy.

One of the less popular British officers on the Mission was a Brigadier who used to begin the day, when we wished him good morning, by saying, 'I'll be all right when I get the blood out of my eyes.' He was a pompous little man, who made me interpret for him on a visit to the Mayor, later Austrian Chancellor, to whom the Brigadier was extremely rude, snapping out orders, and not listening when his questions were answered. We were always accompanied by Russian officers, and on this occasion my Brigadier was taken aside. Did he not realize that General Koerner was a friend? Otherwise he would not be Mayor of Vienna. The Brigadier thought he should report this to General Winterton, who dressed him down soundly and ordered him to apologise. I was rather pleased, when we returned to the Rathausplatz, that General Koerner refused to receive him.

A few months later the same little Brigadier was again put in his place, this time by Peter Fleetwood-Hesketh, a delightful Major who was in charge of the fabric of Schloss Schönbrunn when it became the British headquarters.

There was a high level meeting there one day, broken by the arrival of Austrian maids, who closed the shutters against the sun and plunged the meeting into darkness. The Brigadier flew into a rage and summoned Peter Hesketh at once. This was intolerable, he shouted. Besides, the maids were probably spies. Peter held his ground. 'Perhaps,' he said, 'you do not have eighteenth-century silks on your walls at home, sir. Perhaps you do not have miniatures on ivory in your vitrines. I'm afraid, sir, that as long as I have instructions to maintain this palace in proper order the shutters will stay closed against the sun.'

Vienna at this time was a very sad city, though the unquenchable Viennese gusto still survived. I tried to find one or two old friends, among them a very plain lady who told me that she had been inundated with tales of rape. 'It is my last chance,' she lamented. But the only Russian officer to come near her did so to warn her that her concierge was dishonest, and that she had better lock up her silver. 'Too disappointing,' she said.

Finally, the different occupation zones were allotted, and we returned to Naples for a month or two until the allied troops moved in. By the end of the year my military service ended, and might have done so earlier had I obeyed an order to return to England and fight the Louth election I had been expecting six years earlier. But by that time there seemed no point in going back to politics, and I resigned my candidature.

In the last months of 1945 I had no consecutive military work, only a series of odd jobs. At one moment we had trouble with the French who, consulting nobody, promoted the arrival of a Habsburg archduke, to hold a royalist meeting in Carinthia. At others I had to deal with such matters as the destruction of a splendid library at the Styrian abbey of Gurk, where unique manuscripts had been covered with excrement and piled in a cloister; with similar destruction in the city museum of Graz, where early musical instruments had been thrown from the chapel gallery to a marble floor, so that one could have climbed down over the broken carcasses of harpsichord and lute. There were problems in private Schlosses, arising from a Russian tendency to use the inviting flow of a lavatory to wash in, and the equally inviting empty space of a bath for defecation. There was the case of the Archduchess Rosemary, whose Schloss on the Danube was occupied, and whose sleep broken by Russian officers bursting in to her room at night to display a living Habsburg to their friends.

The Russian army, we learned, was cheerfully childish more often than cruel. The fighting troops, as I have said, usually behaved very well. With the Americans we had a friendly but somewhat guarded relationship. We felt a little like poor relations, but also considered ourselves – not always rightly – more experienced and level-headed. In my own sphere of Intelligence it was axiomatic that the OSS were always a nuisance, and seldom useful. But the worst crime against humanity was of our own, or rather, of Whitehall's seeking, when we handed over to the USSR and to certain death the confused remnants of General Stassov's Ukrainian forces. From our local command we protested with vigour, but we were overruled, the poor victims were rounded up, and despatched.

Before I left Vienna I gave, jointly with Michael Dawnay, a dance. We borrowed the Dietrichstein Palace, a ravishing house which had been empty for the duration, but to which a young Tolstoy cousin of Prince Dietrichstein had access. We collected the liquor bottle by bottle – supplies were almost non-existent in the city – and we took our army rations to what had been a good restaurant to be improved. We were forbidden to 'fraternize', so Viennese guests were few. And the wiring failed as soon as the ball opened, so that the rooms were lit by as many candles as we could muster. It was a very pretty party, which would have done credit to Hofmannsthal's Faninal.

At the same moment I became involved in a benign conspiracy to gain an entry permit to Vienna for Clarice Rothschild, widow of Alfons but British born. Her contemporary relations had thrown their hand in. The great family properties in Central Europe, Schillersdorf, Langau, Enzesfeld, where earlier the Duke and Duchess of Windsor had proved difficult and expensive guests, above all the Hohe Warte – a large market garden in the city – and magnificent collections of pictures and furniture, seemed to have slipped out of their hands for ever. But Clarice was a fighter. When the British refused to admit her, I recommended her to apply to the French Commander, who soon did as he was asked. She arrived – to the extreme indignation of her countrymen in office – and before long made a bargain with the Austrian Government which saved the day for the Austrian Rothschilds, at the expense of giving a proportion of their good things to the nation.

Her courage and energy were typical of the non-Nazi Viennese. I recall being invited by Princess Hanau to a palace which had been badly bombed. One climbed a stepladder to half a drawing-room, to be given acorn-coffee along with a dozen others, all gossiping away and behaving as though life in the house were entirely normal. The opera re-opened – in the Josefstadt Theatre, its own home having been partly destroyed – and I saw a certain amount of the stars, Elisabeth Schwarz-kopf and Erich Kunz, in particular.

The Russians played a diminishing part in our lives. Once or twice our mess invited a senior Russian officer to dine, but what happened was that either nobody turned up on the day, or a whole group appeared unannounced, often bringing wives, who were in reality Viennese shopgirls out for the evening.

I also had good times with our principal interpreter, Colonel Peniakov, universally known as Popski. An excellent book about him appeared later, and I shall not repeat its contents, except to say that, like Captain Hook in *Peter Pan*, he wore a hook in place of a hand, that he was in character brave, efficient and unconventional, and that he won the confidence both of the British and the Russian commanders.

One day he took me off in his jeep, with a Belgian driver, to visit Slovakia. We had no right whatever to be there. We asked no permission. We carried no papers apart from a piece of vellum adorned with a strip of red tape and a wax seal imprinted by a British half-crown piece; for he thought it unlikely that the Russian guards could read.

We had already dropped in once or twice on Russian messes in the country, and been received with kindness and surprise – for Popski's Russian was of a stamp which had died out after 1917. On this occasion we drove to a property of my mother-in-law's near Tepla Trenčin, where I found the house exactly as we had left it, and the agent still living there.

In Vienna there had been very little food, in Slovakia there was plenty; the main reason for our journey was to replenish the mess larder. We were hailed at the house, fed and wined; the jeep was filled with ducks and venison; we spent a comfortable night. Then I overplayed my hand. I thought it wise to find our family lawyer, so as to prove we had not lost interest in our property. Next day, we drove from house to house. No, Herr Novak was out. No, Herr Novak was playing bridge. Suddenly, we were stopped by the Russian police, and taken to the cellars of the little town-hall for interrogation.

Nobody, I thought, knew where we were. We had no right whatever to be in Tepla Trenčin. I could not speak a word of Russian, and for half an hour I listened to Popski's voice with growing fear. It seems that he repeated himself many times. How right they were to arrest us. How well they were executing their duty. But he must be given an immediate line to their Marshal. The consequences for our captors would of course be grim indeed. But they could always console themselves by reflecting that they had done their duty. After a time, his message went home. Get out, we were told in effect, get out, and don't come back. We got out.

Back in Vienna, I still had no work; Hitler's Redoubt never existed. So I was delighted to be carried across Europe on a train to shed my uniform on arrival. Also on the train was an elderly Austrian couple, the Wimmers, later appointed to the Austrian Embassy in London, who were convinced that they would be taken off at the frontier, and so proved exaggeratedly grateful when I locked them into my compartment where I knew they would be safe.

Finally I doffed my uniform at my depot, Wentworth Woodhouse, and, joined by Thérèse, spent my first evening in permanent mufti with Osbert and Edith Sitwell at Renishaw.

They made a little occasion of this, and after dinner Edith said, 'Tonight we shall sit in the ballroom' – a room of singular cold. We were lit by an altar candle, and Edith knitted, very slowly and on enormous needles. At her feet lay a kind of stair-carpet of wool, and Thérèse asked what it was. 'It's for the troops,' she said, slowly stabbing into the next loop.

XIV

O<small>UR HOUSE IN</small> York Gate had, I have said, been destroyed by bombs, and we remained in Kent, though for a year or two we shared a London home with the Lennox Berkeleys. They lived in Warwick Avenue, and I acquired a lasting affection for Little Venice, for the eye-catching tower of the church at the end of the street, much later torn down by the Ecclesiastical Commissioners and replaced by an ugly office building; for the oozy canal and its moored barges; for the small shops of Formosa Street and the Victorian splendour of our local pub, the Prince Albert.

My plan had been to resume a pre-war life, and to write a book or two immediately. But a pre-war life meant a return to Vienna and that was impossible. To restore Meidling would have cost a fortune, and, restored, it would have been a very ugly house. In the end it was given to the City of Vienna and converted for use as a children's home. More than thirty years later, I revisited it, on a rainy summer day. The avenues were cut, the park dotted with little villas; I could not even find the shell of the house, and, under a thin drizzle, did not try very hard.

We went to Marienbad in 1947, with my mother-in-law and Frank Wooster. It was a year before the extreme Left took over, but already there were warning signs. The Woosters told us to buy anything we could find – cars, furs, pictures, furniture – under the premonition that they would be expropriated before long. We went to Prague and finally left with twelve cocktail glasses, so bare were the city shelves. It was the end of our old life. True, the Czech Government compensated British citizens. But Eugène de Rothschild, at the very last moment, put in a claim so large that nothing much remained for the odd governesses and nannies who should have been chief beneficiaries, let alone for ourselves.

So we settled into England, and I had to decide what to do. It seemed foolish to depend on an unearned income, and, with a wife and child, I did not want to anyway. So I listened with interest to the suggestion of a new friend, Stanley Morison, that I should join him on the staff of the *Times Literary Supplement*. I was to share a large bare room with two delightful veterans, Edmund Blunden and Philip Tomlinson. In no time I experienced a feeling of home-coming each time I entered that room, perched at the top of a high, dark staircase – the kind of room properly inhabited by a Dickensian scrivener rather than by a modern writer. True, all Printing House Square in 1946 was still Dickensian in feeling. In what was still called the Private House – once the home of the Walter family, Chief Proprietors of *The Times* from its inception until the arrival of Colonel Astor in 1922 – John Walter V, by then in his seventies, still reigned in a dark parlour, rather than office, dispensing tea to his senior employees. The air of the entire building – which was not beautiful but at least better than the packing-case which had replaced it twenty years later – was prim, Victorian, kindly.

The most agreeable, but not the most assiduous, of *Times* editors, W. F. Casey, used to say that all went well with the paper if the staff left its daily appearance to the Geist. The Geist saw to it that the leader made sense, that the news met the eye, that nothing essential had been forgotten. What was fatal was to take thought.

The Geist certainly controlled the presses better than latter-day printers. Misprints were rare. We were told of the obit dedicated to a senior general and pitched rather high. It referred to him as 'that battle-scared veteran'. This led to a commotion, and to stern words which so vexed the compositor that next day he set a correction: 'It must be obvious to our readers that 'battle-scared" should have read "bottle-scarred".'

Moreover, the Geist spread about all the operations of *The Times* a kind of rubicund benevolence, a supportive friendliness which locked the very different personalities of Printing House Square into a single entity. As readers of *Barchester Towers* will know, this kind of clubbiness does not exclude a certain amount of infighting. We called one another by our surnames only; we led the kind of collegiate life which involved frequent meals at the Garrick Club; but we watched one another like hawks; and in particular we watched Stanley Morison.

Others have recorded his contributions to the civilization of his time. They have stressed his intelligence, his industry, his devotion to causes: to Catholicism, *The Times*, the Encyclopaedia Britannica, fine printing, fine handwriting. They have recorded his penetrating voice and his no less penetrating laugh, which exploded like the bursting of a bad child's paper bag. But no one, I think, has quite captured the essence of a most complex and endearing personality.

Just to see him was impressive. He was tall and very thin. He stooped. He dressed in black, down to a stringy black tie, though on one day of each year he wore a tie adorned with bathing belles. His eyesight was poor, so that he needed thick glasses. They were encased in wire. Surprisingly, he had been married; not surprisingly, the marriage did not hold. He had almost no private life, unless one could call a devotion to Lord Beaverbrook that. But when the unhappy Stephen Ward committed suicide after the exposure of his sexual peccadilloes, Morison adjusted his glasses and said, 'There, but for the Church, go I.'

I relished him. During the fifteen years of our friendship, I never had cause for complaint. He made me think. He also made me laugh. Once, in early spring, he invited me to lunch at the Holborn Restaurant – he was a great expert in unfashionable restaurants with splendid, unfathomed cellars. As we sat down, he said, 'I suppose you, like me, are observing Lent strictly.' I mumbled. 'I am your host,' he went on, 'and I have a cold. I owe it to you to break my fast.' And he ordered two double martinis, oysters, lamb, stilton, washed down by a Château Beychevelle of a good year, and a large brandy. This was done without irony, without a smile, as the discharge of a duty.

He knew what is called 'everybody'. From Downing Street to Cambridge, from Westminster Cathedral to the University of

Chicago, he was to be found as a consultant on diverse problems. His private combination of extreme right and left wing views must often have bewildered those who consulted him, just as his chosen position as grey eminence, so grey as to be all but invisible, awakened suspicion. It was said of him, as he walked slowly away from the seats of power, that he had the most sinister back in London. And indeed he saw nothing wrong in a little intrigue. But he possessed an inborn Glaswegian canniness, an obstinate if pessimistic awareness of the cross-currents which surrounded him – and which he himself had often stirred up – and he was a loyal, if formidable, friend to those he cared for.

He was also extremely sensitive – to ugly manners, for instance, or harsh voices. He never forgave Victor Gollancz his brusqueness to waiters; he winced when Harry Luce boomed at him – the more so because he dreaded bores, and Harry Luce, protected by his deafness, could be a paralyzing bore, pontificating at dinner on such matters as the influence of the Norman Conquest on British character.

Before Morison's time the *TLS* had had two editors only: Sir Bruce Richmond, who set up the paper in 1905, and D. L. Murray from 1938. It had been Murray's hope to popularize it. He shortened the articles, he introduced pictures, he lightened the tone. The upshot was not successful, and when Morison took over in 1945 he would have none of this. By stiffening the contents, he raised the circulation by the following year to 30,000, and when I took over from him in 1948 the manager's office reported a clear financial profit.

I was suspicious of this, and delved into the matter. It was possible to assess the cost of the *TLS* to *The Times* in different ways. We used office space; suppose that space were leased to, say, the *Figaro*? We used the *Times* telephone switchboard; were we to be charged with a proportion of the bill? And so on. After discussion our profit was turned into a noticeable loss. This would not do, I decided, and the matter was gone into yet again, until it was concluded that we broke even. And so we remained for the rest of my time in Printing House Square.

Twelve very happy years passed quickly. I was fortunate in having Morison to turn to for advice, and in having, as my assistant, Arthur Crook, who eventually succeeded me, and who was much better able than I to make a success of office routine. I notice that if my record as an editor ever achieves mention in someone else's book I am usually accorded a knowing wink. I was a nice fellow, I learn, and out to help; but often away, often inattentive. It is true that, without Arthur Crook and a succession of able helpers, the paper would have suffered. In matters of routine I have not progressed far beyond a state of mind noted in an Eton school report from a mathematics master, Hope Jones. 'In practical matters,' he wrote, 'keeping Pryce-Jones up to the mark is like breaking a butterfly on the wheel' – a phrase which gave much pleasure to my tutor and my father. Thus, if I had to explain formally the workings of a linotype machine to the Duke of Edinburgh, it was not often long before a printer piped up: 'Perhaps, sir, it would be best if I took over.'

But I conceived it my job to enlarge the changes introduced by Morison, and, to begin with, to fight the insularity imposed by six years of war and their aftermath. This meant a good deal of movement. I noticed that other editors confined their view to London, Oxford, Cambridge, just as years later I found that the pace-setters of New York or California knew very little of any province other than their own. So I asked myself: how about Swansea, Keele, Durham, East Anglia? How about Budapest, Uppsala, Montpellier? In those post-war years travel was hampered by currency rules, but the British Council proved helpful, and over the years I moved all over the world, often finding contributors on subjects which amply repaid the trouble of unearthing them. I introduced a series of special numbers, so as to cast light on neglected subjects; I introduced the publication of poems; I encouraged young and unfashionable writers. I do not say this to show my editorial prowess – other literary editors of my time, like John Lehmann, Cyril Connolly, Tambimuttu, even, had as keen, or keener, a flair than I. But I had *The Times* behind me, I had a degree of personal independence, and I had an easier possibility than they of covering the whole spectrum of contemporary writing, since it has always been the boast of *The Times* to be the paper of record. An Albanian epic? the work of the Uruguayan Symbolist, Herrera y Reissig? Should we not know something of each at first hand? From time to time, we were amply rewarded. One day two friends came to my office, Eithne Wilkins and Ernst Kaiser. They brought with them a published fragment of a long novel in German, the rest of which reposed in a trunk. It was called *Der Mann ohne Eigenschaften*, and the writer was an almost totally unknown Austrian, Robert Musil. I encouraged my friends to write a long essay on what the published fragment showed to be a masterpiece. To begin with, close acquaintances suggested that, even if I revelled in obscurities, to invent a writer and his work was going too far. But Secker and Warburg thought differently. They commissioned a translation from my contributors, and it was the success of the English version which launched Musil in Central Europe and added a name – alas, posthumously – to stand beside Proust and Joyce and Thomas Mann in the first line of European novelists in our century.

It was also a happy day when I opened a small paper-bound pamphlet of poems by R. S. Thomas. I did so partly because the little booklet had been printed in Newtown, Montgomeryshire, the home of my father's family. At the time I was doing one of many stints on a once-familiar BBC programme 'The Critics' – a programme brilliantly mocked by Peter Sellers on a recording of the 1950s – and I made *An Acre of Land* my book of the week, thus bringing an admirable poet to the notice of London publishers. The paper was also able to act as a forcing-house, in varying degrees, for Edwin Brock, Christopher Logue, W. S. Merwin, G. S. Fraser, Burns Singer, Alan Ross, Philip Larkin. We also tried, not always successfully, to stand behind a category of writers which needs help even more than the young: the old and half-forgotten who deserve better. I made Wyndham Lewis write for us – an arduous experience recorded elsewhere by Anthony Powell. I struggled to extract a contribution from William Gerhardie.

These prose contributions – like all our critical articles – were at that time anonymous. I did not feel strongly that this was desirable, but I could not but perceive that anonymity had its advantages. Publishers tend to be snobs; and they preferred, on the whole, an inferior review by a famous name to a better one from an unknown hand. The good name of Proust was more than a little due to a review by Mrs Duclaux, a critic totally unknown to fame, but so good that his publisher thought, complacently, that Virginia Woolf had written it. This was before my time; but I soon found that certain writers – Edith Sitwell is an example – wrote far more objectively when the pressure of a signature was lifted.

Very occasionally we did print a signed critique: that by Sir Lewis Namier of Winston Churchill's opening volume of *The Second World War* was signed, and I think it was over that critique that I scored a small triumph. The American edition was printed ahead of the British, owing to last-moment changes insisted on by Churchill. *The Times* – the Parent Organ we called it – wished a review to appear as soon as possible, so as to reinforce an opinion which the editor wanted to expound without delay. Accordingly, I arranged to review the Houghton Mifflin edition of the book rather than wait for the house of Cassell to be ready.

I was not surprised when Sir Newman Flower, Chairman of Cassell and Co., exploded. In a day or two I received, from Colonel Astor's secretary, his letter demanding that I be sacked for impertinence to a distinguished British firm. The secretary told me that Colonel Astor was away, and asked how she was to answer. It gave me great pleasure to write to Sir Newman, pointing out that, since I had to answer his letters to our chairman demanding my ouster, it would save trouble all round if he confined his correspondence to me.

When I became editor, Morison buttonholed me one day by saying that he had only one instruction to give me: I must honour a tradition by joining the Garrick Club. Later I found out that he had invented the tradition on the spot, but I was none the less flattered and happy to observe it. And in time I was invited by him to dine there on my first evening as a member. We walked along the Embankment, past the sagacious chambers of the Temple, so quiet and so rosy. All the way, Morison regaled me by planning dinner. Oysters, he thought, and a little Pouilly Fuissé. Then perhaps saddle of lamb and a bottle of Musigny, or a Rauzan-Ségla. Finally, Madeira rather than port. We arrived, and found only one or two at the central table, presided over by an old gentleman who appeared either embottled or asleep. Both, I believe, described his case. However, he shook himself, called for a waiter, indicated me, and said, 'A new member. I think. Barker, bring us tankards of the ordinary.' Morison was outraged. His plan had been counter-manded, and he was not consoled by a tankard of champagne. However, the old gentleman had sunk back, his eyes closed once more. Uneasy talk turned towards the prospects of a general election. The old gentleman – he was the painter Frank Salisbury – bobbed to the surface again. 'The trouble with this country,' he intoned, 'is that it is inhabited by fifty million fools.' This was too much for Morison. 'Don't forget,' he thundered, 'that it is those fools who pay you to paint their relations. Come on, Pryce-Jones, we're leaving. I look on dining in this club as an exercise in Christian charity at the best of times. But this is too much.' And we moved to the Savoy Grill.

The waiter on this occasion deserves a word. He was a small elderly man, of melancholy demeanour. And he was always in love. The objects of his love were male, and his disappoint-ments made him mournfully talkative to sympathetic mem-bers. Now, the Garrick was and I presume is, when sex rears its head on Garrick Street, far from permissive. However, a unique exception was made for this old fellow, so that High Court Judges of iron respectability and Puritan leader-writers would exchange solicitude. 'Have you heard what a terrible time poor Barker has been having with Harry?' Then, 'Poor old Barker. Harry was bad, but he was nothing compared with Dick.' And they tapped off their cigar-ash with thoughtful sadness.

I have never been much of a clubman, although I cling on to my memberships, complaining, as elder members do, of col-lapsing standards, disgusting food, and ever duller and less distinguished members. Not that the Garrick's standards have declined. But I miss Morison's laughter. I miss the celery-coloured cheek of T. S. Eliot mournfully silhouetted against the street. I miss the conviviality of Hamish Hamilton and the elegance of John Carter, who for many years guided us through the mazes of the rare-book trade and once, by capturing the marked catalogue of a most distinguished bookseller, enabled us, for a time, to break the 'ring' which had been nobbling the rare book trade at auctions.

When the Garrick palled, there was always the Travellers, and the Beefsteak. The Travellers has played the largest part in my club life, chiefly because for many years its secretary was an old Oxford friend, Robin McDouall, who managed as successfully as possible to make the transition from a smallish pre-war club which fulfilled its title by catering to travellers and diplomats, to a much less selective community struggling to survive in a society which no longer cared much for the memories of Talleyrand enshrined in an Italianate palace. I am just old enough to remember its former state, when Lord Algernon Percy, who regularly lunched at a table by the door, used to hit out at fellow-members with his napkin, crying, 'Get away, sir, get away,' if they lingered on his rectangle of carpet. At the Beefsteak, which is founded on compatibility and therefore on conversation, things were livelier. The convention of the Beefsteak requires members to be discreet, so that should the Prime Minister or the Bishop of Rumtifoo feel inclined to relax in good company he can do so with safety. When Harold Macmillan was Prime Minister, he used to lunch there from time to time, and so more often did his Private Secretary, John Wyndham. At the time of the Profumo scandal the rights and wrongs of the matter were much discussed at the single long table, but the Secretary never saw fit to report what was said to his innocent employer.

The talk occasionally became surreal. One day I was sitting between Arthur Onslow and the Italian Ambassador, Gallarati Scotti, when the former, leaning across me, began to describe the effect of a slight hangover, 'You know how it is: one wakes up, worried and lost; one can't find anything in the dark; one's fingers don't touch what they expect on the bed-table –' At which the Ambassador interrupted him. 'Ah, dear Lord Onslow, I know so well. You are searching for your crucifix, you need your rosary. Ah, I so understand.' 'Well, I wasn't exactly meaning that,' said Lord Onslow.

XV

IT WAS IN 1950, with Gallarati's words in my ears, that I
finally became a Catholic. Morison, except as a silent
example, played no part in my decision. I needed order, I
needed logic, and in the Church of England I found neither. I
had loved St Cyprian's, Clarence Gate, St Mary's, Bourne
Street, even a particularly hideous High Anglican church in
Tunbridge Wells, for years attended by a French maid of ours
under the belief that it was Roman Catholic. Nobody relishes
the idea of changing an inborn adherence, and I knew, moreover, that to do so would cause distress. So I chose to be
instructed by the Jesuit Father Martindale, thinking to myself
that it was an advantage to find him uncongenial, so that I
could not possibly be swayed by his personality, as I might have
been by the more appealing approach of his colleague, Father
d'Arcy: Father d'Arcy, about whom the Dominicans of the day
used to recite a little rhyme:

> Are you rich and highly born?
> Is your soul with sorrow torn?
> Come, and we shall find a way:
> I'm Martin d'Arcy, sir, S. J.

Martindale was old and frail. He lived in the uniquely
unattractive Jesuit house in Farm Street, surrounded by a
waste of brown linoleum, brown deal, leatherette, and peeling
paint. To instruct me bored him; no doubt he conceived that, at
over forty, I ought to need prompting rather than instruction.

One day, stretched on his shaky iron bed, he suddenly said that I could be received that very hour. I had not discussed the matter with Thérèse, nor with my parents, and the suggestion struck me, foolishly, as Godsent. My mind had been made up for me, I simply had to follow the path laid down. And an hour later I walked out of Farm Street a Catholic. I remember that at the time someone in the street was playing the 'Eton Boating Song' on a penny whistle. It gave me a little pang, as if it were a wistful intrusion from the past.

Thérèse, when I told her, was passionately hurt. She was by temperament a Voltairean Deist. After the war she had told me of her intention to join the Church of England as a gesture of thanksgiving for our survival. I dissuaded her, on the grounds that the only reason for changing one's religion is a change of conviction. Now she felt excluded. She had not been consulted – although she knew of my intention – above all, she had not been present. She went straight to Martindale and accused him of breaking up a family. To me, all that had taken place was a gesture of tidiness. In my own eyes, I was a tributary rejoining the main stream. But when I saw the genuineness of her grief I was appalled. I had hurt the one person whom I wholly loved, and had done so through insensitivity. Because we did not discuss this area of feeling I had made the trivial assumption that she would be indifferent. I had not conceived that she would feel lonely, betrayed, as if I had acted under an irrational impulse. Not long afterwards – by which time calm had been restored – the Assumption of the Blessed Virgin became a matter of Catholic dogma, and then it was I who felt betrayed. I was commanded to believe that an event had taken place for which there exists no shadow of evidence: an event acceptable as a pious legend, but deeply embarrassing as a revealed truth.

I had already found that my defection, as they conceived it, had greatly hurt close friends like Rose Macaulay and John Betjeman. And I began to ask myself if I had indeed defected. At this time I concluded that there are two reasons for becoming, or remaining, a Catholic. One is the unquestioning unintellectual confidence of the Sicilian or Irish peasant; one is the need of a strong and disciplined structure of belief, unaffected in its essentials by time or circumstances: a Rock of Ages. I suppose that such a need becomes rarer as its Victorian satisfactions recede, but if I have remained a Catholic it is because I am aware of my own vacillations, trivialities, mistakes, and I need to be in sight of the Rock of Ages, even if I dare not presume, in Toplady's metaphor, to hide myself in it.

I was not to foresee, in 1951, what would happen only a few years later. I could not guess that an excellent old man would be so feckless, so inane indeed, as to dismantle nearly two thousand years of Christian experience in pursuit of an *aggiornamento*; to set aside the grace and dignity bestowed by the human imagination on liturgical music and words for the sake of cheap pieties sung to an electric guitar; to attenuate whatever in Catholic life requires effort or skill in order to tempt other denominations into the fold; and above all to vulgarise, to pare down; to show largeness of mind by appointing to distribute the communion wafer a middle-aged lady in sensible tweeds.

By now, attendance in a Catholic church is often an affliction to the minority who resent the transformation of God the Father into God the Pop, while the majority look elsewhere for what the Church once had to offer. Had I remained in the Church of England I should have undergone much the same deception within a few years, and in either communion I suppose the only consolation is to exchange the one-time delights of any church for the solitary meditations of an oratory.

Some of the melancholy induced by such thoughts was dissipated by my first visit to the United States, on behalf of *The Times*. Thérèse came with me, and we both had much the same reaction: an instant renewal of vitality and hope, a reviving sense of enlargement. We were lent an apartment on 66th Street, between Madison and Park Avenues. We were taken under the wing of a new friend, Betty Pirie, sister to Mrs Adlai Stevenson, whose family connections took us to Chicago. We spent happy days on the dunes at Southampton and in Cambridge, Massachusetts with the Philip Hofers, and also round Boston with delightful members of the publishing house of Houghton Mifflin, whose British activities depended to some extent on me: the Paul Brookses, Lovell Thompsons, and Dorothy Santillana among them. We experienced a New York Thanksgiving in style, first in a Fifth Avenue church, and then at a large luncheon-party in the apartment of a Belgian friend, Renée de Becker. We had sat down some sixteen or twenty, to the rituals of turkey and cranberry, and pumpkin pie, when it occurred to someone to count the number of Americans in the room. There was not one.

On our very first evening in New York we were given a cocktail by the expert art-dealer George Dix. During our visit he was called to the telephone by a Boston lady unknown to us, who warmly invited us to stay for a week-end. In the ensuing days, she tracked us down to repeat the invitation, always in vain, until we reached Cambridge, where the Hofers informed us that we were to dine with someone they took to be a close friend. 'We hear that Mrs McLean is rather eccentric,' they told us. 'She is in fact shut up from time to time. But we also hear she has a fine house and an excellent cook.' We were returning from a visit to Edmund Wilson in Wellfleet, and were aware of an impending storm of dramatic violence. As we left Cambridge for Pride's Crossing, it began to rain, and when we reached our destination, we found a great many guests assembled in a room like Toledo Cathedral, but no hostess. Storms upset her, and she had not come down. After a very long time, and many cocktails in the Cathedral for the guests, she appeared at the top of an operatic staircase, and led me, as a foreigner, into dinner beside her. Her doctor, knowing her allergy to storms, soon called her to the telephone and, while she was out of the room, the tempest outside became such that a barrier broke, and water began to pour into the house. One by one the guests left.

When at last she returned, we were alone with the Hofers, and water in the corridor was ankle-deep. But she made no comment, as we splashed on, merely saying, 'You must see my Picassos. No, the pictures in here are by me. Come along, come along.' By the time we reached the car a flood had topped the hub-caps.

Before we returned to London we had decided to miss no chance of getting to know the United States better. In my heart I had undergone a second, a secular, conversion, and one which Thérèse willingly shared. It was not a reaction against England. I have never wished to be other than the Englishman I was born. But I felt, and feel, about England much what I felt for the English Church. It is warm, comfortable, often a rich satisfaction in terms of aesthetic experience. It is also touching, in the sense that children and old people are touching. What it is not is alert, expansive, challenging. I could love it better at a distance. I had no plan, then or for many years, to leave it for good. And when I did so the break, as in another context at Farm Street, was the response to an unexpected push. I knew that I should sadly miss much that I loved in England: the Constable skies; the village calm; the chilly smell of damp and hassock when one finally opens a church door – now too often locked; the kindness of the familiar; the presence of old friends. For these, downtown Indianapolis, or the gas-glaring bayous of Texas City, would be an insufficient exchange. But with luck one can do better than that, and again with luck one can count on frequent and very different surprises, like New England winter sunlight, an almost universal wish to be helpful, and a spurring sense of enterprise.

For the moment, however, all future plans were held back by disaster. For fifteen years doctors had told us that Thérèse should not again become pregnant. During the war years, when she was separated from her family, we found this advice easy to follow. Her moments of breakdown always cast a shadow but at last she felt compelled to start a second family, perhaps in part because her younger sister had married Elie de Rothschild, a prisoner in Germany throughout the war, and Thérèse soon found herself with a small nephew and two nieces. When she got her wish, however, I could see that she was frightened, though she never said so. She did foolish things, such as driving over rough roads in the Forest of Chantilly in a pony-cart. And she had a miscarriage. Not long afterwards, the abominable sequence began: of operations, spread over almost two years, hope, disappointment, more surgery, leading to death in Paris. It would be morbid to recount in detail an experience by no means unique – the slow death of someone still young and adored, not only by her husband and child, but also by a wide-ranging company of people united by affection for her. But, if I forego to speak of a sorrow which has remained dark for thirty years, I should like to justify that sorrow by trying to set her in focus.

She was small. She had a round and expressive face, marked by large, dark eyes, which her sisters described as 'coming out on stalks' when she was roused. She was not fat, but partridge plump, yet quick and neat; an excellent dancer, and with witty, eloquent movements when she talked. She was not athletic, though she skied well; her interests were more Latin than English (how could they not be?). But, in France or Austria or England alike, she had a natural gift with people of every kind – highbrows, country neighbours, servants, Tyrolean Jaeger, politicians. She was as much at her ease with Queen Elizabeth at Hatfield as with a Hungarian gardener trying to kiss her hand. She was shy but not daunted, very funny, utterly loyal, and extremely fierce on matters of principle. Those who knew her have not forgotten her, and for those who knew her well – her family, that is – she is as much alive today as ever she was. She had read a great deal, she was an excellent critic of books and of painting, she created rooms with skill, using the best talent of the day, Stéphane Boudin, through his London partner E. G. Lehmann. It happened that both of us inherited from our families furniture and objects unfashionable when we were young, but much appreciated many years later, so that we had a small collection of Directoire and Regency and Charles X pieces to which Thérèse added, and which she knew how best to display. Her father had been a dedicated collector, at Royaumont and in Paris, and she inherited, as did his other children, an excellent eye. But it was not in what she did but in what she was that she achieved excellence.

Bravery and justice were two of her characteristics. She must have known for a year and more that she had cancer; but she never spoke of her knowledge, never complained. Her care was to make life bearable for us who surrounded her, so that when at last she died very peacefully – eased into death, I believe, by the solicitude of a doctor who did not want her to suffer – her nurse, Joséphine Ricord, mourned her as much as any of us.

In the last year or two of her life we had bought the lease of a house in Cavendish close, beside Lord's Cricket Ground. It was a square, free-standing house in a pleasant garden, but it had been badly damaged in the war, and at that time there was a very low ceiling set on the amount of money which could legally be spent on building.

Against Thérèse's advice I retained Ernst Freud as architect, because he was well-liked by the Marylebone authorities. Thérèse repeated that she knew her Viennese, and that she could foretell disaster when I told him what I wanted done, but at the same time begged him not to fly in the face of the law. He reassured us, and the work was almost complete when the law descended; at which Freud told the authorities that he was only a colour consultant and that I had acted illegally quite on my own. Luckily the law changed before I was taken to court, and in the end we found ourselves in a handsome house but with a short lease which the Eyre Estate, our landlord, would only renew on terms very different from those they had forecast, so that in a few years I moved to Albany, when I leased the two top floors of the main building, facing south into a sunny courtyard. Once again the house of Lehmann went to work, in spite of the fact that while they were restoring Cavendish Close the last of the truly Dante-esque London fogs fell on the city, just as Mr Lehmann was helping to move a grand piano, spurred on cheerfully by Thérèse, who gave a hand herself. He went home and died.

Albany, in the 1950s, was still run in patriarchal fashion, through the care of a centenarian Mr Stone, who owned most of the freeholds. No money changed hands at that time when a lease was reassigned, only tenants thought 'suitable' were admitted, and the secretary of the building acted as a more or less benevolent dictator, under a board of trustees. My predecessors in A 5 had been the Malcolm Muggeridges. Downstairs lived Graham Greene. Harold Nicolson was up another staircase, likewise my brother Adrian. Dame Edith Evans and G. B. Stern added a theatrical note to the tenants, and an old Eton friend, Peter Coats, the garden expert, soon founded a centre of hospitality on the ground floor.

It was only now, in my forties, that I came to know my brother. After the war, he went into the world of cinema, impelled by a brother-officer, Terence Young, and for some twenty years led a successful career with Carol Reed, Otto Preminger, and other good directors, working on such movies as *Moulin Rouge* and *Summertime*, but never given the chance of setting up film on his own. To direct stars needs a special temperament; and it is on the first assistant-director that this need falls with special harshness. He had to calm the star's tantrums. He had to set up a location in, say, Tobago. He had to undertake prodigies of organization. And to this Adrian was not really suited. He was very efficient and very well-liked. But the strain of constant movement led him to drink a little, then to add pills to vodka, then to drink a lot. Finally, he was going from nursing-home to nursing-home, too often becoming engaged to a fellow-alcoholic on the second floor.

What can a brother do? I tried cajolement, tyranny, warning, sympathy. And at times all went well. Adrian was a delightful companion, he was unexpectedly shrewd, but years later, towards the end of his life, I remembered the advice of an American friend who had worked on *Horizon* with Cyril Connolly, and suffered from a sister afflicted with periodical bouts of drunkenness. 'There is only one thing to do,' Tony Bower had said, 'with an alcoholic. Ask them to stay. Furnish their room with cases of liquor and bottles of pills, and hope it won't take too long' – brutal advice, but comprehensible.

Adrian's situation was made worse by the death of our father in 1952. He quickly faded away, after showing no special symptoms of age except deafness. 'Don't bother to speak to me,' he would say, 'I can't hear a word.' Which made it irritating that when he went to a military dinner, say to the mess of the Gentlemen-at-Arms, of which he was Harbinger, he heard every word effortlessly. My mother, who lived on in Windsor Castle until she died, felt the strain. One Christmas I found her in high agitation. 'After all these years,' she said, 'I've found out that Harry loves someone else.' Her evidence was a letter of thanks from a quiet old lady in an adjoining tower, with whom my father liked to work on a crossword puzzle, and to whom he had sent a year's subscription to the un-erotic *Spectator*.

Into the bargain, my mother, left alone, became more eccentric. One day she announced to me Adrian's bankruptcy. She had given him, she said, all her money to save the day. She had not a penny left. I enquired tactfully of Adrian, to find that he had been surprised by the amount of uninvested cash in her bank account, and had therefore persuaded her to let him invest it for her own good.

Next, bottles of brandy began turning up: under the bed, behind the bath, up the chimney. Again, what can a son do? It is easy to understand the loneliness of a sentimental old lady, who had adored her husband for nearly fifty years, but possessed no inner resources to combat solitude, and no real wish to share life with her children, fond though she was of them. For months I went from home to home, and doctor to doctor, now experimenting with total rest for mother or brother, now with electric shock treatments, until finally I cajoled my mother into coming for an indefinite visit. At this time there was a fortune-teller in Hereford Square, much consulted (I found) by Cabinet ministers and in particular by Lord Salisbury. His technique was to insist that clients must not identify themselves, but to hold in his hand an object they often carried.

I went in total anonymity to Hereford Square and found a most uncongenial sage in a quilted dressing-gown. He accepted a watch given me by Thérèse, and a letter from my mother in a blank envelope, with no writing visible. He spoke of a castle in my life, an odd castle, because so many different people lived in it. 'The part which concerns you,' he told me, 'is named after Henry VIII;' and of course my parents lived at Windsor in Henry VIII's Gateway. He also told me that I was not happy about the impending visit of the letter-writer. 'This is either a child,' he said, 'or someone lapsing into second childhood. Don't worry about the visit. But understand that when your visitor leaves your house he or she will immediately die.'

My worry was only concerned with the fact that my mother was bringing three nurses with her, and thereby straining a small household. However, all went well. First one nurse left because unneeded; then another. And my mother took to seeing a few old friends until the day, a few weeks later, when she announced her wish to revisit Windsor, in order to see that all was in order. She left by car with the remaining nurse, and I waved her off, very content with her progress. She died in the night.

You may ask why I record these melancholy events, why I point what must look like an accusatory finger at a mother and a brother. The answer is that, like it or not, one is totally involved with one's relatives, so that one cannot paint a picture of oneself without also describing them. For instance, my mother was expert at creating very small accidents. The telephone would ring, and she would get up to answer it. In getting up she would catch her foot in the telephone cord. To steady herself, she might clutch the table and overturn a lamp. It knocked the telephone to the floor. Stooping, with the cord still under her foot, she then tottered and slowly fell, crushing the lampshade. Today I find I have inherited the clumsiness. My father was a model of gentle efficiency. He went about all he did without hurry and in a set of orderly sequences. I cannot emulate him. I possess to the full the fine natural incompetence of my mother; and into the bargain I never take a drink – and I often do – without a pang of anxiety. Where will this end? In the suicides of Uncle Alan, of Cousins Lewis, Michael, a second Cousin Michael, his niece Cynthia? I doubt it, since I have a strong Polyanna side to my character – a side which has exasperated two wives, each of whom relished moments of darkness, of cloud in the crystal, and so flinched from too much cheerfulness. But I am aware of a native impracticality, a compulsion to drift, procrastinate, overlook oppressive essentials. I have very much the kind of temperament which vexes me in others, and so more powerfully in myself.

When I think of my mother today – and I often do, for in old age one slips easily into childish attitudes, one longs for the reassurance of parents, one longs to amaze them by some small anecdote, then remembers with anguish that they are no longer there – I think of her idiosyncrasies: of her habit of standing in front of the fire and lifting her skirts higher and higher, to reveal black knickers, while my father coughed deprecatingly from the sofa; of her perpetual cough, which made chandeliers rattle; of the extraordinary sound she made at the back of her larynx when a tickle afflicted her; of her habit of writing fan-letters to Noël Coward or Ivor Novello, all about her hard-worked husband and her wonderful sons (much to our embarrassment when we met the recipients); of her constant resentment that 'Mother's emeralds' had been left, not to her, but, very properly, to her elder brother. For, as she grew older, she developed a sense of martyrdom. Everybody possessed more than my father and herself; nobody but they had Communist maids – in reality the most devoted and apolitical of women – or an ungrateful chauffeur; nobody had such ungovernable nerves.

Yet she could be extremely funny. And at successive Hever Christmases it was she who led the remembered rituals of huge family dinners, who prompted the singing of old carols to see out the dying year. I loved her very much, but I found it almost impossible to make a happy contact with someone to whom the world since 1914 was not only unfamiliar but unthinkable. Nor had it been any use turning to my father in his lifetime because he too had switched off his responses thirty years before his death.

Not that either of them was stupid. The mother I knew when I was a child was imaginative and lively. She had been a very pretty girl, with the kind of prettiness which evokes sympathetic compassion – a quality she never lost. She was also wonderfully tender to her husband and her children. I can see her now, in the firelight of my night-nursery, lying on my nanny's bed and singing me to sleep. I was a spoiled and odious child, who had more fun with my grandmother (for whom my mother never greatly cared) but felt protective in my father's absence at the war; and, later, at Eton. I needed the emotional nursery atmosphere which my mother only sought to provide, and from which wiser parents ought to have weaned me.

My father read a great deal, but kept his reactions to himself. No doubt he suffered from anxiety over a wife who seemed always ill, always dependent on Dr Coué or a famous London counsellor named Dr Leahy, always likely to be unable to face obligations as small as a journey by car. No doubt he was disappointed by sons who shared none of his tastes, though as time passed he hid his feelings behind a screen of exquisite manners and a kind of astonished pride that Adrian and I had not brought our lives to unrelieved disaster. He did nothing at all, beyond perusing the crossword and the newspapers. He smoked endlessly Egyptian cigarettes, and not merely wrinkled his nose but exclaimed in anger if somebody else lit what he called a 'gasper'. He drank one drink before dinner, and, on reflection, he must have been bored to death. We would go for walks in the Home Park at Windsor, and when my son went to Eton his spirits briefly rose. But when he died, soon after, he quietly slipped away into a disembodied Edwardian world of mess-dinners and shooting parties. The world round him had long ceased to exist.

XVI

D URING MY YEARS in the *Times* office I was captured by a host of busy little activities of the kind which fall on the middle-aged, and which, in retrospect, seem to inhibit more valuable activities. Someone has to join committees, raise funds, needle rich acquaintances into charitable activities. And so I found myself with the years a Trustee of the National Portrait Gallery, of the London Library, a Council Member of the Royal College of Music, and of the Royal Literary Fund, chairman of a committee to appoint a French Book of the Month, Board Member of the Alliance Française, President of the Montgomeryshire Society, President of PEN. Such activities bring out a Flaubertian side in us all. We ought to watch ourselves as Flaubert watched Bouvard and Pécuchet, on the alert for fatuity, for a crippling kind of self-content.

There were compensations, of course. The National Portrait Gallery meetings were enlivened by Harold Nicolson, and soothed by the majestic somnolence of Lord Stanhope, who seemed unsure of his whereabouts much of the time. And the French Book committee, which involved an excellent monthly luncheon at the Ecu de France, led to some fine acrimony. One day there was a clash between Rose Macaulay and Ava Waverley, over a novel under discussion, which Ava Waverley tried to end by saying that she did not expect Miss Macaulay ever to understand the book, since for that some experience of marriage was necessary.

One did not with impunity say such things to Rose, then some seventy years old. Her eyes flashed, her thin face grew thinner. 'I do not know,' she said, 'why Lady Waverley presumes that because I never troubled to take a husband I have no first-hand knowledge of what it means to be alive.' And months later, when Lord Waverley died and was buried in a small Sussex church, so small that mourners had to be allotted a seat, she was delighted to find that the names in each pew were written on the back of ancient visiting-cards forgotten by Ava's first husband, and used up as an economy measure at the funeral of her second. 'She doesn't know much about life after all,' said Rose.

Once or twice Thérèse and I had stayed at Long Crichel in Dorsetshire, a house also frequented by Rose, and of which I treasure memories. It was run jointly by Raymond Mortimer, Eddy Sackville-West, Desmond Shawe-Taylor and Eardley Knollys, each of whom had a separate London establishment, though they found it convenient to share a country house. E. M. Forster might also be there, and the atmosphere was of books, music, and talk. The local village was called Cussage and, because of the celibate lives led by our hosts, Thérèse referred to them as '*Les messieurs de cul sage*'.

What, I thought, can be pleasanter than intelligent country life? After breakfast each member of the party withdrew to library, bedroom or terrace, to read or write. There was much music, though Eddy whose pianism was at concert level, did not care to display his gift except in a brief burst to demonstrate where Serkin had gone wrong, or Gide betrayed himself as a vain amateur. Rose might talk of the steepness of St James's Street which she used to negotiate on a bicycle in wartime, then switch to High Church theology or Cambridge gossip. Once, when she and I were at a Cambridge dinner party, she was amused by the snappish comment of a professor's wife recently transplanted from Balliol: 'In Oxford we should be having *good* conversation.' She was a traveller, like Freya Stark, who feared no discomfort, though on the road any passenger of hers had every reason to fear her driving. She loved swimming, to the point that one day, when I returned from giving a lecture in North Norway in mid-winter, she asked only, 'Did you bathe?' Forster seldom talked of books, but feelingly of music. He deliberately wove a Pooter-like atmosphere round himself: an atmosphere of smoky old clothes, unfashionable spectacles, chairs with springs hopelessly relaxed. Of his private life he gave no hint, though we knew that he had written a novel – later shown to be unreadable – called *Maurice*: which was kept locked away in King's College. I once shared with him a long wait in Rome airport, and an eventual flight to London, and then – the only time we ever were alone together – I saw how companionable, how skittish even, he could be. But his talk left no great trace; he was very much not a show-off; and when we reached Heathrow he refused a lift home. He did not wish it to be known where, outside Cambridge, he lived.

I have always had a passion for country-houses. I buy when I can those multi-volumed collections of plates by Neale and Jones and Co. I buy the designs of Sir Charles Eastlake, and the sepia quartos of ornamental villas or Gothick lodges. I buy Pugin's *Contrasts* and Repton's superimposed aquatint constructions. My curiosity had been aroused when I was small and went driving with my grandmother. As often as we passed promising drive-gates she turned the car towards the house and rang the bell. When someone came to answer it she announced, 'I am Lady Victoria Dawnay, and I was born in this house. I wonder if you would allow me to show it to my little grandson?' And if we were admitted she would reminisce. 'Oh, this dear old library! What happy memories I have of it. Look, darling, there is the conservatory where Aunt Margie let her mongoose escape.' On a good afternoon my grandmother had been born in half a dozen different rooms, and her family legends had been noticeably enriched, to my delight.

So that now, when I look back on my life twenty-five years ago, the part played in it by other people's houses is vivid indeed. At the top, perhaps, comes Somerhill, the home of our landlord in Kent, Harry d'Avigdor Goldsmid. I was in and out of it for fifty years. Somerhill is an Elizabethan house, greatly enlarged in the nineteenth century by the Goldsmid of the day. Turner painted it and on canvas moved the Medway in order to give it an even better setting. But its lawns, its beeches, its bluebell woods, the great cedar beneath which we were given white-napteried afternoon tea, the Jacobethan library in which cocktails followed the tea, the greenhouses hung with incomparable nectarines – a proportion of them grown for Solomon's, the fruiterers by the Ritz Hotel, now long vanished, but in its day the superior of Fortnum and Mason in this regard – then Victorian appurtenances like a laundry in the park, now turned into an elegant dower-house, and, above all, the stream of guests every week-end: Cyril Connolly, Peter Quennell, with their wives of the moment, politicians, racing experts, magnates from the city, beauties like Bridget Poulett – in her day perhaps the most beautiful of all – country figures such as the Abergavennys and the Cornwallises, collectors like the Trittons of Godmersham nearby, gardeners like Sir Albert Stern, who among other throwaway skills was greatly responsible for inventing the tank: Saturday after Saturday they passed through.

I especially recall one early week-end when Harry Goldsmid's father was still alive, and a group of architects turned up in a small bus, having 'done' some of the local great houses, Knole, Penshurst perhaps. By the time they reached the Somerhill cedar, they were non-receptive and slightly drunk – two conditions which did not appeal to Alice Goldsmid, their hostess. The leader of the architects was Lutyens, who had a weakness for puns. Suddenly he piped up, 'I say, Lady Goldsmid, I've got a good one for you. What's the name of the ideal husband?' She looked blank, and not the less so at the answer, spoken fast with the maximum of elision, 'Hugh Geoffrey Knight. Ha, ha, ha.' Born Polish in the late nineteenth century, she was not much of a one for blueish jokes in Kent.

Only a few miles away stood Fairlawne, the home of an Eton contemporary, Peter Cazalet, and his enchanting second wife, Zara. Peter trained the Queen's steeple-chasers, and so there was a good deal of royal life in the house – a life which would, for even the sternest republican, have dispelled any suspicion of stuffiness, while Princess Margaret played and sang with professional skill, and the Queen played foolish acting games until the small hours. What impressed me most, though, was the early morning, long before breakfast, when we staggered from our rooms into the icy winter mist to watch the horses put over jumps: ourselves red-eyed with lack of sleep, but the royals – as non-royal people used to call them – clear of eye, pink of cheek, and perfectly geared to an early breakfast in half-darkness before returning to London and work.

I used often to stay with another Eton friend, Michael Astor, at Bruern, a house where you might meet the Stephen Spenders, or Edith Sitwell, wrapped against imaginary draughts in an old fur cape reeking of moth-balls, the Lennox Berkeleys, or a selection of more or less eccentric sportsmen like Boofie Arran. Bruern was almost the only house where, in my middle years, I attempted any kind of sport. Michael and I used to play golf, but usually laughed too much to complete the course; and we used to shoot the Ditchley woods. The comical side of this was to be placed next to Boofie. Like another excellent shot, Tony Lambton, he never dressed as convention-al sportsmen do, but wore some exotic colour of velveteen. While waiting for the pheasants to come over, he showed every sign of nerves. 'Oh God, I want to pee. Oh, I haven't got a handkerchief.' And he paced up and down, very fast and with the kind of disarticulated jauntiness which indicates distress. Then came the sound of shouts and beating wings after which, having reduced my own mediocre skills to zero by his play-acting, he brought off his right and left with repeated authority, totally at ease.

Each of the Astor brothers had been a friend, if not a close one, since I grew up. Bill, the eldest, was the least amenable. As eldest, he had been exposed more than his siblings to the personality of his mother, who combined knock-out charm with a rare capacity to devastate. After his father's death he used to lend her Cliveden from time to time, and I stayed there several times as her guest. Then, at a large dinner, she would abruptly say to Dean the butler: 'Just look at his Lordship sitting there. God knows his father was a dull man, but he's worse: doesn't say a word to that pretty girl on his left. You'd better leave him and come to me.' This was said with no intention of wounding: it was simply what the Mitford family called 'a tease'. Just as when, at the height of the war, Bob Menzies, Prime Minister of Australia, was called to Chequers in the midst of a house-party built round him, she saw him off in his car and shouted after him, 'If it's a peerage you want you can have ours for half what we paid for it.' To tease was instinctive to her. But she was also endlessly generous and kind, not to say extremely funny. I had not known her when my cousin Angus MacDonnell fell in love with her – she was still Mrs Shaw at the time – but she must, as a young woman, have been utterly irresistible. And even at

171

eighty her trim little figure on the golf-course or walking down to the Thames through extravagant gardens gave the impression of a debutante rather than a grandmother.

One week-end Bill had a number of his relations in the house, one of whom had asked Stephen Ward and a girl or two, and his cousin Alice snorted that though it was possible to have a brothel in your park you did not usually invite the girls to meet your mother. Knowing nothing of Stephen Ward, I thought this merely an example of the astringent talk common to Nancy Astor and her family. However, it turned out that Nancy had taken a great fancy to Stephen Ward's friend Christine Keeler. She would be ravishing, we heard, if only she were dressed up a little. And so, after tea, she was brought early to Cliveden, and sent upstairs to be dressed by the lady's maid, who despatched her to join the party dripping in diamonds and applauded by her hostess. The Profumo scandal broke a week or two later.

In a subsequent essay, A. L. Rowse writes of a dinner given at about that time by Nancy Astor in her Hill Street house, but, though he gives a racy account of it he is unaware of the whole background. A few days before the dinner I had been invited one afternoon by the Duchess of Marlborough; my fellow-guest was the Queen Mother. The Queen Mother asked me if I were going to the dinner. She said, 'Nancy tells me I have very dull friends, so I am to meet hers for a change. What do you think this means?' On impulse I told her that Dr Rowse would probably be there, and just as probably would make her a little speech on Queen Elizabeth I. She smiled politely.

The evening of the dinner was star-studded. Knowing their mother's teetotal habits, Nancy's sons had set up a bar in a bedroom, but we were given champagne in very large glasses during dinner, so that some of the guests acquired a glazed look. Dr Rowse was indeed among us, and after the coffee we were sent two by two into a drawing-room where the Queen Mother had been installed with her lady-in-waiting, Lady Spencer. Dr Rowse and I were sent in together, and the Queen Mother caught my eye, remembering my silly joke, and gave a small laugh. As there was no apparent reason for this, Dr Rowse looked disconcerted, and tried to break the silence with an intelligent remark. Unluckily, the remark contained a reference to Elizabeth I, at which the Queen Mother broke into open but inexplicable laughter. Dr Rowse, I think, was surprised rather than pleased.

I used also to stay with another Astor brother, Jakie, at Hatley near Cambridge. He won my heart by making remarks such as before a visit to the stables, on the eve of a race, 'Let's go and take some wrong decisions.' He was an admirable host and once allowed me to bring a Viennese woman friend who had arrived at short notice from Austria. The friend was very nice, very clever but also very plain. As a conscientious organizer Jakie asked me if he ought to put us in a lonely wing of the house, to ourselves. I reassured him, but evidently he did not believe me, because after dinner I was reproached, 'I know,' he said, 'that you are no great catch, but surely you can do better than this.'

The third Astor brother, David, played a part in my life both as friend and as editor of the *Observer*, for which, when much later I left *The Times*, I served as theatre critic while Kenneth Tynan went to the *New Yorker*. In much older days I had been taken up by the Garvins, with whom I used to stay, and I owe a debt of gratitude to J. L. Garvin, one of the first editors to promote my cause, and the founder of a connection with the *Observer* which has lasted over fifty years.

At this time, however, my days were taken up by *The Times* and by the BBC, for, thanks to George Barnes and Harmon Grisewood, I did a good deal of work for the then new and lively Third Programme: work which brought me into delightful contact with one of the more enterprising producers, Anna Kallin, a Russian polymath, who introduced a proper sense of fantasy into the staid studies of Broadcasting House. The more arcane the subject the better she liked it. At one moment, with the collusion of Martin Cooper, we even invented a composer, Fillink, who had made his name with a ballet, *Unesco*. The *Musical Times* printed an article on Fillink. These early years of the Third Programme were a delight and a stimulus. Unlike some other sections of Broadcasting House, the staff was determinedly anti-Philistine, and for a time developed a kind of family feeling among those who took part. In the course of work one also learned a few practical lessons. One of my projects was to discuss with Ilse Barea the possibilities of translation: what it could, and could not, do. We were given a studio and unlimited time, to prepare a forty-minute talk, and when we emerged it was with the self-satisfied thought that our recording would be very hard to cut, for it seemed so literate, so balanced and fluent. The tape was played back to us and we might have been two baboons, incoherent, stuttering, repetitious. We had to start again from scratch, pencil in hand.

This lesson was especially useful to me, because, partly from laziness, my instinct has always been to plump for the impromptu. When I gave lectures I was so afraid of boring myself as well as my audience that I usually scrapped a prepared draft as soon as I reached the platform. I now learned that Ruskin's was the wiser plan, as exemplified in *Sesame and Lilies*. No public gesture needs to be so carefully rehearsed as an impromptu.

My insufficient skills were also used by the British Council year after year. I still remember spending my fortieth birthday alone in Liège, giving a lecture, sharing an immense casse-croute with Gabriel Chevallier in Lyons just before an immenser luncheon, spending an evening with Neruda at Isla Negra in Chile, dodging a bullet on the steps of a Buenos Aires hotel at the moment of Peron's dethronement, addressing in Spanish (how rash!) the Ateneo in Seville, in German an audience of nuns in Munster, in Italian a Milanese university group. I am not a good linguist. I make impressive progress for the first three lessons in a new language, and then stop for good. But some residual vanity, or challenging folly, had often made me tackle what I should have let alone. And I consoled myself by reflecting that in the Argentine or Norway, in Portugal or Brazil, I was likely to gain first-hand experience which would be useful to the *TLS*, to discover new themes, new contributors, all the more vividly if I were operating among them, rather than just paying them a visit from a foreign land.

The totally dedicated writer, the Walter Scott, or Simenon of his day, can sit at his desk and excrete prose like a silkworm: lesser men become entangled in a web of fantasy as they struggle to pit their little talent against the clock, the bank manager and the oculist. Thus, I found myself on more than one Anglo-French jury, one of which was to choose the best translation of the year. To my embarrassment I found that I had won the prize with a version of Supervielle's *Voleur d'Enfants*. Perhaps for this, and for a translation of his play *Schéhérazade*, commissioned for the Third Programme, not to speak of committee work with the Alliance Française and more or less close association with a number of French writers such as Montherlant, Jouhandeau, Gabriel Marcel, and the world of those admirable periodicals, *Commerces* and *Esprit*, I was awarded the one public honour I coveted, the Légion d'Honneur, only to be sent for by the French Ambassador, René Massigli, who appeared constrained when I was shown into the room. He showed me my ribbon, then said, 'But I am afraid you can't have it, though it has already been gazetted. Sir William Haley says no member of the *Times* staff may accept an honour.' As Sir William, deservedly, sported at the time ribbons both French and Dutch, I thought this a little hard; but my Légion d'Honneur was put back in its box and not heard of again.

Journeys for the British Council held compensations and surprises. Once, in Belo Horizonte, in Brazil, I was told that there lived in the city a Central European couple who would like to greet me as an old acquaintance. I tracked them down, and they turned out to be Hungarian Hohenlohes. The Princess had been a Batthyáni, and a famous beauty. In the tiny adobe cottage where they lived in severe poverty there was one memorial of the past, a slickly dashing portrait of imposing size, by Lászlo, with ropes of pearls carefully shadowed to indicate opulence. The Prince at that time was making a tiny livelihood by carving wooden statues of saints. They seemed perfectly happy.

Such assignments corrupted my standards of travel. Arriving in Buenos Aires, or Ankara, or Tokyo, I came to look for the special kind of Rolls-Royce, immense, aged but pristine, which seems to be accorded British ambassadors. There were never Customs formalities; a dedicated man with a moustache would always be on hand to take my passport through a side-door. I was deposited at a local Ritz, or, more rarely, at some monument to the picturesque, such as a Japanese inn, complete with wooden pillow and tank of boiling hot bath-water which it would be impolite to cool. But at times I was given a room in the Embassy, furnished in Office of Works Sheraton with a mushroom-coloured carpet, and shepherded from place to place as though I could not be expected to survive by myself outside the confines of the City of Westminster.

There were occasional setbacks. Once, in Lisbon at the inauguration of the Gulbenkian Museum, I was asked by a friendly stranger, glass in hand, what I thought of the building. Remembering the exquisite little palace of Oeiras which had initially housed what it could of the collection, I replied that I thought Mr Gulbenkian might not be pleased with so sternly functional a setting had he lived to see it. 'A pity,' said the stranger, 'I am the architect.'

XVII

Y EARS LATER, WHEN I have attained, if any standing, that of
a patriarch to whom strangers write, asking if I have letters
from Evelyn Waugh or if I ever met the Sitwells, I well may ask
myself if the process of aging is much more than a growing
perfection in the art of wasting time. To live life at concert pitch
for even an hour or two a day is beyond the usual human range.
In public activity there have been many more Asquiths than
Churchills; in the private realm of the creative artist territories
may lie fallow for months or years on end. Yet we fill the blank
spaces of living with a show of bustle, a strut of self-importance.
Thus when, soon after peace was restored in 1945, Emerald
Cunard ordered me to dine with her, so as to discuss a project of
hers, I fell in with her plan. The project was to design a season
of opera in English at Covent Garden, then in the financial
empire of Boosey and Hawkes, the music publishers. My task
was to translate *Der Rosenkavalier*, the existing English text of
which dated from thirty-five years earlier, and had been cast in
the Gadzooks-Egad style of 1912.

I did not envisage a contract as a means of making money,
but had I foreseen what occurred I should not have accepted
one anyway. For having assigned, against a cheque for twenty-
five guineas, the copyright to Boosey and Hawkes, I found
that they had parted with this sum most reluctantly, since
they had on their shelves a whole edition of the superseded
translation, which they proceeded to sell during performances
in the opera house. This meant that I received a stream of
letters from strangers, complaining that my text was hopelessly

superannuated. It also meant that, with no printed text of mine in existence, no singer wishing (rashly) to sing Strauss in English could find access to an approved version, so that I would discover over the years a variety of rubbish printed over my signature representing a conflation of both versions. Never was twenty-five guineas more hardly earned – there had been no question of a royalty – and when, years afterwards, Michael Hamburger, preparing a collected edition of Hofmannsthal, in English, asked for my translation, my request to buy back the copyright was refused. I do not record this out of paranoia, but simply as an instance of absurd conduct on the part of a publishing house which in theory had the interests of opera at heart.

However, a more rewarding operatic venture came my way a few years later, when Lennox Berkeley asked me for a libretto. I assumed that he had something domestic or whimsical or pastoral in mind – something which might stem from the example of Ravel, with whom he had worked as a young man. I began to speak of taking a subject out of Turgeniev. But not at all. He wanted a heroic theme, and so we hit on a classic conflict between love and duty: the story of Nelson and Emma Hamilton.

The difficulty of writing an opera libretto is to keep literature at bay. The writer is tempted to write beautifully, to spread his wings, whereas the only wings which should be encouraged to spread are wings of song. I was fortunate in my composer. He knew what he wanted. He was also a man who combined an instinctive knowledge of his craft with a delicate imagination, a Gallic practicality with West Country lyricism. We chose to plan our opera on unfashionable lines – this was before *The Rake's Progress* or *Lulu* – to revert to the manner of musical storytelling which is expressed in solos, duets, trios, rather than in the vocal and symphonic surge which is Wagner's legacy. Once or twice a problem arose when Lennox thought that what had been designed as a trio would go better as a quartet. 'But who is the fourth person?' I might ask. 'And how do we get her on stage?' 'That is your problem,' he would answer. But he was the least demanding of men and we never faced a problem which proved insoluble.

The first night took place at Sadler's Wells in 1954. George

Devine was the director and showed, I thought, less than his usual skill. Once again I underwent the odd sensation of taking a curtain call. You step forward, blinded by footlights, so that the audience is invisible. You feel, unless you are a Noël Coward or an Ivor Novello, like the statue in a public park, bathed in light, and trying, from your plinth, to look thoughtfully, gratefully, modest.

The critics were reassuring next day. But I was clear that any success *Nelson* achieved was due to the composer, not the librettist. Rose Macaulay confirmed this by saying later, 'But your text has poetry in it.' If true, this pointed out its weakness.

Shortly after, I was given a promising invitation. Gerry Wellington had inherited a handsome property – though not a handsome house – originally bestowed on the first Duke by a grateful Spain. The warmth of my pleasure was a little cooled when Gerry explained, 'You are one of the few people I can count on to pay their own fare,' and added that, although he would pay our expenses in pesetas, 'of which I have quite a few', he expected reimbursement of my share in pounds, 'of which I have not nearly enough'.

This seemed a sensible arrangement, and we started our little journey at the Ritz in Madrid. When I came down in the morning, Gerry was paying the bill. 'What's this?' he asked. 'Your bill is bigger than mine. Ah, I see you had orange-juice. And mineral water. Quite unnecessary.' When later his Spanish lawyer joined us for the drive to Granada he was warned: 'We can't have Alan ordering luncheon, he's far too extravagant.' My excesses had amounted to, perhaps, two shillings.

At Granada we were met by an English major, the agent, who had improvidently set out a bottle of local wine and a few nuts. 'What's the meaning of this spread?' Gerry protested. And he repeated, 'Quite unnecessary.'

As the week progressed he took me riding. That is to say, we walked dispirited horses among the olives until I became impatient and gave my mount a gentle kick. 'Look what you're doing,' said Gerry. 'It'll break into a trot.'

One evening Violet Trefusis arrived for a night or two. Many people found her magnetic, irresistible even. To me she was an extremely tiresome woman, with too calculated a wit, and a depressing tendency, with the years, to drink too much. I recalled with pleasure her sister's joke when asked why Violet had been given the Légion d'Honneur. 'I think,' said Mrs Cubitt, 'it was first her Resistance, and then her knowledge of French Letters.'

Gerry evidently shared my reservations because, as Violet's car drove up to the door, he murmured to me, 'I can't be left alone. I think she is out to get me.' He had lost his own duchess, we used to be told, because whenever they fell out his pledge of reconciliation was yet another bust or portrait of the Great Duke, on whom, however, he used to comment, 'I can't imagine why they call him that.'

To distract Violet and me he organized a display of caracul lamb skins from his farm. The good skins, he told us, were sold to Madrid furriers, but those which remained were quite good enough to make a rug. There were about twenty passable skins, one of a different colour, and one hairless, as if eaten by mange. Violet was not interested, but I offered to buy the passable skins. 'The other two cost the estate just as much,' said the Duke. 'If you won't take them too, I'll have to raise the price.' Somewhere, to this day, there lies in store an unused motor-rug.

We ended our journey with a final night in Madrid. This led to talk of where to dine, and I suggested a restaurant called the Jockey. 'Impossible,' said the Duke. 'Last time I wanted to dine there they said there was no table.' I suggested telephoning myself in my own name. 'That is not at all the same thing,' he observed.

However, we went there in the end, were treated most kindly, and as a final gesture given the visitors' book to sign. 'This is most difficult,' the Duke said, having executed a commanding 'Wellington.' 'I suppose I should add "Ciudad Rodrigo".' And he did. 'Then there is Portugal.' He reflected. 'I think I should give the Portuguese "Victoria". And of course one can't forget the Belgians. That would never do.' And so the page was finally filled: 'Wellington y Ciudad Rodrigo y Victoria y Waterloo.' 'One must always be careful not to hurt anybody's feelings,' he concluded.

It is a curious sensation to be fifty years old, a widower, a father, a comparatively successful man in the worldly sense, and yet to feel as though life were still in the embryo, still a show of possibilities. Shall I decide to become a bishop, a statesman, a poet, a man of business? I do not remember stopping to think that it was too late to be any of these things, any more than I had anticipated the death of parents. Without much thought I took myself to be a creature of infinite promise, sealed into the security of a dear and affectionate family.

At fifty, one experiences a small pang, less than at forty or sixty but strong enough to make one put away deliberately the sensation of aging. I recalled Eddie Gathorne-Hardy, many years before, saying, 'Look at me carefully. I'm twenty-eight today, and I'm going to stay twenty-eight *for a very long time*.' It is easy to do so. One is not yet breathless; one does not, as Harold Nicolson used to say, gobble turkey-like at the follies of the young. I even at fifty or more climbed the spiked gate which links Magdalen College to the Isis. I did it at midnight, regardless of spikes, because my young host was locked out at that hour and I did not want to pull age and rank on him by ringing the bell for myself. One can still pick up new interests. When Kenneth Tynan accepted a year in the *New Yorker* office as guest critic, I took his place on the *Observer*. It was just the right time to do so: the year when John Osborne had given the theatre a shot in the arm with *Look Back in Anger*, the year when Harold Pinter's name became known. I also took great pleasure in a television programme called 'The Bookman', which gave me a free hand in presenting after my own fashion two or three books at a time. There was *Lolita*, for one, which for an hour or two was expected to lead to Nabokov's arrest for writing so shocking a novel. After we recorded our programme there was a studio luncheon at which the exemplary Catholic, Douglas Woodruff, told me that he would not shake Nabokov's hand. We were only eight at table, but I was able to conceal this harsh reality from Nabokov through cocktails and three courses.

There was also, on a higher plane, the triumph of persuading Ivy Compton-Burnett to give an interview in her house. She supposed innocently that this would involve no more than a Leica camera, and yet put up with the horrid disturbance to Braemar Gardens of a crew, of thick cables, of heat and light. There was new talent to support on other days, such as Edna O'Brien and James Kennaway. Above all, perhaps, there was the satisfaction of working with a supportive and intelligent producer, Guy Verney.

But the most agreeable aspect of my middle years is bound up with a set of friendships which had always existed but deepened measurably at that time. My grandmother, Victoria, had an elder sister who died young of puerperal fever, leaving three small children. The third, of whose birth she died, married in due course William Lascelles, by whom she had two daughters, Mollie and Diana. They too were orphaned early and grew up partly under my grandparents' eyes, but chiefly with a step-aunt, Lady Moyra Cavendish, at Holker in Lancashire. They also had a devoted governess, Miss Mallam, who lived with them in a tiny flat out of Eaton Square. They were older than I, and to me (and to others) extremely glamorous. I used to be taken to tea in Elizabeth Street when they were teen-agers and I nine or ten. Or they came to play in Belgrave Square where their only rival in my eyes was Diana Fellowes, who used to sit me down in a summer-house on top of the central mound, and tell me stories in French, of which I understood no single word. All three meant to me the promise of a grown-up life and I was immensely impressed by them.

In the fullness of time they married. Mollie became Lady Dalkeith, Diana, Mrs Bowes Daly, and Diana Fellowes Mrs Henry Broughton. All passed out of my life. Diana Broughton died before the Second World War, Diana Daly lived in Ireland, and Mollie Dalkeith, subsequently Mollie Buccleuch, was caught up in her husband's public life. In later years, however, we came together again and I was made free of a world which, without rejecting the twentieth century, preserved unflawed memorials of the last three hundred years.

This world embraced three exceptional houses, two of them gravely beautiful and the third no less of a treasure-house than these. One, Drumlanrig, is a baroque castle built of rose-coloured sandstone, flecked with mica which throws off, from time to time, a firefly glitter. The castle is wonderfully placed, at the end of a long avenue, high above Nithsdale. By contrast, Bowhill, in the Vale of Ettrick, is, if a palace in size, an unbuttoned palace. It rambles. It hesitates before making a grand gesture. To my mind the most alluring of all is Boughton in Northamptonshire, a house of brick and stone built round several courtyards, to enlarge a monastic plan to which is pinned, with a gesture almost defiant, as entrance front an echo of Versailles, where its builder, the first Duke of Montagu, served as Ambassador.

The life lived in these houses was, and still is, much the same. There is the outdoor world of horse and gun; there is the indoor world of formal duty, of hunt-balls, and garden-parties and political gatherings. There is the family world of children and grandchildren, growing up among established treasures taken not exactly for granted, but as treasures long familiar, intimately loved. None of these houses was open to the public until many years later, but those who cared for such things were always welcomed. And there were innumerable guests: not only ambassadors and royal duchesses, but off-beat writers like Brian Howard; museum experts; dogged American millionaries who required a nap after luncheon, soon tired of Raphael cartoons, Carlin writing-tables and Isfahan carpets, and wondered anxiously why there was no golf-course in the park.

The royal duchesses were collectively known as the Mammals, because of the respectful 'ma'ams' slipped into drawing-room conversation. Of the ambassadors the most frequent visitors were the Winthrop Aldrichs and the Massiglis. In particular the Aldrichs came to play a growing part in my life. Winthrop Aldrich's characteristic as a diplomat was a strong preference for pretty women over eminent men. All the same, he would not have been president of the Chase Bank had he not used a natural shrewdness, even if he were known, when statesmanlike talk became too monotonous, to switch off his hearing aid. Harriet Aldrich was a genial matriarch, bluff, sensible and tolerant. When his ambassadorship drew to its close, Winthrop returned to the United States, bringing with him a Bentley, which his wife disliked. I was staying with them in New York shortly after, and ventured the opinion that Bentleys at that time were not family cars at all; they were designed for rich young bachelors. 'I have spent thirty years,' said Mrs Aldrich, 'reminding myself that that is what Winthrop thinks he is.'

Mollie and I made several trips with the Aldrichs, who owned a fine yacht, *Wayfarer*, which they used in the United

States and the Caribbean, though they preferred a charter in Europe. One year we sailed up the Maine Coast in almost perpetual fog, anchoring overnight in the Bay of Fundy, New Brunswick, where there is a tidal rise and fall of over fifty feet. Winthrop, a former Commodore of the New York Yacht Club, liked to be in command at moments of drama at sea, and plumped himself in front of the radar. In the early morning the fog lifted briefly and revealed us nestling beneath the bows of a cruiser high overhead.

Mediterranean trips were less adventurous. We might travel along the French Riviera, from Bandol to Mentone, while Harriet raked the shore-line through her binoculars in search of a casino, exclaiming in triumph when she thought she had perceived one on the horizon. Then we put in to harbour at once, confident that if the casino turned out no better than a Grand Hotel our hostess would be released for an hour or two from the servitude of the sea.

But it was especially at Boughton that life assumed a strange luminous quality which has never faded. Boughton is a very large house indeed, but it is not aggressive, unlike, say, the houses of Vanbrugh. It might be the palace of the Sleeping Beauty, on a summer afternoon when the company is playing tennis or swimming, and the State Rooms, shuttered against the damaging sun, smell of lilies. The house is said to shelter a ghost – Winston Churchill was very uneasy in one of its bedrooms – but it is above all a kindly house. Its guardian spirit, to my eyes, is the Lord Monthermer whose portrait by Batoni looks down from an easel. Monthermer, heir to the first Duke of Montagu, travelled on the Continent, collecting pictures and furniture. In the Batoni portrait he is holding the score of a Corelli sonata, and clearly he was something of an aesthete, handsome, melancholy, a student of drawing as well as music, and never with enough health to copy the arduous excesses of ducal heirs in the eighteenth century. He died in his thirties. There is something compelling about his portrait, and I have sometimes paused as if I were half-expecting to catch an echo of Corelli in the silent house.

Duke Walter, Mollie's husband, was cut to a different pattern. He was a man of the outdoors, a skilled forester, a huntsman, an excellent shot, a practical man, an administrator. He cultivated a sense of duty, knowing his privileges to be rare indeed. He stood by relations in trouble, he was the exemplification of conscience.

In character, he and Mollie complemented one another. They were totally unalike. She was visibly descended from the Lady Bessborough who cut such a swathe through London society two centuries ago; she would have been perfectly at home in the Devonshire House of 1820. He, by contrast, appeared shy, withdrawn. Neither epithet was precisely applicable. Rather, he was concerned, bent on his own business, a man with little time for fantasy. Yet he knew well, and loved, the beautiful things he owned; he had a sharp sense of possession without being at all a proud man. He was utterly loyal to friends like Prince Paul of Yugoslavia, not least when political fashion turned against them.

It cannot have been easy for him to share a life with someone as mercurial as Mollie. Winston Churchill once said of her that when she entered a room it was as though a light had been switched on. Her progress through fifty years of marriage had been flecked with colour and movement. She had revived three great houses, banishing the buff paint-work of her mother-in-law, attaching to herself experts like John Fowler, creating gardens, libraries and ballrooms with authority. She also attached to herself a huge variety of people – at first sporting and political people mainly, and the ramifying branches of two large families, then later clever people such as Jean Cocteau at one extreme, the Menuhins, the Pope-Hennessy brothers, and a great many more whose friendship we both shared: Roy and Billa Harrod, Patrick Kinross, Brian Howard – against whose waywardness I warned her in vain – Somerset Maugham.

Both Mollie and Walter dearly loved their children and grandchildren, but it was inevitable that their day-to-day interests diverge. Walter was devotedly practical, Mollie never knew the difference between one pound and a thousand. They shared close friends – Paul Maze the painter, Audrey Pleydell-Bouverie – for a time – Odette Massigli, Serge Obolensky. And in the background there was always the severely affectionate figure of Mollie's sister, Diana Daly, watching over them both. But the house-parties, which served as a kind of anchorage to Mollie, for Walter stood as a pleasant interruption to a life built round committees and public duties always given first place. As a couple they resembled their own relations of an earlier period, the Balfours, the Cavendishes, the Bridgemans, the Lambtons, each with a life-enhancing wife – sometimes causing a raised Edwardian eyebrow – and an admiring but diffident husband.

As well as Boughton I took great delight in Drumlanrig. I have old sketch-books of my grandmother's, with careful water-colours of the terraces, of the summer-houses roofed with sphagnum moss, of the bridge by the river below. She used to tell of the four identical staircases in the corner towers, and how each sported a cord of a different colour so that visitors might not get lost. All this was unchanged after nearly a century. The Duke of the day had introduced Labrador dogs into Britain, and there, in the stables, was Mr Humphries, the dog-handler, cherishing the line. Through the woods near the house there were ravishing walks, brilliant with azaleas; a little further off, the ruins of Morton Castle, jagged on its slope. Indoors, according to your mood, you might look up the shooting records of the Buccleuch moors, or you might contemplate an El Greco. But always what counted was the sense of continuity, of an abiding place, silently opposed to the fragility of the twentieth century.

The practical centre of my life in these years remained the Albany – I could never bring myself to omit the 'the', as became fashionable at that time. The Albany, too, was an abiding place in the life-time of old Mr Stone, who had gradually bought up a majority of the free-holds. It wore a patriarchal air, possibly because Mr Stone himself was over a hundred years old. To own a lease, you had to be approved by a committee. Money did not change hands apart from rent and rates – and I note that the going price for a week's rent nowadays (we were not allowed to rent, but the secretary might turn a blind eye if we 'lent' our rooms against a small sum) is considerably higher than a year's rent in the 1950s.

It was all very comfortably inbred. Mr Mercer, the head porter, was a pillar of strength to the whole little community. He tended the courtyard gardens, he controlled (not always easily) the under-porters, at whose activities, as a perfectionist, he tut-tutted from time to time. After a time he married my housekeeper, Mrs Gibbins, the exemplification of efficiency and kindness. It became known before long that Mrs Gibbins was in touch with every good household in the British Isles. Ladies in search of a chef, gentlemen needing a butler, were constantly on the line, asking her help. I came to know exactly which houses it was satisfactory to work in, and which to avoid.

I had enlivening neighbours. There was Harold Nicolson, who was likely to be sharing a drink any evening with John Sparrow, Warden of All Souls. There was Graham Greene, who gave the impression as he walked silently and sensitively by, that he was permanently imprisoned in a thriller of his own writing. There was G. B. Stern, by now a rather galumphing lady who pinioned one with book-talk if one accepted her invitations. Just near my own front door lived Fleur Cowles, who reigned in perhaps the handsomest room of old Albany House, and below were the David Bruces, lately at the American Embassy. The K. Clarks lived along the Rope Walk, a pretty passageway which divided the building of the Albany, and the art critic John Richardson lived close to Ted Heath on the corner of Savile Row, at the opposite extreme to Peter Coats the garden expert. Possibly the total atmosphere of the building was a touch claustrophobic. We all knew more than we needed to of one another's business. But we made up a small, secret community remote from the fume and polyglot energy of Piccadilly.

And there was amusement too. One day I was hailed out of a taxi in the courtyard by Jane Clark*, who said something to the effect that we met too seldom. 'And now,' she went on, 'we are off to Sweden.' I tried to be helpful, and suggested they should try to visit Elghammar, the home of the Fouchés, who descend from Napoleon's minister and possess superb Napoleonic objects. 'Oh,' said Jane, 'do give us a letter. We should love to meet some ordinary people. We never see anybody in Sweden but the King.' And she drove on.

The Albany courtyard, incidentally, is flanked by low buildings, now offices, but in Edwardian days a brothel run by a once-famous Mrs Jeffreys. Which is why an extremely respectable friend of my father's, General Jeffreys, was always known as Ma. The garrulity of age prompts me to remember that

* m. Sir Kenneth. Later Lord Clark.

General Jeffreys married the widow of Lord Cantelupe, who died young, after a few months of marriage. She refused to abandon her title, and my parents were delighted by embarrassments caused, in those prim times, by General Jeffreys and Lady Cantelupe booking into the same hotel room.

We even had a ghost in the Albany. Among its inhabitants was a rather sad young man, John Phillipps, who was drowned in early middle age. He drank more than he should, and presented a dejected front to the world. After his death he was seen more than once in his former rooms, always by someone who had never known him in life – a maid, or a delivery man – but who was struck by his *farouche* appearance.

It must have been in 1958 that I made friends with two visitors from the United States, ambassadors from the Ford Foundation, McNeil Lowry and Chet d'Arms. They were in charge of that section of the Foundation concerned with the Humanities and the Arts: a section which at that time disposed of some fifteen million dollars a year. Their task was to justify spending a great deal more, and so, among their extravagances, they decided to employ me for six months as an adviser.

At that time I had been a drama critic for a year; but Ken Tynan was ready to leave the *New Yorker* and to take up his job with the *Observer* once again. My son had recently married, and I was tempted, being free of any tie, by the prospect of half a year in New York. I did not foresee that my life up to the age of fifty-two would close abruptly; that I should spend the rest of my days in another country; that, without feeling different from the middle-aged Englishman of partly Welsh extraction I was resigned to being, I should experience an immense enlargement of living over the decades to come, should remarry, should discover myself equally at home on either side of the Atlantic.

And so, on May 19, 1960, I flew to New York.

XVIII

I STARTED MY new life at the Gladstone Hotel – a welcoming mid-town hotel. Not too grand and much used by high-brow Europeans, partly because Alice Pleydell-Bouverie, once von Hofmannsthal, and Harding, born Astor, lived, and indeed died, there.

This was 1960, and transatlantic exchanges were still looked on as unusual. As a British resident, you crossed the ocean on business, perhaps, but unless you were a lecturer, a photographer for *Vogue*, or the Duke and Duchess of Windsor, you rarely did so with enthusiasm. The Nancy Mitford view of Americans still held. They had extravagant names, they drank too much, they were mostly Jewish; either they knew their place and were amusingly sycophantic to the European Establishment, or they were just amusingly brash. The Kennedys were still unknown outside Embassy circles and it was not thought odd when a British peer-to-be – even though he had an American mother – climbed on deck on the *Queen Elizabeth* planning to visit his rich relations after the war, took one look at the New York skyline, returned to his cabin, and only disembarked on reaching Southampton again.

I, by contrast, was instantly pitchforked into New York life. My first evening there was Ken Tynan's last, and he was celebrating it by giving a large party. There before me stood the ranks of the *New Yorker*, of the *Times*, of Condé Nast's innumerable magazines. There were suddenly embodied names, Katherine Anne Porter, Marianne Moore, Tennessee Williams, glass in hand, abundantly human. It was the first evening of a period in which I wasted time absurdly. In New York, I at once found one is not tired. I soon concluded that I could survive without strain on an hour or two of sleep.

But the days were delightful too. The Ford Foundation offices were not far from the Gladstone. One walked out of a cool hall on to a hot, brilliant street, lined with buildings to which Nancy Mitford might have allocated the names; Chock Full of Nuts and The Full Beli Deli, say. But were they really more bizarre than Parisian storefronts like Nik et Pouff? One stepped back into the cool on Madison Avenue, shot up to the nineteenth floor and settled into a glittering little office – very unlike Printing House Square – to await events.

At first I had no idea what I was supposed to do. When I was told to present myself in May, I answered that, on a six-month assignment, I should be wasting other people's time and money, since from July onwards less and less potential colleagues would be in New York offices owing to the long distraction of an Eastern summer. Later I was told that my timetable had been set for budgetary reasons only. A fixed sum had to be spent by the Foundation before a certain date. As usual my masters were perplexed by the need to spend; there were just not enough schemes afoot. And at least I was not a notorious left-wing figure in my own country; my presence in New York need not embarrass the Ford Motor Company.

Hitherto, I had imagined that Henry Ford and his fellow directors were impelled to sustain the Foundation simply because they were very rich and very generous. I soon discovered that, however rich and generous, they were also wary. An ample Foundation was one means of keeping control of company shares. The worst that could happen was that the heads of the Foundation, as distinct from the company, might feel the power behind their millions and promote causes ungrateful to a motor magnate. This indeed happened; and by 1960 Henry Ford and his Foundation were poles apart.

However, they could spend a few thousands a year on me and so help modestly to postpone a situation which made the Foundation apprehensive. One day on my way to the elevator I heard two pundits discussing our budget. 'It is bad enough with four billion in the kitty,' one said, 'but if we go to six or seven we are sunk.' We did not go to six billion, but it was soon confirmed that we were not in need. I was encouraged to lease an apartment and transfer books and furniture from London at the Foundation's expense. Any reasonable expense incurred on its behalf was met at once. We were not extravagant; we were not spoiled by our motor millions, but we were used with great consideration. The secretaries were admirable, the rooms were jalousied and quiet. As far as it could be said of a totally modern building, much later to be superseded by a discreet palace of crystal, built round an interior courtyard garden, and close to the United Nations Headquarters, our offices wore the aloof and meditative air of a latter-day cathedral close.

To these rooms came a bizarre assortment of visitors. A lady of sixty with a hundred thousand words of unfinished fiction in her desk needed five thousand dollars to finish the job. A lithographic studio in California needed only a few more millions to revive the art of lithography. A large modern theatre was needed in Texas. The symphony orchestra, in a grand general sense, could do with a hundred and fifty million. The ballet was more modest, twelve millions for Balanchine would do. And there was the opera question. Why did the Metropolitan Opera not commission three American operas, for which the Foundation would underwrite the expenses – the composer to choose the subject and ourselves to contribute nothing but a cheque? The Metropolitan replied coldly that there were not three composers in the country capable of writing to their standard. So the Foundation, stung, commissioned twelve operas spread over the country. One was performed in San Francisco and one in Chicago, but before the scheme collapsed Rudolf Bing, who had dismissed it in the first place, changed his mind and an opera was commissioned for the Met from Marc Blitzstein. The subject he chose was the Sacco and Vanzetti trial. Perhaps as a joke, Bing in later conversation said that Sacco and Vanzetti sounded to him like a safe Renaissance pair: the Viscontis and Strozzis or the Guelfs and Ghibellines. No great thought was given, therefore, to the press release on the subject and nobody stopped to reflect on the extreme left-wing politics of the composer. When Blitzstein was murdered by a sailor in Martinique before completing his opera, I wondered in an irresponsible moment whether we or the opera house should be held responsible for suppressing a composer who might have caused an irreparable breach with the Ford Motor Company.

One day an unannounced visitor wished to see me just as I was going to a meeting. The secretary explained the case and he left; but the following day I was given a note written apparently on lavatory paper in a very childish hand. It was a note of apology. The writer should have telephoned first, he said, but he had heard that I was interested in architecture, and while he was briefly in New York he had hoped to discuss with me 'some of the houses built by Lloyd Wright for myself and my family'.

There was a notable contrast between the look of the note and the invocation of Lloyd Wright. I was interested, and tried to get in touch, but he had left the city. However, some months later I was in Tulsa, Oklahoma, in order to see an eccentric but brilliant architect, Bruce Goff. Hardly had I left the plane when I was paged and ordered to the airline counter. As nobody, I thought, knew me to be in Tulsa, I was doubly curious. A youngish stranger with a black eye – he had been playing handball he told me – was waiting, with the news that he was to drive me to call on Bruce Goff. He set off, and I noted that the driver had an impediment of speech. Suddenly he asked, 'C-can you tell me why I stammer so when I'm so r-r-rich?' I said we had a drive of some sixty miles during which to find out. And then I discovered that he was my New York visitor, and that Lloyd Wright had indeed designed houses for his family, whose fame in the world of engineering appeared to rival that of Cartier among jewellers.

His own house, when we stopped there briefly, was not by Lloyd Wright. It resembled an upturned Siamese imperial boat, gilded, I seem to remember, and set, without any amenity like a garden, on a rough patch of ranch land. Inside the house there were windows edged with white fur-like rime on a branch – to match the white sheepskin of the walls, which tilted back like airplane seats. There was no furniture, only innumerable cushions, and there was a conversation pit from which, at the touch of a button, a bar and a sound system rose to table height. Much of the ceiling was covered in white goose feathers, which moved to the rhythm of the air-conditioning, and the walls were either of coal or glass residue, dramatically lit. I should have been more impressed had I not spent a night or two just before at the Loël Guinness house in Florida on the coast at Manalapan. That house itself was a simple yellow building, of classical design. But it is so built that a main road runs right over it, planted out in order that no tarmac be visible, and with the space between tarmac and drawing-room ceiling filled with steel wire and cement. There was never the least sound of traffic overhead.

These were early examples in my experience of an ever-fascinating American trait: the urge to try things out. This is an Elizabethan virtue which in Europe becomes daily rarer. Nobody would build a house under a main road at Margate. Yet nothing could be quieter or more comfortable than life on the Guinness terraces.

I did not want to stay long at the Gladstone Hotel, so I accepted an offer from Clarice Rothschild while I was looking for a flat of my own. 960 Park Avenue turned out to be a throw-back to Europe, a comparatively modest setting for what was still a splendid collection of pictures and furniture. Clarice must have been some seventy years old. Both her daughters had married American husbands, and in the evening of her days she, the most European of dowagers, changed her lifestyle completely. Her rooms were typical Park Avenue rooms, low-ceilinged boxes of no particular distinction. But she had been allowed to take enough Rothschild pictures and furniture out of Austria to create a small museum, and there she held court, still beautiful, still formidable, but delighted by the novelty of what must have seemed a restrictive life, populated by a few ramrod-stiff elderly Viennese barons, a French dowager or two, an opera-singer here, a minor poet there. I found her warm and funny. To see her at all brought back memories of Meidling; and our best moments were when we both woke in the night and as though by homing instinct met in our dressing-gowns round the kitchen table, milk in hand, and soon afloat on a rich tide of gossip. Clarice spoke in a voice of dark velvet, a vibrant cozy voice which in the end spared nobody. If her affections were deep and totally unsnobbish, she could also be a dangerous friend with a verbal karate chop at her disposal.

She liked to play with fire. But while she did so – and while he lived – she was devoted to her husband. Alfons. Of the three Austrian Rothschilds in her generation, Alfons had been the intellectual. When forced to talk parish business to a Hungarian priest, he preferred to do so in Latin rather than Magyar. Now, without him, she looked about her afresh, and soon formed what she called her 'Mother's Meeting' – a small group with which she had very little obviously in common. There was Brian Urquhart, already a dominant figure in the secretariat of the United Nations, Brian's first wife Alfreda, Robert Rushmore, a life-enhancer who wrote a good book or two, John Richardson, the art critic, Speed Lamkin, the southern playwright, and a host of more or less nebulous friends who floated in and out of their lives. Robert eventually wrote his best novel about Clarice, aptly called *A Passion for Meddling*. Meddle she did, with the dexterity of a puppet-master. Her grand coup was to invite those members of her Mother's Meeting locked in the densest emotional tangle, all to stay with her in Austria together. She then set about a divorce here, a remarriage there; and I still have her telegraphic progress reports, usually on a note of triumph, as she guided her guests from bed to bed, towards a final magisterial re-grouping.

Life at 960 Park Avenue was tiring at times, and I was glad before long to find an apartment just off 5th Avenue on 55th Street. It was the top floor of a once one-family house opposite the St Regis Hotel. I went to see it with Robert Rushmore and a foundation member of the Mother's Meeting, Harriet Meredith. We had come from the piers, after seeing a friend off to Europe on the *France* and we still carried with us bottles of champagne which there had been no opportunity to open on board.

The apartment had not been furnished though there were rugs on the floor. And there we perched, stretched out on the rugs, Harriet aged about sixty, I over fifty and Robert in his forties. We opened the champagne, we chatted happily, when suddenly there was a loud knock on the door and the sound of a turning key. The building's superintendent had heard talk and laughter in an apartment which he knew to be empty, and I have not forgotten the look on his elderly, respectable face, as he looked down on three mature recumbent figures in an empty room, with a small line of empty champagne bottles behind them.

Once the rooms were furnished, I asked Mrs Henry du Pont,

a dowager hardly less embattled than Clarice, to visit me, because I had heard that as a small girl she had lived in the house with her grandmother. She told me that from my bedroom window, then a nursery window, she used to look across the street at a charming little girl, so charming that she wished to scrape acquaintance. 'No, darling,' said the grandmother, 'I am afraid we can't know her.' Why? The grandmother evaded the question but at last Ruth du Pont wrung from her an explanation: the little girl was called Vanderbilt, and upstarts like the Vanderbilts would not in 1900 be welcomed by an old-fashioned New York lady in her eighties. I remembered a tart retort of Lady Astor's when she thought some Vanderbilt lady was pulling rank on her: 'Never forget that we Astors was skinning skunks years before you Vanderbilts began pushing ferries.'

It did not take long before the social distinctions upon which New York society rests obtruded themselves on me. London, Paris and Vienna had been organized in a manner comparatively simple. There was an *'erste Gesellschaft'* – a First Society – and there were the rest. The First Society in Austria, Germany, France, Italy and Spain was much older than that in Britain and gave itself higher airs. A mediatised prince in Vienna was still somebody, a pre-revolutionary French peer still outranked a colleague ennobled by the Bonapartes. But America was supposed to be a classless society. Nevertheless, it clung with anxious obstinacy to a class-structure of the utmost complexity.

Throughout my lifetime, and especially in Europe, it was hard not to acknowledge the extreme distinction of certain elderly Americans, mostly women. Henry James's friend Ethel Sands was a pre-eminent case. Not beautiful but elegant; lively, not witty; with a rare addiction to fine things; talented (she painted elegantly), crisp, she made many of her European friends look slightly tawdry. Madame Balsan, born a Vanderbilt, totally gave the lie to any criticism implied by Mrs du Pont's grandmother. And a whole slew of American wives, too often married for their money, gave lustre to the noble houses which embraced them.

True, by my time the traffic of peer and millionairess had dwindled. There was a Barbara Hutton or two, but the steady stream that flowed from Minneapolis to the House of Lords and the Paris Jockey Club was drying up. This was only one of many signs that America was standing on its own feet. It had become rather old-fashioned to need the reassurance of Europe. American painters and writers and musicians no longer felt as Emerson had felt before Carlyle, MacDowell before Raff or Mary Cassatt before Degas. The younger generation knew themselves to be leaders in their own right.

Should they stop to think, however, they might still envy Europeans one thing: a homogeneous society diversified by odd sports and grafts on to a parent stock. The United States by contrast has no parent stock by now: it displays nothing but diversification. New York hates New Jersey, the East flinches from the Middle-West, all non-Texans look askance at Texas. Locally, every American society is like a cat's cradle. The strings are pulled this way and that between Anglo-Saxon Protestants, Greeks, Italians, Jews, Puerto Ricans, Germans, Irish Catholics, Blacks. Give an extra tug and the whole society threatens to fall apart. Yet each little section of it is sustained by the same prop: a happy self-confidence between set limits. I am a Boston Catholic, so I'm all right; I am a Chinese on Mott Street, New York, and I need never leave my neighbourhood. I am the black mayor of a great industrial city; I've got there and I'm staying there. I have fifty million and my wife has two Presidents of Yale in her family tree: thank God we're safe. These little echoes are rolling round the homes of America, very few of which care a rap for what used to be called the Old World.

When I lived in Europe, before the war, I used to think of Europe as a Camembert cheese, left out too long – runny at one moment and smelling high, then suddenly dry as plaster. Now, as I edged my way into the United States, my first reaction was a keen pleasure in finding an apparently free society, released from centuries of inhibition and disappointed hope.

XIX

I HAD NOT been in the country long when it entered a period of
effervescence: the Kennedy election was upon us. Towards
the end of the war I had watched Americans in action. I had
briefly been attached to General Patton in Normandy and
formed for him not only immense respect – he was perhaps the
outstanding fighting general on our side – but also a liking.
There was no reason why he should have shown more than the
briefest courtesy to a British major during a lull in the fighting.
But in fact, while I ate in his mess, he went out of his way to be
agreeable. During my Bletchley days, I had occasional meetings with senior American officers, and I have not forgotten one
such: when J. L. Austin, the philosopher, was called to describe
in front of Eisenhower and others the slope of the Normandy
beaches. Austin was an austere figure. He wore fierce little
spectacles; he dressed only in issue uniform, eschewing the
more comfortable shoe or shirt in favour of an army hand-me-
down. He spoke unsmiling and to the point. When he had done
so a Lieutenant-General questioned his judgement. Was he
absolutely sure he was accurate about the slope of the beaches
at Arromanches? He stiffened. After all, he was a Professor of
Moral Philosophy. In a thin voice he replied, 'The trouble with
you senior officers is always the same. It is not that you will try
to run before you can walk. You will try to walk before you can
stand.'

By this period of the war, in the British Army, the amateurs
had taken over from the professionals. Men of no previous
experience had shown themselves better at the job than regular

army types. Although this was not so in the American army where the amateurs were anyway in the majority, the senior Americans present looked stricken. They apologized for doubting Austin's word. They winced.

During the weeks before the Kennedy election much the same thing happened. Disguised as an amateur, Kennedy proved far more professional than his rival. At the climax of the campaign, Caroline and Ian Gilmour arrived in New York, and we spent evening after evening with a little group of Kennedy enthusiasts, sitting up late into the small hours and hardly daring to hope for the victory of our hero. It was for me rather like watching American football. I achieved enthusiasm without ever quite understanding what went on. Ten years before, in Washington, one of my sisters-in-law and I had cheered a winning side to the echo. Why? We never knew. And so it was with the Kennedy election. The Gilmours at least moved among the Kennedy clan, and I supposed their keenness was infectious. It seemed as if a new political world were struggling to be born.

True or false, this belief added to the excitement of living in America. Its power could be gauged three years later. On November 22 I was booked to give a lecture at a convent school in the former Otto Kahn house on East 92nd Street. The subject was totally peaceful. I think it was an analysis of *Pride and Prejudice*. Just as I was about to begin, an agitated nun told me that a shot had been fired at the President. I sensed that my audience was restive. The Kennedy connection with the school was a close one. And so I broke off and told the girls to listen to a radio if they wished. A voice said dully, 'The President of the United States died an hour ago.' Pandemonium broke out. The nuns knelt and I, from the platform, was uselessly concerned with the problem of which direction to face as I sank to my knees. A few moments later in the street there was total silence but for the tolling of bells.

More than twenty years later, and after a torrent of ink has been poured on the subject, it is still possible to feel that the three Kennedy years held a promise of a Golden Age. No matter if the Kennedys themselves were aggressively human in their faults: John Kennedy had managed to light a flame in the Western world. The times were drab. The world of Eisenhower and Macmillan revolved around the golf course and the grouse moor; and suddenly there was talk, however unsteady, of Camelot. Camelot was never built, but the prospect of it added to the American dream.

Politics in the United States are a dusty business. Nowhere in the modern world do politicians elicit enthusiasm. We do not remember Wilberforce, Gladstone, General Marshall, as enviable examples. We see politicians as ruffians to react against, such as Batista or Somoza, or as ruined up-thrusters like President Nixon. We read of their doings in the papers: a little graft here, a lie or two there, a tantrum, a sophistry. We learn that they wreck their careers for a small bribe, a still smaller sexual exploit. It is not that American politicians are any worse than the rest, only that less is expected of them, so that the public comes to greet their antics numbly. When, therefore, a promise of Camelot flashes up it is as though footlights have been turned on. Everything is transfigured, the old pockmarked scenery is flooded with a fresh brightness.

From my safe eyrie above Madison Avenue, I did not contribute much to this spirit of hope. It was one of the rules of the Ford Foundation that nobody working for it could lawfully break into print. We had to show that while we were forking out our millions, we were ourselves above the battle, unswayed, unadvantaged. After my six months were up I had been asked to stay another half-year, and then another year, and then forever. I had the sense to point out that if this were fine for me it was probably not fine for the Foundation. For each of us was supposed, by our possible clients, to have uncounted millions in our pockets and if this were so what on earth were they to make in Tulsa of a foreigner approaching sixty and speaking in a strange plummy accent, to Tulsan ears that of an unfrocked bishop, I feared? Then a new hitch appeared. In the small print that went with my visa was a warning that when it expired I could not apply for another until three years had passed. This was designed to staunch a flux of academics into the United States, thus vexing their countries of origin. The fact that I had never been an academic was apparently irrelevant.

The only exceptions were confined to those whose presence was held necessary to the United States. Not surprisingly, therefore, my case, when submitted, was thrown out. This set the Foundation on a high horse. The President wrote to the Attorney General, Robert Kennedy, saying in effect that if the Foundation wanted me the whole country must want me too. And the Attorney General capitulated. I was one of a small handful whose visa status was changed. Overnight I became the owner of a green card, which admitted me to gainful employment in the United States.

Naturally, I was extremely grateful to Robert Kennedy. But gratitude never turned to liking. I have not forgotten a dinner in the house of the Jock Whitneys, who had as their house-guests Lord and Lady David Cecil. The dinner was totally non-political, but it included the Mayor of New York, John Lindsay – this must have been in 1964. Robert Kennedy was placed next to Rachel Cecil and I on her other side. He did not address a word to her, so that she was reduced to rare platitudes such as: 'We're here for such a short time. Is there any play we ought to see?' In reply, he was talking across the table to Mayor Lindsay, on matters of local politics. And there was a day when I was invited by the headmaster of a school near Washington. It had been a wet spring and the headmaster suddenly saw two figures, a man and woman, jumping their horses over his hedges and tearing up the grass. He ran out and seized the bridle of one, to be shouted at: 'Don't you know I'm Senator Kennedy?' The financial damage was large, the trustees of the school were suitably indignant. But in the end one of them told the headmaster that to ask for compensation was too dangerous. It might be the end of the school. And so the trustees paid and said nothing.

It was about this time that I resigned from the Ford Foundation. The pretext was a slim one. A London friend of mine, Robin Pitt Miller, had the fancy to make a musical out of *Vanity Fair*. He was much younger than I and conceived that I was likely to be more experienced than he – a notion open to question. We set to, however, and confected a script. The division of interest eventually turned out to be that Robin concentrated on the lyrics and I on the spoken text. He flew with our work to London and very soon reported that it had been taken by the producer Geoffrey Russell and that Julian Slade, whose *Salad Days* had been a great hit in 1954, had consented to write a score.

This led to a confrontation with my employers. I clearly could not break their rule of silence and continue to work for them. Had I been the intellectual trufflehound they thought (briefly) they were employing, I might have hesitated. I know my own slothfulness. I know, too well, the extent of the conflict between a sheet of white paper and the words to put on it. But I did not hesitate. I wanted to part friends with tolerant and amicable bureaucrats who had given me large cause for gratitude. But I also wanted to break the silence. I might have soldiered on, just as I might have stayed indefinitely with *The Times*. In one case I should have fetched up as an elderly literary knight, I presume; in the other a sheltered and prosperous Manhattanite. In both cases, I think I was right to clear out in time.

Nobody who has not seen his play worm its way onto the stage can appreciate the heavy farce which marks its progress. When I worked with Lennox Berkeley on *Nelson* all I had to aim at was to content the composer. Now I found myself having to fence with a producer, a director, a lyricist, a composer, four or five stars, and the clock. I had to be on duty in London, Oxford, Bristol, Brighton, to face tears one day and misplaced enthusiasm the next. I had to combat outbursts of amateurism, including my own. An admirable actress, but not obviously a Becky Sharp, had been engaged, Frances Cuka. Then, to add weight, Sybil Thorndike, whose eightieth birthday we celebrated on stage in Bristol, was chosen as Lady Crawley. Upon which Ken Tynan commented, 'Sybil – that means rave notices and a closure on the tenth day.' After twenty years I remember the nice things: Sybil playing the part of an even greater lady in real life, chatting about Cuba, about Sicilian ruins, accepting a cup of tea as though it were a chalice; working with a somewhat nervous stage director at all hours in Belsize Park – nervous because he was more experienced as a television director than on stage. I remember lively sessions with Sybil's husband, Lewis Casson. Her I had not seen except on stage since her spectacular performance in *St Joan* at a revival some thirty years before. Now, at eighty, she was astonishing. She even insisted on singing a song. Her husband at nearly ninety, spry, wise, funny, watched over her and over us all. I remember above all the shy but reviving presence of Julian Slade. One day while we were in Bristol, I drove him by the entrance to the American Museum near Bath, at Claverton Manor. It was closed for the winter, but we ventured up the drive, and at last perceived a number of tweedy people behind the glazed door of the house. 'Come on,' I said, 'Let's try to join them.' He faltered. 'We can't,' he said. But I opened the doors and was greeted, to my consternation, by someone who exclaimed, 'We were getting quite worried, sir. Did you have difficulty finding us?'

I saw that I was supposed to be someone of consequence whom the company had assembled to meet. And I brazened it out. I had none too much time, I said. Could we make the tour at once? So, while Julian crept round like a condemned prisoner, I tried to impersonate someone possibly royal, dreading, each moment, his appearance. The worst moment was on being brought a visitor's book at the end. I dashed in a typical royal signature, splashy and illegible, and we got away in time.

I remember kind hosts and hostesses suffering with me at provincial try-outs: Nancy Lancaster, with whom I stayed at her exquisite Haseley – a house which the Laurence Oliviers had tried to sell unrestored to Thérèse and me many years before at a price, I think of £2,000; a kindly Clifton housemaster whom I had known in the Army and with whom I stayed during our try-out in Bristol; and the tolerant friends who came to see the show, before it reached London, Robert and Alfreda Rushmore, now married through Clarice's machinations, Mollie Buccleuch. They must have been tolerant, because the show underwent all the classic misadventures of rehearsal and then some. The leading lady, in tears, was to be dropped one day and congratulated the next. The choreography was a disaster. The director was threatening to walk out. The lyric-writer became unnerved; the producer was at his wits' end. Still, we opened at the Queen's Theatre, Shaftesbury Avenue, with Princess Margaret in the house, and we did not close on the tenth day, though before long an interminable strike darkened the theatre and ended a run not, in my view, too soon. It should be added that Robin Miller subsequently wrote a show without my help, *Dames At Sea*, which did very well indeed both in London and in New York.

Back in New York after this sobering endeavour I found myself caught up in two new jobs: as book critic for the *New York*

Herald Tribune, and as drama critic for a serious monthly, *Theater Arts*. As well as that, I decided to buy a house outside New York, as an escape-hatch from a time-consuming existence.

I had immensely enjoyed my years at *The Times*, but I was no less happy at the *Herald Tribune*. *The Times* possessed a certain imperial aura, as though any one of its editors was expected to don at times an ambassadorial frock-coat. People came from all over the world, from India, Russia, Australia, Japan, Turkey, from no matter where, in order to have commerce with *The Times*, and it was part of the business of the house to meet them halfway. At the *Herald Tribune*, which occupied a run-down building on West 41st Street, nobody disturbed our solitary, bookish calm. I and an agreeable colleague, Maurice Dolbier, lived in a dusty rectangle filled with new books. We got on with our jobs unpestered by management.

After a very short time there, I was asked by the British Government to open an exhibition in Tokyo. They gave me a first class round-the-world ticket and asked only that I give as well a few lectures in Japan. Nervously, I asked the *Herald Tribune* if I could accept. My calculation was that, if I accumulated a few pieces of prose in advance, I could keep up with my obligatory three columns a week during a month or so of absence. The paper applauded. 'Why come back so soon? Why not go on to Bangkok and Delhi? Of course,' they said, 'your columns will reach us; and nobody else will ever offer you a first class round-the-world ticket.' I went; and my pieces duly arrived.

Tony Powell, the novelist, was in Bangkok and I flew there to meet him, trying to digest my first contact with the Far East. What struck most forceably perhaps was the precise equation between Japanese painting and Japanese landscape. I had always supposed that the mistiness of Japanese painting was a convention; but I found that in fact the air of Japan is constantly opaque. As in England, clear skies are at a premium; the atmosphere is as cloudy as milk of magnesia. Next, I was surprised by the unfailing, even unnerving good taste of everyday objects. The smallest package even was in itself exquisite. On the other side of the world, I had noticed much the same thing in Finland. I came to long in either country for something ugly to offset the enduring impression of just-rightness.

I had not expected to feel at home in Japan, nor did I, though the extreme courtesy of the Japanese made personal contact very easy. Only once did I come up against a problem. The Rector of a provincial university had invited me to what turned out to be a large formal dinner. When we had sat down his interpreter told me that to his regret the Rector's only European language was German – the more so because he would have enjoyed discussing with me the foreign policy of Neville Chamberlain. The interpreter enlarged on this. The Rector, he said, had felt much at home in Germany. It was a thousand pities that he could not talk to me as man to man. I replied that I had lived in Austria for most of the 1930s and that I should be delighted to speak German with him. I thought I detected a slight rictus on·his face and I launched off, piling on the sub-clauses in which German abounds and stretching my syntax as far as it would go. As I suspected, the Rector could not dig up a single German phrase and I felt that in an unnecessary contest I had won.

A minor embarrassment overtook me in my Tokyo hotel. There was a health centre attached to it, and I had tried on the telephone to make an appointment for a massage. Just as I was about to leave my room the door opened and a very pretty masseuse appeared, and firmly chained the door behind her. She spoke only Japanese, and I could not explain that I had expected to visit the centre rather than to be called on. She had my clothes off in a trice, stretched me on the bed and began a treatment of the greatest dexterity in which the most vulnerable parts of my anatomy were spared by a fraction of an inch. I realized that my fine manners must match hers, but what exactly was expected of me I also wondered? *On ne veut par être mufle*, but on the other hand . . . Later I was told that had I shown the smallest anatomical interest in my massage it would have been a disastrous breach of courtesy. I had done the right thing by preserving calm under threat.

XX

I DID NOT use my round-the-world ticket to the full, because my mother-in-law, who now lived permanently in Florence, wrote that she particularly wanted me to visit her there on a date which meant curtailing my trip. I flew to Rome, therefore, and immediately took the Florence express, only to be greeted after a twenty-two-hour journey by a hearty octogenarian laugh. She couldn't remember why she had wanted to see me, but since I was there I might as well stay.

Florence at this time was made memorable by the presence of Bernard Berenson. For many years he nourished a love-hate relationship with my mother-in-law, partly founded on her habit of referring to an unfortunate moment many years earlier in Vienna. They had both been lunching with Prince Lanckoronski, who had a fine collection of pictures. One of them caught 'B.B.''s attention; he crossed over to it, scrutinized it, and then asked, 'Why in the name of Heaven do you call that a Severo da Ravenna?' Or whatever it was labelled. 'Take it down,' said the Prince patiently. 'Look at the back.' A letter was pasted to the frame, attesting the picture twenty years earlier and signed Berenson. It gave my mother-in-law great pleasure to remind him of this when he became too dogmatic.

At ninety he was still a fascinator. He thought me much more knowledgeable about Central Europe than I was, and constantly quizzed me. As his mind also darted with breathless rapidity from one aspect of a subject to another, the thread of talk unwound after this fashion. He might begin speaking of Kleist, then move on to the merits of Kleist's *Penthesilea*. This brought

205

him to Othmar Schoeck's opera on the theme. Had I been to the first performance in Zurich, in 1921, wasn't it? – No – he did not greatly care for music but he was playing up to his guest – passing briefly over Schoeck's settings of Lenau and Mörike, he skipped to the influence of Swiss scenery on the Swiss imagination, paused to reflect on the pleasurable horror inspired by the Alps in relation to romantic poetry, and by the very different horror which excited the mind of Fuseli – not that Fuseli was any good, of course; switched to John Martin's somewhat superior madness; paused again to wonder if any mad poet were the equal of Hölderlin; and finally returned to Kleist as an atypical suicide.

A few years earlier, I had thought that my son David, still at Eton, might enjoy a rather rarefied experience. Ancient monuments, I concluded, usually persist; one can visit them at any time; whereas ancient human monuments vanish. So I took him to visit four. We began by staying at the Villa Mauresque with Willie Maugham, then went on to Max Beerbohm at Rapallo, to Berenson, and to Percy Lubbock at Lerici. When he returned to school he wrote, I was told, an essay on his visits, and apparently assessed the monuments accurately: Willie Maugham to be used with guarded respect, Berenson a brilliant old rogue, Percy Lubbock a period-piece of secondary interest, but Max alone worth the whole journey. Max had endeared himself to us by leafing through the celebrated section of his small library which consisted of doctored illustrations – doctored to turn some quite ordinary portrait, say, into a dizzying grotesque. And then he had boasted of the exceptional harvest that year on his tiny property – three whole bottles of oil and two of wine.

After Lady Beerbohm's death he had been cared for by the widow of Gerhart Hauptmann, at her suggestion. And I remembered that, when Max himself died, the lady had written to Tom Eliot, since she evidently felt a vocation to tend elderly men of letters, suggesting that she come to London to look after him. Much later, having refused her offer, he told me that in Paddington Station he had seen, to his alarm, Frau Hauptmann descending from a train. She has come to get me, he thought, and he hid behind an iron column until the danger passed.

With Percy Lubbock I recall only one other meeting at about this time. Diana Cooper had been lent the Niarchos yacht, *Eros*, and she invited me to spend two or three weeks on board, along with Frank and Kitty Giles, and Paddy and Joan Leigh-Fermor. We passed halcyon days, clouded if at all by the routine reluctance of the crew to take the trouble of hoisting sails – *Eros* under sail is a spectacular sight – when they could taxi along on the engines.

We reached Lerici, and the Gileses, who were old friends of Percy Lubbock, wished to bring us all to visit him. Diana did not want to go. One of her admirable qualities was a high degree of disregard for her own beauty – in her sixties, and for years to follow, she was still outstandingly beautiful. She used to pour scorn on looks like her own, fair-haired and blue-eyed. Could she only look like her sister, Marjorie Anglesey, who was no less beautiful, but dark. So, on the yacht, she led a gypsy existence, barely doing more to her appearance than comb her hair, until we put into harbour, when, with no help and a tiny cabin to hold her possessions, she would, in ten minutes, clothe herself with the kind of elegance which makes strangers suddenly halt in their tracks.

She preferred herself, however, in her gypsy role, and had to be persuaded to join the little group which set off to the Lubbock villa. Lady Sybil Lubbock was dead, and the old gentleman was not only almost blind but had let himself go to some extent. He was sitting on a terrace in a quilted dressing-gown, a very portly old gentleman at that, with on the table a great flagon of wine which he was attacking with zest. Perhaps in reaction to the world he once had shone in, the world of Henry James and Edith Wharton, he had also adopted a mildly Marxist attitude to other people, and now, fortified by the wine, he started to belabour Diana on political grounds, prefaced by phrases like 'I suppose people like you think . . .' or 'Of course reactionaries like you and Duff have always believed . . .' Since she did not hold the opinions wished on to her, I could see her beginning to boil. At last he suggested that she might like to see round the house. 'Not in the least,' she replied. 'Ah, I know that since Sybil died I have let things go,' he sighed. To which she continued, 'But I like it as it is: almost a ruin, isn't it?' She wore the most genial expression. 'Like your garden. A dust-bowl without a flower in it:' all with a ravishing smile. We did not stay long.

Perhaps Diana cut a better figure in her own house near Chantilly. She had friends – a Prince and Princess Ghika – who as Roumanian ex-diplomats had fallen on evil days, and lived in an old folks' home on the outskirts of London. Their annual treat was a visit to Chantilly.

One year Princess Ghika, exhilarated by the glory of it all, fell into her cups at luncheon, and suddenly sank to the floor just as coffee was being offered. Without hesitation, Diana descended to the floor beside her. 'It's so much more comfortable down here,' she said, peeking up from under the tablecloth at her conventional guests.

XXI

LITTLE EVENTS LIKE this, remembered in the thinner air of New York, came to seem very odd indeed. Many rich Americans in the 1960s, if they thought nostalgically of Europe, still had not emerged from the social approaches of the Edwardian home counties. They preserved conventions which in Europe itself had long been dead. They were lavish in their use of doilies and finger-bowls, they worried over fussy details as if they were modelling themselves on Carrie Pooter. They were all superficial talk, immensely but often disingenuously kind. Speaking to some ancient in the golf-club they might enquire after 'your lovely wife', heedless of a saddening appearance. And they were deeply worried by the frankness with which Europeans spoke to and of each other. The kind of verbal tennis which might amuse a dinner party in Belgrave Square would cause the greatest alarm on Park Avenue.

More than once, after listening to what seemed to me a bout of normally abrasive talk between two British friends, an American has said anxiously, 'After that I suppose they will never speak to one another again.' But in relaxed moments the same Americans let their defences fall. 'His lovely wife' becomes 'that silly old bitch' when the finger-bowls are put away.

Americans in Europe were very different. They swept the Pooters from their own ground and replaced them with a world from which boredom was banished as far as possible. London was never the same after it had been stormed by Lady Cunard, Chips Channon, Laura Corrigan, Lady Granard or Mrs Simpson. Winnie de Polignac in Paris and Marguerite Bassiano in

Rome were only two of many American wives who helped to rejuvenate life in Europe, by using their money to commission new music, restore old palaces, or run intelligent magazines.

During my first years in New York I underwent the usual experiences which beset visitors from Europe. I received great hospitality and great thoughtfulness. Americans do not suffer from the shyness which afflicts Europeans in front of a foreigner. One may spend weeks in London or Paris without overcoming a widespread fear of being intrusive on the part of the natives. But Americans do not in the least mind being intrusive so long as they intrude to a good end. By nature they are generous and helpful. The only mild reproach I sometimes make them is that they deliver too much on a first meeting. Their wells, so to speak, have not much water in them. You let down a bucket and very little comes up, so that you will not reliably bask in that most delightful of experiences, a ripening friendship. At a first encounter, you may have got as far as you will get.

English friends were always turning up in New York, and I crossed several times a year to England. But a degree of fissure little by little divided my ageing from my younger self. At first I thought myself unchanged: I had merely altered my dwelling and my destination. I could easily, I thought, change both entirely, and take on American citizenship. But after a time I found that I was living in a version of Atlantis, poised between two continents and belonging to neither. An oath of loyalty to America would mean abjuring my past. Yet the past is only valuable if it nourishes the present. And by degrees I saw that there was no continuing link between Buckingham Palace Gardens and East 55th Street. I had been happy in both; but the fissure between them widened every day.

One afternoon, Anne Fleming, who did not take kindly to the New World, said that she wanted to see some literary New Yorkers. So I collected together Tennessee Williams, Christopher Isherwood (a temporary Manhattanite) and Wystan Auden among others, and we all gathered in my flat on an occasion on which Tennessee felt moved to explain what love meant to him, and cried so hard that his tears soaked a sofa cushion. I noticed how different Annie was in New York and in

London. In London she was sprite-like – sprites can be dangerous as well as winsome, and Annie, like Tinker Bell in *Peter Pan*, could develop a hard rattle when she chose – in New York she became a cross between columnist and governess, avid for local celebrities, and then losing no time in telling them where they had gone wrong.

Inevitably, my flat became a European meeting-house. Elizabeth Bowen used to indulge there a taste for salmon caviar, Randolph Churchill and Cecil Beaton, who both stayed at the St Regis opposite, loved New York hospitality, and put me on my mettle. Not long before he died, Randolph suddenly telephoned at one in the morning, begging me to come over and see him. I dressed, and found an unfamiliar Randolph, lying in bed, all charm and nostalgia, wanting to remember old days, and totally unlike the noisy, vituperative nuisance he had become. Nobody had greater possibilities than he as a young man, nobody threw them away with greater alacrity; nobody, not even Brian Howard, could be so appealing on a good day, or so lethal on a bad one.

At about this time, both my jobs vanished. The *New York Herald Tribune* lost so much money that Jock Whitney, its proprietor, closed it, and created instead an amalgamation, the *World Journal Tribune*. Much later he told me that he had made a mistake. He had been making good his losses from the wrong pocket, and, had he used another, could perfectly well have avoided a closure. I joined the new paper, but before long a lengthy strike closed that too. Meanwhile, *Theater Arts* came to a ludicrous end. During a holiday weekend, the owner sent trucks to clear the offices, and when the small staff arrived one morning they found a set of empty rooms: an end more appropriate to the Wild West of the nineteenth century than to a respectable New York monthly.

There was some talk of my joining the *New York Times*, for which I had written intermittently over the years, but I decided that, having killed two newspapers, I ought to spare a third. A *Newsday* syndicate then employed me until that paper changed hands, and at last I decided to claim my freedom. Many years before, Harold Nicolson had said to me, 'Never get caught up by journalism. It will change any fire you have in you into a small pink light.' Journalism had been kind to me, but I concluded that at almost sixty I would do better to keep away from datelines.

However, I also concluded that I needed to extend myself and find somewhere to live as an occasional escape from New York. My earliest thought was to buy a house on Long Island. In my first New York summer I had spent happy days with Diana Vreeland and her husband, and with a splendidly indomitable hostess, Adelaide Leonard, who later spent years of unconsciousness as a consequence of a stroke. A mutual friend went to call on her after she had been silent for a year or two, when suddenly she spoke. 'I have it,' she said. 'Eight at one table and fourteen at the other.' She did not speak again. Diana Vreeland was not yet at the apogee of her career as an arbiter of New York taste, but she had long perfected a style all her own, as though she were stunningly shaped out of lacquer rather than flesh and blood.

My first thought, then, was to buy a house at Watermill, just outside Southampton, the centre of Long Island summer life and the possessor of one of the loveliest beaches imaginable. However, a week-end in Newport, Rhode Island, staying with Nin Ryan, changed my ideas. She ordered me to buy a house there, and gave me a list of possibilities. I knew nothing whatever of Newport, except that in my *Times* days I had been fascinated by a book on its architecture – Maurice Bowra had spoken of it with awe as 'Compton Wynyates leaning up against the Grand Trianon, each on half an acre of land'.

I had also been asked by the then editor of *The Times*, Sir William Haley, to confect a series of dialogues for the paper, and as in those days anonymity was the house rule I chose as a pseudonym 'George Cloyne', after Bishop Berkeley, whose *Alciphron* dialogues I admired and who, coincidentally, had been Vicar of Newport in the early eighteenth century.

Armed with my list, I set out. Maurice Bowra was not totally accurate, but I discovered that in the nineteenth-century section of the city there was a whole group of very large houses on very small properties – notably the huge Genoese palace of the Vanderbilts, The Breakers, which in Europe would have been set in a two-thousand acre park, but in Newport, standing behind immense gates, towered over a paddock-sized enclosure.

Naturally, I was not in search of a palace. But, as well as these once-fashionable monsters all standing together on a promontory, there was an earlier city built round the harbour, which had largely been created in the 1750s by families escaping the summer heat of the Carolinas. By 1960 this older city was very run-down. It was dependent on a naval base, and inundated by neat white uniforms in August. And there, on a street descending to the water, I was shown two small houses, the earlier built in 1770, for sale at $2,500 the pair.

Round them both was planted a hedge higher than the roof-line. The houses were joined by a muddy yard, littered with broken bricks and glass shards. Inside each house was a mass of broken furniture, old dresses, torn curtains: a tiny derelict estate which had been abandoned by an old lady, long living alone behind locked doors, and now finishing her days in a home for the aged.

These were the first Newport houses I saw, and I bought them at once, with the thought that so very small an investment could hardly be called rash. If I were to cut down the hedge, pave the yard, add another bathroom, sand the wide eighteenth-century floorboards, I should have a manageable property of some ten rooms, with the possibility of creating a garden. Much later, by buying the house next door, I extended the tiny garden over two levels, and also acquired one fair-sized room by knocking out partitions. For nearly two hundred years the whole rectangle, which stands on a street corner, had belonged to the Martin family, after whom the street was named. A contemporary Martin was kind enough to give me, among other papers, a plan of the whole as it had existed in the 1820s, and I saw that all that was missing was a bee-house, whatever precisely that may have been.

Over the years I have had great pleasure out of my little houses. At first they were shaded by two large elms, which sadly died of elm-disease. Two trees: I was reminded of a conversation between Walter Buccleuch and Winthrop Aldrich, after severe storms had ravaged both Scotland and New England. Winthrop lamented his loss in Providence – four trees blown down. Walter commiserated. He too had lost trees. How many? Winthrop asked. About two million, said Walter reluctantly.

Newport has been much written about, notably by Thornton

Wilder. For many years it has ceased to be a theatre of conspicuous spending, as once it was. But it preserves a unique continuity of atmosphere. American families tend to be nomads. They suddenly become much richer or much poorer, and in either case they move. In Newport, however, families often persist from generation to generation, restrained only by the lack of endurance which marks American successions. The Astors offer a typical example. In the United States they have all but disappeared in the male line. A single Astor, however, who became naturalized in England in 1899, has left an abundant descendance nearly a century later.

The Newport I now discovered was divided into three parts. There was the Navy, whose presence was severely curtailed during the Nixon years; there was the City proper; and there was the summer colony. All they had in common was a remarkable number of eccentrics. Newport had long been a centre of writers who do not write and painters who do not paint. Hot in summer and piercingly cold in winter, it nevertheless has a benign climate, in which the inhabitants survive to a great age, cultivating their idiosyncrasies. Just before my time there was an old gentleman who played golf every day at the Country Club, addressing himself with dedication to the choice of a putter and an assessment of the prevailing wind. He did not, however, use a ball.

There was a tribe of old ladies, like an exaltation of larks, each very much herself: Mrs Guy Cary, radiantly equipped with Turkish trousers and a twirling parasol; Miss Alice Brayton, diminutive, brilliant and outspoken; Mrs Stephen Wiman, who stood even less nonsense than Miss Brayton; Mrs Sheldon Whitehouse, who reigned over her private empire at ninety as efficiently as ever she had. These were only four, all alas now dead, but representative of a continuing line.

I particularly relished Miss Brayton, around whom gathered an encrustation of legend. She was very pleased to be a cousin of the celebrated murderess of Fall River, Lizzie Borden, who 'with an axe hit her mother forty whacks'. I once asked Miss Alice if her cousin had been guilty and, if so, how she had got away with her crime. 'Of course she was guilty,' said Miss Alice crossly. 'But she was a Borden from Fall River. You couldn't execute her, and it would have been very expensive to keep her in jail. Far better leave her be and not invite her to luncheon.'

She was an expert in lifemanship. When the father she had tended, not very willingly, for nearly three quarters of a century, died, leaving her a rich spinster rising seventy, her friends encouraged her to visit Europe for the first time. Reluctantly she agreed, and took a cabin on the *United States*. She came on board early, she settled in a deck-chair. Then a succession of stewards came into action. Flowers for Miss Brayton. A hamper for Miss Brayton. More flowers. A parcel of books. She became a centre of attention on board, and immediately was claimed at the Captain's table. She did not say that she had sent the flowers and the books and the hampers to herself as a means of gaining notice among strangers.

In her talk she occasionally used a kick like a mule. One day she asked me if I did not find Mary McCarthy very malicious. I replied that she had never done me any wrong. 'I'm glad to hear you say that,' said Miss Alice. 'I've never heard her say an unkind word about anybody.' Then after a pause, 'There's nobody she cares enough about.'

During my first years in Newport Elizabeth Bowen came up more than once to visit me from New York or Washington. One day I took her to tea with a somewhat menacing dowager, formerly Mrs Van Alen, who lived in a house copied from Wakehurst in Sussex – I had spent week-ends as a young man in the original house with my Loder cousins. In her latter years, Mrs Van Alen had married an attractive but impoverished neighbour called Louis Bruguière. They were a devoted couple, I was told, and spent much time and much of Mrs Bruguière's money equipping the Rhode Island Wakehurst with everything a huge house could possibly need, including a hunt-breakfast set in gold for thirty-six, although there was no hunt, and indeed barely a horse, for many miles round.

Mrs Bruguière wore wire spectacles, through which her lance-like gaze alternated benevolence with disapproval. There were only the three of us – she was again a widow – and we were set up round an assertive silver kettle. A note of formality had been struck, and formality at tea does not permit silences. Silences, however, there were, and one was broken by my hostess saying how fond she was of my sister-in-law, at that time living in Washington. 'I must visit Hélène,' she concluded. 'I shall fly down for luncheon. After all, it only takes an hour.'

The silence resumed, until I broke it feebly by saying that it had seemed to take more than an hour when Elizabeth and I flew up a few days previously. Mrs Bruguière adjusted her spectacles and her tone. 'Perhaps,' she snapped, 'you travel in public planes.'

Another afternoon we were invited by Mrs Cary who, as a Roche by birth, was delighted to entertain another Anglo-Irishwoman. The same routine had been organized: the purring kettle, the cucumber sandwiches, the chocolate cake. Suddenly Mrs Cary, then well turned eighty, announced that she had left her handkerchief upstairs, and disappeared for a few minutes. Very shortly after she found that, on fetching her handkerchief, she had forgotten her glasses. Up the stairs she vanished once more. After the third or fourth climb I noticed that she had a little difficulty in negotiating the steps. I put this down to age. But, trained to Irish ways, Elizabeth was on to the facts in a flash and, when we left the house, turned to me with indignation. 'I too like martinis,' she said. 'And all *we* were offered was tea, which I detest.'

One of the treasurable aspects of Newport life turned – and turns still – round the Beach Club: Bailey's Beach, in the eyes of its members the only beach in the city. It had been rebuilt after total destruction in a hurricane, and its key had always been kept deliberately low. The fashionable mode of enjoyment here might be thought odd. The mornings are deserted, while the members stay imprisoned in their beds at home by the telephone. At precisely 1 p.m. they flood in. They dip ardently in the ocean if the winds and tides have not brought too much seaweed to shore. They have a sociable drink or two, and then stand in line for an extremely modest meal. By two the exit has begun. The golfers are off first. And by the time a delicious afternoon light is transforming the bay into a picture by Kensett or Winslow Homer there is not a soul there to enjoy it, apart from a nanny or two.

Much as I relish Rhode Island I can never drive down to New York without a lift of the heart as its towers loom into sight. From Connecticut they appear beyond one of the saddest townscapes in the world, the South Bronx, a vast tract of New

York apparently dedicated to ruin. The industrial suburbs of most cities are a disaster, but the outer ring of American cities is uniquely a waste-land of broken glass, pock-marked brickwork, single squinny trees fighting for life, mountains of old motor-tires and rusting gas-pumps. But there, beyond the Bronx, probably against a clear, aquatinted sky, winter or summer, are the towers, dove-grey in the distance and commanding.

You cannot, in New York, separate its buildings from their tenants. Paris or London or Vienna or Rome can be remembered simply as so many streets and squares, memorable in their own architectural right. New York, by contrast, depends for its flavour on the astonishing mix of its inhabitants, to whom the buildings supply only a backdrop. New York is not Times Square or Fifth Avenue: it is the Haitian cab-driver, the Latino bell-hop, the Chinese laundryman, the pious bag-lady sheltering from the cold in a Lexington Avenue pew.

Quite apart from the real New York of the streets, the wrangling, scuttling, bawling crowd – Irish, Jewish, Black – there is the New York which gets into the society columns, and of that I had a taste before I had long lived there. Truman Capote gave a fancy-dress party at the Plaza, and for weeks this party made the news. The guests were to be masked; they had been whittled down to a couple of hundred from a list of all that was glamorous in the city. My friend Evie Backer, a lady of imagination and charm, was to plan the décor; in brief, the city was agog.

We all went. The entrance to the Plaza was blocked by TV cameras. We were pushed about, annotated by gossip-writers, glared at by those who had not made the evening but all the same came to stare. We found a rather under-decorated ball-room. Truman had been allowed to write the fundamentals of the evening off his taxes as a business venture, but his accountant did not approve additional extravagance. And so there we were, with not much to eat nor drink, no room to dance, and a tremendous din to contend with. I left before midnight, with the poet Marianne Moore – why was she there? – and drove back with her in a taxi to Brooklyn, enchanted, as always, by her talk but above all thankful to have escaped.

I might have recollected other such evenings when I was young and in England. There had been a country party in

Kent, where someone got drunk and was killed in a car-crash, while all next day benighted guests turned up, dazed, asleep in haycocks in the park. There had been Brian Howard's party in a swimming bath in the Buckingham Palace Road; Elsie Mendl's circus party at Versailles on the eve of the war; another circus party, given by the Hultons just after the war ended – the last occasion in our lives when Thérèse and I stayed up all night. It was this party, I believe, at which Emerald Cunard put a barbed question to Chips Channon. Carried away by the flash of diamonds, he had exclaimed to Emerald, 'This is what the war was fought about,' and she had answered demurely, 'Are they all Poles?' There had been a ravishing party of the Arturo Lopezes in Neuilly, to celebrate the building of a shell grotto – a party adorned with great towers of plaited larkspur. There had been the notable Beistegui ball in Venice. There had been the absurd parties immortalized in the early novels of Evelyn Waugh.

The point is that all successful parties are absurd. They play on the silly streak which afflicts party-goers to make them forget that they would have a better time were they to take Pascal's advice and stay at home. But Americans in America usually lack a sense of fantasy, adept though they may be under the stimulus of Europe. They tend to mix business with pleasure, like a New York host with whom I dined on one of those evenings at which thirty people are crammed into a dining-room which can comfortably seat twelve. He abruptly informed us that his wife divided their dinners into categories for tax purposes. He had caviar dinners with distinguished guests who justified a larger rebate than the ordinary folk who were given mulligatawny soup. We all looked nervously at our plates and at our neighbours. Similarly, the Truman Capote party was spoiled by the fact that it was essentially a business proposition, not so much concealed as emphasized by the masks we wore.

XXII

URING THE 1960s I travelled constantly in the United States. The Ford Foundation encouraged me to help spend their money from New England to Texas, from Colorado to California. One day I might be in the City Lights Bookshop in San Francisco, enquiring what money might do for little magazines, the next in Cincinnati making plans for a possible theatre. Later, once more a newspaper man, I became conscious of the extent to which different states are autonomous. The writers of the West know very little of what goes on in the East. A group of intellectuals in New Mexico barely looks beyond the boundaries of their state. New Yorkers assume that nothing of interest occurs outside New York; Texans, with shining exceptions, assume that nothing of interest occurs anywhere apart from making money.

One or two cities stand out. I went often to New Orleans, where I fell into the friendly hands of an exceptional couple, the Leclare Ratterrees. They lived in the Garden District, a couple with four growing children. Leclare was part-Mexican, his wife came from Houston, Texas, and both were devoted night-owls. I was told that I passed as a guest because I needed so little food, and indeed they and their children seemed to exist on peanut butter and, for the elders, an occasional oyster. They knew 'everybody' and 'everybody' was delighted by Leclare's wit and intelligence and by Shirley's vitality. When in his middle years he was baptized he chose me for a godfather – a status we celebrated in the steamy jazz parlours and dubious bars of the city, a Cuba Libre in hand. In those days Mardi

Gras was a light-hearted street festival in New Orleans. There were processions organized by the numerous city krewes; there were balls, at which one was supposed to sit in a box and never to dance. One might, though, find oneself dancing in the street with Ethel Merman, dressed as a lettuce. One took the street-car named Desire, carrying a plastic jug of Cuba Libres, and visiting open houses in the Garden District. And it was five in the morning.

Again, I pressed on further, to Houston. The atmosphere there was very different. I stayed with the John de Menils, an outstanding couple who at that time occupied themselves with a Catholic university in the city, St Thomas. Mrs de Menil was a Schlumberger, therefore a senior partner in an industrial empire. Not only was she a great collector, she was also a devoted scholar, who organized exhibitions of such things as African masks, or ironwork, and herself prepared catalogues which I am still happy to have kept.

Dominique de Menil represents a side of America which fascinates foreigners: the rich citizen whose civic generosity seems to have no limit. Admittedly, American tax laws encourage private spending on the arts to an extent unthinkable in Europe, but the American scene, throughout the country, has been enriched by individual donors who use money as a magic wand. The Mellons are matched by the Heinzes, the Astors by the Rockefellers. And there are isolated givers, like Otto Kahn or Judge Irwin Untermyer, who have made possible institutions such as the Metropolitan Opera and the Metropolitan Museum. True, lavish benefactions can be a means to a social end: There have been terrible magnates and worse wives who have won a grudging acceptance from the community because the wife in question has compelled them to give, give, give.

But, whereas in Europe there is a tendency to withhold private generosity on the grounds that in the end the public will pay, Americans dip into their own pockets with fervour. These differing attitudes can be noted in small matters like tipping or returning hospitality. Not all Englishman are as extreme as Willie Maugham who, towards the end of his life, persisted in tipping in French hotels as though a pre-war currency still persisted, so that, when he offered the head-waiter the equivalent of less than a shilling, his secretary Alan Searle had always to be on the watch, supplementary purse in hand. But it seldom struck British visitors to the United States that they might perhaps manage on their own. I noticed that visiting notabilities – and more conspicuously their wives – seemed unaware that hotels and restaurants exist; they needed to be invited to American homes. Whereas in England the American, should he penetrate an English home for a night, sometimes astonished the maid by pressing into her hand a hundred pounds.

All the same, there were a number of popular Britons who visited the United States regularly, and even kept a flat in New York. There was, for instance, John Foster, who had been captain of my Eton house until just before I was sent to school, in 1922.

John Foster was a colourful man who had made a name for himself in Washington when he was serving in the Army. He never smoked nor drank, and he perfected a stoat-like approach to women: an approach which visibly worked well, because all his life there was a regiment of them each of whom thought, 'I am the one he really loved. It is just kindness of heart which leads him only for the moment to pretend that he likes this *creature* better.'

He never married, but spent his days until she died with an aged former governess who had disapproved of his parents' neglect and herself more or less adopted him, sending him through Eton and watching with pride as he won important scholarships, was called to the Bar, entered Parliament and became Minister for Commonwealth Relations, although, since the conversation of men, and especially of serious men, bored him, he did not last long.

It was Tony Powell who made the chief contribution to my factual knowledge of John Foster. 'Have you ever looked him up in *Who's Who?*' he once asked. 'He says he is the son of General H. B. Foster. Doesn't that strike you as odd?' 'Why?' I wondered. Tony explained: 'A full General without so much as an OBE?' Anyway Tony, who is a patient and accurate researcher, had not been satisfied, and eventually dug out of the Army List not a full General but an Indian Army Lieutenant-Colonel. We both thought it peculiar, since you list your own entry in *Who's Who?*, to upgrade your father by five military ranks.

221

As peculiar as the case of Lord Bracken, a contemporary who, years before, wishing to impress Honor Philipps, had invited her to inspect his old home in Ireland one Dublin afternoon. They had driven out to a fine Gothic pile, its furniture under dust-sheets. Brendan had enlarged on the life of the house twenty years earlier, and at last pulled out of a sheeted cabinet a silver-framed photograph of himself as a small boy. It threw him into a sentimental reverie. Much later she learned that he had visited the house for the first time that morning. He had no Irish home; but he had tipped the caretaker generously and placed the photograph carefully in the cabinet. Not even my grandmother Victoria could have lied more convincingly.

A large part in my New York life was played by Alfreda Rushmore, formerly married to Brian Urquhart, a pillar of the United Nations secretariat. Alfreda was in some ways a tragic figure. Her mother, a formidable friend of my parents, had written an extremely gifted novel, *Madame Solario*, which was published anonymously and reprinted with equal success decades later. Her father, Constant Huntington, was a leading Anglo-American publisher who spent many years in the Manor House of Amberley, Sussex. Alfreda was an only child, and found herself hampered, surprisingly, by an acute intelligence. For that intelligence was rudderless. Had she been an ordinary prosperous wife and mother she ought to have been a happy woman, for she was surrounded by friends in the United States and in England. But just as her mother, to whom she was less than devoted, could not bring herself to sign her name to her one book – which has evoked comparison with Henry James – so Alfreda could not bring herself to take any action whatever. Her second husband, Robert Rushmore, used to deplore her habit of leaving a keen intelligence totally at rest, and daily waiting for darkness to fall: a darkness enlivened by a cocktail or two and a delicious dinner – should she herself cook it.

She died before she became old, partly because she was acutely aware of potentialities lying fallow, so that she could impose no coherent pattern on her life. This made her doubly sympathetic to me. Year after year, in Europe or America, I cleared my decks for action, and then found myself essentially inactive. In vain I reminded myself of Jack Squire's very visible faults, which forty years before I had deplored. I reminded myself of sad evenings with Cyril Connolly. I counted the Enemies of Promise in my own time, and mourned, now that I was nearing sixty, that I had not fought them more effectively. Jack used to warn me that we were both in danger. We were enjoyers. We liked the human race, we liked movement and comfort and late hours; we did not like to confess that it was only a certain facility, a triviality of mind, which made it possible for us to forget these disabilities.

The anatomist of sloth makes disconcerting discoveries. I have always known that, with a deadline ahead, I could force myself to meet it. But it took me years to discover that sloth is an artificial state of mind. It is likely to begin with a sense of fatigue. '*Morgen, morgen nur nicht heute, Sagen alle faule Leute,*'* Thérèse used to quote to me. I was too tired. In the morning I could not bring myself to work. I practised the Schumann Fantaisie, I tidied desk-drawers, I walked to the post office, but work I could not. Only at the eleventh hour – and this was the spiritual legacy of Jack Squire – could I buckle to, if need be until late into the night. But after years of cringing to my own fatigue I found, in New York, that I only had to sit down and begin, and the fatigue vanished. Better organized and less self-indulgent men find this out at the university. But at Oxford I did no work whatever, and it was more than thirty years later when I made for myself the discovery which most people take for granted: that Stravinsky was speaking the truth when he said that the Muse must be seated on her chamber-pot every day at the same hour; otherwise nothing will emerge.

At sixty, one finds that one's friends are beginning to die off. Luckily, they only begin. But one becomes wary. Those who, only a few years before, were in the prime of life are starting to fail. The heaviest losses come later. But during the 1960s the process for me started to accelerate. One of the first to disappear was a painter friend, Robin Ironside, who had designed our production of *Der Rosenkavalier* at Covent Garden in 1947. He had also been assistant to Sir John Rothenstein at the Tate, and from time to time presented a small, exquisite exhibition of his own paintings. Robin was the most charming of young men

---

* 'Tomorrow, never today: that's what lazy people say.'

in the years before the war when he lived quietly in Paris, studying to be a diplomat. I knew him well in those years, and was proud that he adopted me as a kind of guru. Years later John Lehmann once asked me what disciples I had had in life, and I was appalled by the question. Disciples? *My* disciples? Clearly, and rightly, there had been none. But Robin Ironside was, perhaps, an exception. Mutual friends noticed that he modelled his own small affectations on mine. And although the last thing I wanted was a disciple, I was flattered to be chosen as a pattern by someone as engaging as he.

The death, in 1965, of Willie Maugham was much more reasonable. Not long before he died, turned ninety, British Television organized an interview with him at Cap Ferrat, and put me in charge of it. By now he was in a wretched situation. His body, thanks to Swiss skills, was in good order, but his mind had betrayed him. Things were not yet as bad as they were to become, and for two or three days he was kept both occupied and cheerful. I was put up at the Villa Mauresque – for the last time after nearly forty years – and the technicians at a hotel. The old gentleman was not only lucid but funny: also rather touching.

It is common knowledge that with the years he had turned against his daughter. But at this time, I remember, he had reverted in mind to a happier past and talked of her with much affection.

After the war, he had suffered financially from the fact that, as a resident of France, his ability to transfer money to England was blocked. His daughter, Liza, had married as her second husband Lord John Hope, and a story went around that a plan had been promoted, with kind intentions, that Willie should make his daughter a substantial wedding present. She did not need the money, but it would provide a legal means of making an English income accessible to her father. According to the story, Willie's response was simply to say, 'I, too, have read King Lear.'

It may be relevant that he had greatly liked Liza's first husband and was not well disposed to the Hope family. There was the further complication that Willie's secretary and friend of forty years, Alan Searle, made a totally different impression on different members of Willie's family and circle. To some he appeared an intriguer, a schemer with a keen eye to his own advantage, a troublemaker. To others he was a peace-loving friend attentive to Willie's every need and anxious only to smooth the last years of a by-now half-mad old man.

I had known Alan since the 1920s. In my experience, he was out to help Willie rather than himself. Over the years he and I spent a good deal of time talking about the difficulty of Alan's task, about the growing impossibility of ever leaving Willie, and about his own future. After Willie died, I saw him in New York, by this time very fat, very self-indulgent. Willie had left him comfortably off and his only pleasure was to entertain old friends like myself in the best restaurants, stuffing himself with foie gras. His theme was his sense of loss. If impossible, Willie was also irreplaceable. It was now too late to return to Alan's first love – surprisingly the Discharged Prisoners' Aid Society. He had incipient Parkinson's Disease. He was bored to death; he disliked Monte Carlo, where he lived his last years; his moments of mild content were spent on visits to George Cukor in California; he was impotent, he said, he had become a voyeur. But I never heard him in the role of troublemaker, and in Willie's lifetime he often returned to his anxiety to bestow peace, since he saw that Willie's irascible tantrums were a form of mental illness, not a calculated malevolence.

Two of Willie's latter-day friends were the Graham Sutherlands, who spent time in Villefranche and brought vivacity into his dimming old age. One day they arranged for the Anglo-Irish painter, Derek Hill, to visit Willie, who had long heard of him but had never known him. Mrs Sutherland, who at times has a run-away-tongue, prompted by an imp of mischief, later asked Derek if he would like to know the impression he had made. This is one of the questions which should never be given an affirmative answer. But Derek, fortified by confidence, said yes, only to be told that Willie had been greatly disappointed by a man whose legendary charm and humour he could not perceive.

When this came to Alan's ears he was, he told me, much distressed. Willie had, in fact, been full of praise, and Mrs Sutherland's report was totally beside the mark. But, he said ruefully, he could not clear the matter up nor soothe Derek's feelings without creating a breach between Willie and the

Sutherlands, and now at almost ninety Willie needed their goodwill. He walked up and down in agitation, I remember, wondering how to make peace. This was not, I think, the reaction of a troublemaker.

Similarly, just after Willie's death he discovered, on returning to the Villa Mauresque, that the servants had made off with some of the contents, and he was above all vexed by the implied disloyalty of doing so. Unlike his predecessor Gerald Haxton, who struck me as an odious charmer (he delighted in humiliating Willie), Alan appeared to be a bewildered, but at heart benevolent, life partner: it seemed appropriate that his chosen vocation should be that of prison visitor.

XXIII

I HAVE SAID that when I lived in Vienna before the war I grew apart from most of my writer friends. After I set up in New York this chasm naturally widened. I had not expected to remain in the United States after my time with the Ford Foundation came to an end. Indeed, I kept my flat in the Albany until I found that to do so while I lived in New York would expose me to double taxation. For a year or two I leased it; at first to Michael Duff, and then to the Gladwyns. Michael astonished my housekeeper by always bringing with him during his brief visits from his Welsh home two breakfast eggs in a paper bag and returning home with a handkerchief or two in the bag so that they could be washed without expense. Finally I handed over my rooms to Isaiah and Aline Berlin, not without sadness.

For I found myself in an unusual situation. At first I thought that in my middle fifties my outward circumstances were irrelevant. I should always be the same, wherever I lived. Too old to bear arms, but by now an American taxpayer, I saw no need to change nationality, yet my heart warmed to American living. Technically, I might be an expatriate, but so were those earlier Englishmen who migrated to Kenya or Rhodesia or South Africa – as my father had decided to emigrate in 1919, until a brother-officer came a financial cropper there, and my father, taking fright, relinquished land he had been about to buy in the Orange Free State, without ever seeing it. I thought of Wystan Auden, Gerald Heard, Aldous Huxley, who were unjustly accused in the late 1930s of fleeing from Europe out of fear, whereas fear played a far smaller part in their actions than a wish to preserve a threatened civilization in a continent still unviolated. I did not flatter myself as a kind of temple-guardian, but I did make an equation between two styles of living, the American and the European. In Europe, I reflected, one's gaze is fixed on the past. Even Soviet-based life reposes on 1917 with no clear aspiration beyond the vague hope of world revolution. In America, on the other hand, you will find the constant thrust of aspiration towards greater good even when that good is overlaid by ignorance, brashness or insincerity.

It would have gone against the grain for me to relinquish my British passport, but I greatly relished my American life. Unfairly, perhaps, I found England so changed from what I had known of it as a young man that I barely regretted moving away, except at sentimental moments. An English village, the damp chill of an English country church should I be lucky enough to find it unlocked, little streets in Islington or Chelsea: these were as I remembered them. From Nottingham north-wards England was still recognizable, but the Home Counties, and above all London, had become foreign to me. Not that I could wish the England I had been brought up in to persist; not that the vulgarization of England was much different from what was happening elsewhere; nor that I could reasonably want a state of things to endure in which all the pleasures and promises of life were in the hands of a small minority.

In the America I was now discovering there had for long been no place for such a minority. The America of Edith Wharton and Ethel Sands first migrated to Europe and then vanished. What survived and grew was an America of the very rich, which would have filled the Edith Whartons with horror. One year I was flown in on a charter plane to Fort Worth, Texas, where the Amon Carter Museum was to have a grand opening. Among the ceremonies of a packed weekend was a party in a pool-house, at which the hostess, late at night, took against her husband, picked up a bottle, revolved it like an airplane propeller, and discharged it. It missed the husband, but hit a Modigliani: not, I believe, a gesture which Ethel Sands would have approved.

Yet one of the delights of the United States was the almost universal kindliness of plain people. One night I met a French couple at a Manhattan dinner party. They urged me to take them to Harlem. This was not a reasonable wish in the Sixties, but at last I did. We were the only white people in the dance-bar I chose, but nobody rubbed the fact in. When we left, the couple took a taxi and I hailed another going north from 135th Street and driven by a black driver. As I got in, I counted my money and found I had spent all but a dollar or two, so I asked the driver to drop me at a bus stop. He refused. He insisted on driving me eighty blocks in what was for him the wrong direction, saying that one day someone would help him out in London. He would not accept a cheque nor give an address.

As the years passed, more and more British or British-based visitors flocked to New York. Elizabeth Bowen died in 1965, but Nadine Gordimer and Lawrence Durrell, Maurice Bowra or Harold Nicolson had already set a habit of travel, followed by many more, from James Pope-Hennessy to Stephen Spender. There was one noteworthy evening when John Sparrow, still Warden of All Souls, wanted me to take him to *Who's Afraid of Virginia Woolf?* and, before that, to a typical obscure restaurant as unlike as possible the Four Seasons or the Grenouille. I chose a gloomy little box in the West Forties, at which not once but twice something unique in my experience occurred. The police rushed in, collared a little man in a back room and dragged him out screaming. John looked sage. 'Just as I expected,' he said wagging his head sadly. When we settled in to the theatre he found that Edward Albee's play had been given an academic setting. 'Very unlike All Souls,' was his comment after one act and we left before the end.

Maurice Bowra, by this time, was very deaf, and shouted louder than ever. I was delighted to watch him operating outside an Oxford which still held him, after forty years, in awe. His fires were not damped; he behaved as though in his own University, expecting, not in vain, to gather a crowd round him, waiting for the loud explosion of a joke.

Many of his jokes have been recorded, but some can be added. When Tom Boase, a retiring, uncompetitive, slightly spinsterish don, was elected President of Magdalen, Maurice boomed, 'Extraordinary thing that the Fellows of Magdalen should choose as their President a man of no public virtues and no private parts.'

Or again, when K. Clark and his wife were in full, even vertiginous circulation in London, he adjusted a quotation to 'Jane and Sir K. in all around I see'. And, as a parallel to his famous 'Buggers can't be choosers', 'Nobody makes more trouble for his friends than the normally-sexed nancy.'

Although I had left Oxford under a cloud it was no denser than the clouds which briefly hid John Betjeman and Evelyn Waugh even in War. The latter had alienated his American friends before my time in New York and, although John Betjeman kept saying how greatly he looked forward to seeing the Newport versions of the Grand Trianon and Compton Wynyates, I knew he would never make the journey. It made me unhappy that a friendship which had lasted unfaded for some forty years should be broken. When we again met in England until the day of his death it was always as though we both were still undergraduates: the same silly private jokes, the same shared aversions – as to C. S. Lewis, Dean of Magdalen in our time – the same aesthetic responses, in which he was the leader.

His open Morris Cowley became for me a chariot during my short Oxford days. He would show me the 'Scholar Gypsy' country, the little eighteenth-century church of Chislehampton, the splendid remains of Rycote Palace, the quiet waters of the Windrush, the statuary at Rousham. A few years later, an unlucky incident occurred when an eccentric fox-hunting scholar called Maurice Hastings leased Rousham and one day made his guests drunk, so that they found it amusing to fire rifle-shots at the private parts of the statues. Maurice Bowra was among the guests and, although a very poor shot, did his Oxford reputation no good by taking part. It was at Rousham, too, when John Betjeman had left Oxford, that the four of us – he, I, Maurice Bowra and Maurice Hastings – went for a walk in the park. We were discussing what John was to do with his life. At that time he had briefly taught at a school in Cockfosters. He was games master, although he could play no game but golf, at which he excelled; and he left school when he found a maid, who had spilled a mountain of boiled potatoes, scooping them off of a muddy floor and piling them back in the dish.

What could he do? Nothing, he said. He would have to live off a hundred pounds a year grudgingly offered by his father.

Maurice Hastings' family owned the *Architectural Review*. Could John not be an office boy? He feared not. He could not run a lift; he could not tip his cap as a restaurant doorman. Forty years later, when he was Poet Laureate and one of the most beloved figures in the country, I remembered that walk.

John's appearance was slovenly. Unexpectedly, he was easily disgusted. A speck of dirt, a nasty smell unmanned him. He did not trouble to brush his teeth or change his shirt, yet he knew very well how to cast a spell. He was all response, like a piece of litmus-paper; and to people he responded brilliantly. It was not to be expected that his future father-in-law, a Field Marshal, would appreciate him, but at length he did; though at first he had a harder time with his mother-in-law. She was reported to have wondered why her daughter Penelope had 'thrown herself away on a little middle-class Dutchman'. Whereupon John wrote a letter which he circulated to the daily press, to the effect that he had heard of British inhospitality to foreigners, but had himself been given, with few exceptions, a heartening welcome. He clipped each of these letters from the paper as it appeared and sent it, signed 'A Middle-Class Dutchman', to Lady Chetwode.

He lived, as poets must, on his nerves; and he cannot have been easy to live with. Generous to a fault, compassionate, modest, he was incapable of putting himself in another's place, so that what to him was a light, bantering comment might cause the victim acute pain. He was mercurial, now exalted, now in the depths. Perhaps he was at his best when he made personal contact through an impersonal medium. His television performances later in life made listeners by the hundred thousand feel as though he were their intimate friend, and when he died his death was experienced as a personal affliction by the strangers who sent flowers and telegrams to the hospital.

His funeral was less sensational than that of his father, which took place in Chelsea Old Church. John was an only child, and while he and his mother were waiting for the ceremony to begin a scene occurred like that in the second act of *Der Rosenkavalier*. A second, unknown, Mrs Betjeman suddenly irrupted with a second family, and it turned out that for many years Mr Betjeman had lived a second and hitherto secret life.

During his father's lifetime I was asked more than once to

dine in the pretty green-painted house in Church Street where the Betjemans lived. They were known to their son as Ernie and Bess, and when I first met them all relations between the generations were tense. John published an account of these tensions under the name of Archibald Dixon in the *Oxford Outlook*. This was a playlet entitled *The Artsenkrafts*, of which I have kept a copy. So far as I know it has never been listed among his works nor reprinted. Yet it remains an essential document for a biographer. As time passed, John's attitude mellowed and, from behaving to his parents as to a tyrant and a lachrymose victim, he ended by treating their old age and above all their memory with a kind of sorrowful affection.

But before his marriage a dinner in Church Street was an uneasy function. Mr Betjeman was very deaf and John's frequent aim was to persuade him to make me play the piano. The old gentleman would then open the piano lid and lower a speaking-tube towards the wires, while John, standing behind him, made grimaces and danced about. This did not enhance my technique.

Just beyond the confines of Church Street there was already a crowd of Betjeman-fans, and we formed a closely linked group. It included Billa Cresswell, who drove us about in a tiny little car, on the dusty back of which was long inscribed with her finger an ineffaceable slogan, 'Alan is a pansy' – I hasten to add, a tease and not a comment. There was Camilla Russell, a beauty and a delight, and her brother John who, as a diplomat during the war, broke up a difficult moment in negotiations with the Russian government by leaping onto the desk and dancing a gopak. There was the Fleetwood-Hesketh family, each with a distinctive family drawl inherited from their American mother who years later, at the time of the Anschluss, routed from their Austrian doorstep a German platoon, single-handed and in a dressing gown, simply by using her drawl. It was at the end of a summer – a season in Austria when flies take command at dusk and you may envisage her on her terrace, swatting lazily at one importunate insect and murmuring, 'Poor little thing. Just a bundle of nerves.'

There were, as I have noted earlier, Joan and Graham Eyres-Monsell and the Lygon sisters. There was Edward James, the collector of surrealism, with whom and Randolph

Churchill John shared a house in Culross Street for a time. There was Patrick Balfour, later best man at my first wedding, whose house in Yeoman's Row, at one time shared by Cyril Connolly, was a crowded centre of late-night life where you might find Evelyn Waugh, Brenda Dean Paul between brushes with the police, Harold Acton, Bryan and Diana Guinness, Nancy and Peter Rodd.

As the years pass, just to name old friends is like playing an electronic game in which shapes dart across the screen in a dizzying pursuit feebly controlled by a master lever. They collide, they explode, they are present for a bright flash and are then engulfed in darkness again. From the very different ambience of New York I came to see my past as a succession of splinters, as bizarrely illogical as the objects in Edward James's collections.

Take Nancy Mitford, later Nancy Rodd. I have a clear vision of *my* Nancy Mitford, but it is not in focus with other people's, and who should say which of us is wrong? Short of a love-affair with everyone one meets there is no means of working through to the final reality of other people. Many found Nancy formidable, heartless, snobbish, trivial. We all could agree on her beauty, her wit, her grace, but was she not also rather childish? Or was that childishness a slightly calculated innocence? If so, she was evenly matched by her first love, Hamish Erskine. We all stayed many times with his parents, and there my role was that of go-between, pinning notes from one to the other on their pillows. I do not think either was capable of profound feeling, but Nancy hid her feelings so cleverly that they were hard to discuss. Her tolerance was severely tested by her eventual husband Peter Rodd; a man of extreme good-looks, some literary talent, but little else. They became engaged at a ball. Peter was drunk and at the same ball was accepted by a second girl as well. In the morning, therefore, he found himself in a pickle. But he remembered that, although the second girl had a great fortune coming to her, she only had her parents' goodwill at the moment, whereas Nancy had five hundred pounds in the Post Office Savings Bank. Five hundred pounds was what he needed, and he married her.

Much later, after their marriage ended, she used to complain that he had an extraordinary gift of divining where she had hidden money. In the lining of the curtains, under the tele-phone directory, at the back of the linen cupboard, he went to it, when he came to call, unerringly.

Or take the Flemings, Anne and Ian. Ian had been my exact contemporary at Eton, and, although we were very unalike, we remained friends throughout life. I found him much more congenial than his more obviously outstanding brother, Peter. His was a curiously secretive character. If he did not marry until middle age it was partly because a long love-affair held him back. His love was older than he and spent much time in a ravishing country house filled at weekends with mutual friends, most of whom were quite unaware of the love-affair. Women found him attractive, most reasonably; men were often bored by him. I was not for a moment bored, but I could see that he had a moody, solitary temperament, streaked through by a degree of sexual voracity. He must have been very hard to live with, and he made a mistake in marrying an extrovert, reckless wife with a genius for energizing her friends, sometimes to the point of terror. She loved dilemmas, verbal clashes, irresistible forces meeting immovable posts. She was all glitter and para-dox – a wonderful friend not to have an affair with.

I spent quite a lot of time with them at St Margaret's Bay in Kent where they lived in Noël Coward's former house under the cliff; in Austria; but above all in their London house which became a show-case for Anne's virtuoso social life, led to the great distaste of Ian. One evening we were all three asked to dine by Tom Eliot and his invalid friend John Hayward. The sixth member of the party was Willie Maugham. There was no reason why the evening should not be a success. Willie liked the company of attractive women, and knew himself to be amusing. Tom Eliot seldom talked much, but he listened attentively like a priest in the confessional. Ian, if he consented to come to a dinner, played admirably the part of a slightly tired man of the world, and he shared with John an informed delight in fine printing, good books, publishing, and women – in John's case, since he was not only paralyzed but deformed and in a wheel-chair, the last to a pathetic degree. But the evening was ruined by the extreme nervousness of the hosts. We were served by an elderly housekeeper who had to manoeuvre a barrage of mur-mured criticism. 'No, no, not those forks,' John might say, heaving out of his chair like some ship's captain in a sudden squall. 'I told you, we begin with white wine. The red comes later.' Tom then came in as though assessing a sequence of sins: 'Port before brandy. Yes, Annie dear, what did you say?' We were out of the house before ten.

For some reason Annie and I and James Pope-Hennessy fell into the habit of staying up half the night after a more relaxed dinner party. Men usually preferred the company of Annie's sister Laura, whom I knew much less well; but the three of us were perfectly adjusted to one another, taking it in turns to be the shuttlecock to Annie's battledore. In those days James was still a unique companion. I had first known him in the War Office as a welcome contrast to the usual run of wartime officers. Then, while he was going through one of many financial crises, I arranged for him to have a job on the *Times Literary Supplement*, a staid office in which he caused distress by confiding the details of an exceptionally rackety private life to unappreciative listeners. By 1965 he had written books not only successful but good. He had impressed an enigmatic but fascinating personality – enhanced by a touch of Indonesian blood – on the most diverse friends: Peggy Crewe, Clarissa Eden, Cecil Beaton, his cousin Nolwen, much later Lady Clark, as well as on a Falstaffian crew of hangers-on. And then, by the time we came together in the United States ten years later, a lurid sunset was touching his horizon with scarlet. Hitherto, he had kept up a habit of work. In the last years of his life he drank too much and worked too little. The old friends became concerned, often angry. And at last when he was murdered in his own rooms those who had known him in better days were unhappy but barely surprised.

However, in the years when the Flemings lived in Victoria Square, he had a great deal to offer. And even when he misbehaved he was saved by a quality shared with another notable misbehaver, Hamish Erskine. At the news of some fresh enormity the friends would exclaim, 'Poor Hamish. Poor James. He's done it again. Isn't it typical!' Thus does the possession of charm bedevil judgement.

During these years I lost two old friends after an estrangement. The first was Osbert Sitwell. By 1960 he was a very sick man. He used to eat alone in the Oak Room of the St Regis

Hotel, because the violent shakings of Parkinson's Disease made him unwilling to share a table. Finally he retired altogether to Montegufoni, his father's gloomy Tuscan castle, and there I used to visit him on my yearly visits to Florence. Just before one of these, Edith's unfinished biography, *Taken Care Of*, had been published posthumously. I thought this a mistaken venture, since she had gone considerably to pieces while writing it, and it painted a self-portrait which did not do her justice: it made her appear, indeed, a very silly old woman, which she was not. I talked of this to Osbert, and found that he agreed. A little later I wrote a review of the book for the *New York Herald Tribune* and said there what I had said to him. A little time passed and I received from him the following letter. 'Have you been bitten by a bat? I am told that when bats meet skunks they engender a poison most dangerous to the human race. Having known you so long I suppose I should not be surprised by this disloyalty. Yours truly, O. Sitwell.'

My first instinct was to pass the matter over in silence. He was after all, very ill, very lonely and anyway likely to indulge a taste for a row. At last, however, I answered. No, I wrote, I had not been bitten by a bat. But it was most kind of him to enquire. All the bats I knew were safely lodged in the belfries of my friends. And now, having got that one out of the way, I begged him to remember that we had passed the same verdict only a few weeks before. Why then should we quarrel? He did not answer. He never wrote again. And when I asked Malcolm Bullock, who was one of his trustees, to help my cause, I was told that Osbert was implacable.

Then I fell into disgrace with Malcolm, himself growing old and testy. I had invited him to dine in Paris not London and I received a Proustian reply. Why should I suppose he could find time for an English friend in Paris when Madame de Villeparisis, the duchesse de Guermantes and Madame de Stermaria were fighting for the privilege of his company, whereas I did not even invite him to dine at the Beefsteak? Hostesses might well fight over him, for he was extremely good company; very large, slightly lame from a war wound, with an unexpectedly delicate head. As the son-in-law of Lord Derby he had for many years held a Lancastrian seat in Parliament; he had delighted and alarmed a host of friends by the sharpness of his tongue; he had made an infinity of mischief. And he had showered hospitality, first in a large house in Lowndes Square, and later in a Lutyens country-house outside Cambridge, full of cloisonné work, Rowlandson sketches and sparkling talk. He and his wife Victoria, also a vivid personality, lived at Six Mile Bottom near Newmarket until she died in a hunting accident. They were latter-day Edwardians, with instinctive access to thirty years of gossip, comfort and scandal. The art of Edwardian conversation has by now died, but in Malcolm it survived for another generation. It was a rich upholstered art, matching the rooms in which it first took place. There were endless little stories in it, cruel little comments, bright little explosions of fancy. Few of those who figured in its annals were poor, seriously unhappy or unsmiling; none was prim. Malcolm possessed devoted American friends, but they tended to treat him as an historic curiosity as though as he were on the same plane as a true Edwardian, Harry Melvill, who lived by his own conversation until Osbert Sitwell killed it with a hammer-blow in a ferocious short story called *The Machine Breaks Down*.

As a diplomat, Malcolm had been attached to the British Embassy in Paris during the tenure of Lord Crewe. One evening there was a dinner at the Embassy, during which Winnie de Polignac was overheard by her hostess saying to a dinner-partner, 'I don't know what to do this winter. I'm sick of Virginia. I may try Sicily for a change.' There was a pause, broken by Peggy Crewe's dark contralto, 'Cecily who?' For, as well as a famous musical hostess, Winnie de Polignac was a famous lesbian. This was the kind of incident in which Malcolm revelled.

He also enjoyed teases. One night in Paris not long before she died, Thérèse and I were invited by Guy de Rothschild to the eightieth birthday dinner he was giving for his mother. We took Malcolm with us and on the way he said that of one thing we could be sure: an excellent dinner. When at length we all trooped into the dining-room in front of each chair there was a grapefruit, and I believe that each guest, noticing this, must have felt a pang of disappointment. A second glance showed that the grapefruits were of porcelain and filled with caviare: a good silent joke.

XXIV

M<small>Y APARTMENT ON</small> East 55th Street came to a miserable
end. Over several years it slowly grew in good looks.
And, while it was doing so, I discovered an antique shop, which
always seemed to be closed; yet the stock, which was of a kind
that attracted me, changed from week to week. Next door to it
there was a laundry which I used regularly; and one day I went
there at an unfamiliar hour, to find the shop open and its
proprietor in command.

He was a Texan in his early thirties, not extrovert and
confident, as Texans often are, but mutely shy. After several
visits I had bought a few tables or chairs or lamps, and, having
won, I hoped, his confidence, discovered that he lived in a Black
Hole of Calcutta under the pavement below the shop, with no
bath and no perceptible ventilation. I was about to leave for
Europe, and on impulse invited him to live in my apartment
during my absence and repel the burglars. At least he would
find a bath-tub and an air-conditioner. He accepted, and
stayed nearly seven years – the most thoughtful and undeman-
ding of guests, nearly always invisible. He had considerable
flair, and he was also a talented painter, so that I profited by his
presence. But he possessed, too, a fatal kindness of heart, and
one day told me he had been moved by the plight of two
teenagers who had come to him in search of an odd job, such as
cleaning out the cellar of his store. The youths were penniless;
they had had brushes with the police; both were in flight from
hopeless parents.

Unwisely, I let myself get involved, after one of them had

tried to escape from New York by climbing on to the roof of an electric train. He had no address of his own, and was brought, badly burned, to my apartment in the middle of the night, in search of his benefactor, the antique-dealer. A doctor was fetched, he was cobbled together again, and the question then arose, Where was he to go?

With the help of Mrs Vincent Astor, a large-hearted phil-anthropist, I found a place for him in a boys' home; but they would only accept him with the consent of his father, whom he refused to contact.

He was a decent kid, a natural victim. The second youth, though I had no reason to suspect it, was heavily on drugs, and took his friend for a ride, with other young people, in a stolen car. They were stopped by the police, but contrived to run away, with the exception of the decent kid, who had lost his toes from frostbite and could not run. He was arrested, and within a few days died.

This left the addict not exactly on my hands but certainly on my conscience. Whether or no he thought that I, or perhaps our antique-dealer, had let him down in some way, he chose to break into my apartment in my absence, and smashed it to pieces. Jades were broken with a hammer, the backs of eight-eenth-century chairs were ripped off, shards of porcelain and glass were lying about; and he vanished into the limbo of the city for ever.

I cared less, because, on the turn of sixty, I again fell in love. The circumstances were unusual. John Carter, Sotheby's rare-book expert, whom I had employed as a bibliographer on the *Times Literary Supplement*, used often to visit New York, and there he struck up a friendship with Mary Jean Thorne, a Texan writer who had the rare distinction of having been a war correspondent for *Vogue* in China. Her marriage to Oakleigh Thorne had ended some years before. She was both beautiful and intelligent. Jake Carter had left an American wife in London. They were childless, and both carried on successful careers. It was also clear to Ernestine Carter that her marriage was not under threat if her husband used his temporary liberty with tact in New York. Nevertheless, Ernestine fell victim to that dire and recurrent figure in life, the friend who knows better. She was given a talking-to. She must stop not only an embryo scandal, but a scandal bad for the British image in America. (Believe it or not, this was actually said.) After two or three assaults Ernestine gave way. She told her husband that, if their private lives were to be a subject of international debate, he must choose. And so he chose. He did not see Mary Jean again.

Up to this time, I had spent many evenings with them both. I had my own view of Mary Jean: that she was lovely to look at, certainly, but also a difficult character, to be explained by a difficult background. Her family, the Kempners, had arrived in Galveston, Texas, from Europe in the second half of the nineteenth century, and they had done well. Mary Jean was an only child; she adored her father, but felt little more than dutiful towards her mother. Her mother, Jeane, was already nearing ninety when I came on to the scene, and I could see that she felt uncomfortable in Texas. It helped to be rich, but just over the horizon stood more than one El Dorado – Paris in particular – where it might have helped to create livelier things than Galveston could offer. And so, in a city where money still went hand in hand with simplicity, Mary Jean was brought up in a style which struck herself as absurd. She had a governess to hold her hand when she crossed the street. She was sent out in white stockings when all the other little girls wore sandals. And above all she was discouraged in whatever she undertook, even by a father who loved her dearly but was dominated in his own home by his wife. Mary Jean wanted to work in New York; this was forbidden. The older generation in her immediate family could be daunting. Her maternal grandmother is on record as saying to her when she was a shy fifteen or so, 'Never forget that you come from a line of beautiful women, each generation less beautiful than the last.'

With time, she fell in love with one or another young man; none of them was approved. At length she did marry, and had one son, who was at St Paul's in Hew Hampshire – one of half-a-dozen schools each claiming to be the best in the country and leading comfortably towards Harvard, Princeton and Yale. But her marriage did not work out, her father died, and by the time I knew her she was a woman in her fifties, at odds in most respects with life.

She would do her duty, certainly she would. She would do the right thing by a mother for whom she did not greatly care. She loved her son, and deeply, but having had an unhappy childhood herself she was suspicious of the role of mother. She had a number of devoted friends, both men and women. She wrote well and successfully. The surface of her life was smooth and glowing. But perhaps because she lacked emotional fulfilment she struck people as formidable. She spoke her mind, she was utterly loyal, both to chosen people and to chosen ideas. And as an American she must have seemed doubly formidable to those who did not know her well because she had been moulded by experiences very unlike theirs. At one time, she bought a house in Peking. Year after year she leased the Villa Foscari, the Malcontenta, in the Veneto, and from there moved each year for a few weeks to Portugal, to the Quinta da Capela near Sintra, a delicious house used as a winter home by her Malcontenta landlords, the Landsbergs.

I came to know her through Jake Carter, and when he went out of her life I felt very sorry for her. But I also perceived her to be difficult, without at the time reflecting that all my life I have been drawn to difficult women and bored by darling ones with a golden disposition. I remember saying to Cécile de Rothschild one day in Lisbon that I was unhappy at the Quinta because I found Mary Jean so harsh to those whom, I knew, she loved at heart. And then one day after a long summer evening of talk the climate of our friendship changed. I concluded that her difficulties arose from being starved of affection. She had become suspicious of the world, and from feeling sorry for her on one plane, as an Ariadne deserted by her Theseus, my sympathy broadened. Here, I thought, was a delightful, very responsive woman who needed to be reassured by life. Might I not supply the reassurance?

Within a month or two we were married, and shortly after that I was introduced to her native Galveston, and to her family of cousins. I found an appealing island city connected to Texas only by a causeway and built on a spit of sand which had been swept away by an especially dangerous hurricane in 1900, so that what had been a rich community had largely been destroyed and six thousand of its people drowned, after the breaking of a sea-wall. From being a centre of successful enterprise in the nineteenth century, when Houston, its now-powerful neighbour, did not exist, Galveston sank into the doldrums. It became a red-light city; many of its Victorian houses, built along straight avenues lined with palm and oleander, were ripped down; and not until some twenty-five years ago did an effective change for the better bring new prosperity – a change largely activated by three families, the Moodys, the Sealys and my in-laws.

My father-in-law had commissioned a house, using as architect the Britisher, Alfred Bossom, about whom Winston Churchill has been quoted as making a typical Churchillian joke*. There my mother-in-law reigned, already very old and not reliably well disposed towards her relatives, so that she was much alone. I got on well with her, and I was touched that she should maintain an old-fashioned standard of living whenever I was with her. We might be just the two of us at dinner and I should not have been in the least critical had she come down in an old dressing-gown. But not at all. She always wore a Paris dress – I see her in red velvet – with exactly the right jewels for a lady of almost ninety. She seemed to have established a small, static empire under her roof. And indeed a decade after her death it still survives, a Southern empire with a black citizenry of great competence and kindliness: Mr Mackey, who drove tiny Mrs Kempner about in an immense Cadillac; Twine the cook, Bernice and Pearl, and Johnnie the gardener.

Our happiness was not destined to endure. Less than a year after our marriage, Mary Jean died in Paris.

* 'Bossom. Bossom: a very odd name. Neither the one thing nor the other.'

XXV

Now, when I look back over nearly eighty years of living, I conclude that the most fortunate element in those years was twice to have known a happy marriage and twice to have achieved an enduring alliance with my in-laws. This double sequence took place at a time when family relationships on both sides of the Atlantic were notoriously running into the sand. One was half expected to apologize for anything so feeble as happiness. I thought from time to time of my black New York maid of over twenty years. One day, dusting by some invitations on the chimney-piece, she had said sharply, 'You had better make the most of this life. You have too good a time, and you'll be sorry in the next.' I have indeed over the years had a good time, and even in the last decade I have managed to enjoy myself.

After a year or two I sold the apartment on Beekman Place where Mary Jean and I had lived, and moved my centre to Newport. Even in this I was lucky. I had been introduced to a Japanese, with the comment that he had a pleasant small apartment, looking over Central Park. He invited me there, and when I said to him that it was pleasant indeed, and that I envied him, he offered it me on lease. His father, he told me, was a very conventional man who had never left Japan. The father was concerned that he had a son in his thirties but no grandchildren. The son told me that he had only lately earned enough money to marry, but that now, to please his family, he had decided to accept their choice of a bride. She had never left home; she spoke no English; she was likely to detest New York.

243

Would I take over the apartment until his marriage failed, when he could return to it – for it was not large enough for two? His marriage did not fail, and I have stayed in possession for some ten years.

I also travelled. With Cécile de Rothschild I made annual trips. In earlier years she had kept a boat in Greece, a specially designed caïque on which we had made trips to the islands and down the Turkish coast. Now we explored Guatemalan lakes and the splendid ruins of Tikal; we experienced vertigo in Macchu-Picchu and apprehension in Colombia when our host in Bogotá warned Cécile not to trail her wrist on the window of a car because of the likelihood that someone would notice a ring or a watch and cut off the wrist with a machete. Incidentally, the host, who had been Colombian Ambassador in Washington, reassured me when I crossed his garden to a guest-cottage after dinner, that armed men under the trees were there to guard, not molest, me. Yet a day or two after we flew out of the country he was seized on a Bogotá street and shut for weeks in a cellar while his ransom was being fought over.

In Colombia and in Greece, and often in France, Cécile and I had with us Greta Garbo, still in her seventies a unique beauty. Her genuine wish to pass unnoticed made her a demanding guest in a world of *paparazzi* – for how could we guarantee her privacy? One day, near Mycenae, she and I were walking on a dusty main road when suddenly she noticed that my shoe-lace was undone, and knelt down in the dust, grumbling, to tie it up. For once, to my deep relief, there were no *paparazzi* lurking in the bushes with a camera.

Another year, Cécile and I went to New Zealand and Australia. If I had been happy, years before, to escape being a South African, I was now unhappy not to pass a second lifetime as an Australian, so engrossingly delightful did I find what I saw of that continent. And spring after spring we found ourselves in the Bahamas or Kenya or Florida, with shared friends, Jack and Drue Heinz, in whose Florida house I am today writing these words.

Meantime, while I moved about, the life of my first mother-in-law, Mary Wooster, was slowly ebbing away in Florence. Frank Wooster had died in 1953 and after his death she turned to two forms of solace: a growing sense of infallibility and a very personal form of mysticism. She had always been far more intelligent than Frank, whose handsome head was almost totally empty. After years of marriage he began to bore her, and not long before he died she told her children that she was planning to leave him.

Although they had not at first welcomed his presence, they had become fonder of him with time, and they pointed out that it would be cruel indeed to leave him when age was beginning to tell. She did not do so, and when very suddenly he died she remembered only happier times. She also discovered to her own satisfaction that physical death had not separated them. She stayed in touch, she believed, to the extent that it became habitual to her, years after he died, to say casually, 'I was talking to Frank last night,' or 'I find the irises do much better since I took Frank's advice and had them moved to the South border.'

Under his instructions from beyond the grave she became deeply involved in the oecumenical movement. And so, when at last the Pope and the Archbishop of Canterbury met together in England, it was with a shiver that we learned of the meeting. It had been in the Wooster Room which she had presented to Canterbury Cathedral. Could her intuitions be exact? Was she, as she would have wished throughout life, assisting the movements of the universe?

By the time of the Pope's visit, she was no longer alive, and it was too late for me to indulge a fancy anyway hard to execute: the bringing together of both my mothers-in-law, so as to discover which of two adamant old ladies would survive the encounter.

In the nature of things my teleological questions must soon be answered. But while I am still in this world I pause to remember a day when I was sent out by my parents with a riding-school to Hyde Park. I must have been about twelve. The riding-master warned me to beware if a child hopped by on a pogo-stick, an instrument then in fashion and uncongenial to the pony. All went well until, in a compact group, we rode out of the park at Stanhope Gate. Suddenly a pogo went into action among the bystanders, and there, in the middle of Park Lane, quite close to my birthplace, I almost met a symmetrical end as the pony carried out a series of terrified double-bucks. I stayed on, not gracefully, I suppose. And I reflect with gratitude that all these years, though I have run into a pogo from time to time, even if grace has deserted me, I have not yet been thrown.

INDEX

255